Science of God

Science of God

Truth in the Age of Science

Kevin Sharpe

ROWMAN & LITTLEFIELD PUBLISHERS, INC.
Lanham • Boulder • New York • Toronto • Plymouth, UK
OCM 64592033

ROWMAN & LITTLEFIELD PUBLISHERS, INC.

Published in the United States of America
by Rowman & Littlefield Publishers, Inc.
A wholly owned subsidiary of The Rowman & Littlefield Publishing Group, Inc.
4501 Forbes Boulevard, Suite 200, Lanham, Maryland 20706
www.rowmanlittlefield.com

Estover Road
Plymouth PL6 7PY
United Kingdom

British Library Cataloguing in Publication Information Available

Library of Congress Cataloging-in-Publication Data

Sharpe, Kevin J.
  Science of God : truth in the age of science / Kevin Sharpe.
    p. cm.
  Includes bibliographical references (p.) and index.
  ISBN-13: 978-0-7425-4266-2 (cloth : alk. paper)
  ISBN-10: 0-7425-4266-1 (cloth : alk. paper)
  ISBN-13: 978-0-7425-4267-9 (pbk. : alk. paper)
  ISBN-10: 0-7425-4267-X (pbk. : alk. paper)
  1. Religion and science. 2. God. 3. Theology. I. Title.
  BL240.3.S54 2006
  201'.65—dc22   2006007306

Printed in the United States of America

∞™ The paper used in this publication meets the minimum requirements of
American National Standard for Information Sciences—Permanence of Paper
for Printed Library Materials, ANSI/NISO Z39.48-1992

I dedicate this book to my wife, Leslie Van Gelder, without whose love and support I would not have been able to bring this volume to fruition.

Contents

Acknowledgments

Many thanks are due to the numerous people who have helped me over the many years this book has been in the writing. Ruth Page, Karl Peters, and Sally Thomason have read parts or all of the manuscript and offered their valuable suggestions. Leslie Van Gelder has done likewise and especially encouraged me to bring this project to fruition. Harris Manchester College, Oxford University, has become my intellectual home, and to the Principal, Ralph Waller, I wish to express my gratitude.

A Failure of Science and Religion

I sat in the audience at an American Academy of Religion meeting a few years ago while Holmes Rolston gave a lecture. His presentation typifies the problems in current science and religion. The well-planned attack on sociobiology conflated and corrupted the language of science to promote a strikingly antiscience, religiously conservative view. Sociobiology— or, as its proponents now call it, evolutionary psychology—says many social and behavioral traits of humans derive from a biological and evolutionary base; lovers of received religion abhor this. Rolston dazzled the packed room with his use of the then-modern technology of LCD projection to present quotes from various sociobiologists out of context and, with them, humorously to criticize their assumptions: easily dismissed paper tigers. He finally arrived at his triumphant opinion that atheism is inconsistent. The room burst into applause. Either you are in the in-group with him, or you are out in the cold.

Conferences and courses in science and religion spring up all over the world—but what do they teach? Most seem to promote the status quo of whatever theology the teachers hold, with a science crutch as its support. Theology frequently calls on science to defend tradition and a monoculture of mediocrity. Few voices look at the science that challenges those beliefs, except to attack the science and those who draw implications from it. Being orthodox—so orthodox as to approach a creationist point of view—is in vogue.

The boundary between science and theology offers power that many people in science-religion crave. For them, the dialogue consists not in exploring or asking fundamental questions of meaning, but in kidnapping science's authority to claim the superiority of themselves and their views over others. Humility has gone and arrogant self-aggrandizement has taken its place.

A summer recently past, I assisted in coordinating the C. S. Lewis Foundation's Oxbridge Conference, which organized much of its content around science and religion. The dominant voices from the podium waxed professorially on intelligent design, the theory that attributes supposed gaps in evolutionary explanations to God's intervention. The more liberal plenary speakers in science and religion were Bob Russell and John Polkinghorne. Russell wants scientists to direct their research to support a specific Christian interpretation of the end times and the physical resurrection of Jesus from the dead. Polkinghorne founds his theology on the idea that God acts in the world by directly influencing chaotic systems with nudges so their outcomes fall in line with God's purposes. He reviews one of my books, *Sleuthing the Divine*, with these words: "More orthodox ideas [than Sharpe's] seem to me to have the toughness that a scientist might expect a truly fundamental understanding to display."[1] He misses the point: it is not toughness for the scientist that a theology needs to achieve, but communicability and truthfulness in this age of science. Both Polkinghorne and Russell end with a traditional theology, and their methods fly in the face of science. They impossibly want a science that makes Jesus' physical resurrection reasonable.

Arthur Peacocke—another leading voice in the science-religion field and, like Rolston and Polkinghorne, a winner of the Templeton Prize for Progress in Religion—told me over a cup of coffee that he fears the subject has come to a dead end. With a smile, he lamented that it has nothing new to do but dot a few i's and cross a few t's. I believe he is right about the current direction of the dialogue. I also suspect he overlooks something more basic; even with his own work, he has yet to apply a critical voice to some of his most fundamental beliefs, especially those concerning the relationship between God and the universe.

I challenge theology and the science-religion field to take science and its method seriously, and to do theology without a division between it and science. Very heavy sighs, loud shouting, or obvious ignoring will resist this appeal. No wonder, because it may call all theological ideas and methods into question. Theologians want to protect their ideas, and those who can want to harness the power of science for their own ends. Theology need not fear my challenge, however. Theology ought to believe that the truth of the "God of truth"—whom theologians believe they serve—will softly float over impostors.

The way of science provides my point of reference and base for comparison. I evaluate from this vision many of the suggestions and debates emerging from the methodological challenge for theology.[2] Many, like creationism, draw on science but fall short of the scientific ideal; the discussion suggests what authorities they unscientifically adopt instead. Chapter 1 introduces these issues.

Does theology describe or does it not describe? Because this decision is a basic paradigmatic one over which theologians can clarify positions but seldom change their minds, I probably cannot persuade anyone that the nondescriptive approach has it wrong. I will instead use the descriptive position to help clarify what theological description entails, and where theology might legitimately describe (and follow science) and where it might not. Then I will develop a method for theology as deliberately constructive (it uses "God" as the central symbol; it uses experience, including scientific knowledge, as data; it tries to explain all), that more adequately follows the method of science.

I will lay out each discussion in the historical context in which it came to me, and I will construct my answers in dialogue with the literature current at the time I developed them. Thus, I will set this book in history, following the development of my ideas about theological method. I will, however, examine the resultant proposal in the context of today's discussions.

Chapter 2 begins setting the stage for a deeper analysis of the problem. It presents a stage in Gordon Kaufman's thinking where he veered from neo-orthodoxy toward liberal functionalism, where he tries to answer the challenge of science and modernity. The issue is methodological: whether authority lies in science or in tradition and, if in science, or partly in science, how to allow room for the wisdom of tradition.

My awareness of the issues and personal involvement with deliberate contemplation on the method for theology began in my days at Harvard Divinity School under Kaufman's tutelage. An exciting and clear teacher, he formed a seminar group, of which I was lucky to be a member, to debate and consider with him his newly written manuscript on theological method, later published as his turn-around book, *An Essay on Theological Method.*[3] Kaufman started his theological journey in the neo-orthodox school with its traditional beliefs, a sense of the utmost transcendence of God, and the separation of theology from science. When he taught me, he had rejected the first but retained the others, the second especially shining through. The sense of the absolute transcendence of God—not a regular type of transcendence where God somehow exceeds the universe, but an absolute one where no one can know anything at all of God—pushes God completely out of reach. It does not merely claim that humans can never know everything about God—as I can never know everything about you or, for that matter, as I can never know everything about myself—but insists humans can know nothing at all about God. This claim constitutes an inherent contradiction (to know no one can know anything of God is, in fact, to know something of God) and wipes away the immediacy, relevance, and spirituality of God, things necessary for the success of religion and the moral direction for a person's everyday and broader cultural life. Worse still, it too easily places absolute authority in the hands of those who claim to know God's will.

The questions I ask of methodological proposals and some of the ingredients for my own proposal arise directly from Kaufman's work. On several central issues, I disagree radically with what he then taught about the way theology refers to God.[4]

Theologians and writers in science and religion commonly adopt an idea for God like Kaufman's. Peacocke, for instance, advocates an otherness for God that radically separates God from the universe. I cannot accept this stance. True, theologians have yet to understand the relationship between God and the universe, but they need not give up on it. Ideas of God must be fully responsible to the life people experience and to the world in which they experience it. That constitutes the chief challenge behind developing *Science of God*.

Chapter 3 offers further historical background to the issue and responses to it, focusing largely on the work of the atheist philosopher Kai Nielsen.

Nielsen believes theological claims try to say something truthful and factual about the world and that theologians ought to subject them to the tests applied to similar claims. When theologians do this, they fail. Believers ought to specify or conceive of the difference between the truth and falsity of a claim about God. They need to do this, Nielsen writes, for the claim to be more than talk "about natural phenomena in a high-toned manner."[5] If they cannot do it, the claim is probably "devoid of factual and cosmological significance."[6]

Nielsen raised a storm in the 1960s and 1970s by publishing innumerable articles, papers, and books attacking theologies. He especially singles out positions that adhere to tradition or else try to justify themselves in the face of the challenge. His response to theology fails to satisfy theologians because they feel it too extreme and because they find ways, they think, to shield their foundational beliefs from the critique of modernity. Unfortunately, they also render their beliefs even more irrelevant to contemporary social problems and ways of thinking.

In selecting Nielsen as the guide for this chapter, I place my confidence in an ardent atheist determined to do his damnedest against religious language in as wide a range of questions as possible. I submit my ideas to one of the most critical attacks anyone can raise against them.

Kaufman and Nielsen face a similar challenge—namely, the confrontation of religion by modernity—but both respond ineffectively. Theologians ought not, as Kaufman does, relegate the supposed reality God to something so far from people's lives and possible experience that God becomes irrelevant to living and theology becomes a system of ideas not descriptive but merely functioning in particular ways. Neither ought the scholar follow Nielsen and throw cold water on theological constructions without attempting to help reconstruct them adequately. Theologians need to face the challenge head on with theological constructions that answer secularity's challenge and that still center on the reality God. That is, theologians need to do theology fully scientifically without losing the wisdom gathered over the past many millennia of human experience and the moral critique necessary to guide and admonish how people live: a difficult, but not impossible, challenge.

Two resources help meet this challenge.

The first is the use of the scientific method for theology. I justify this by establishing in chapter 4 the need for a better-functioning Western society. Current social chaos and uncertainty largely derive from the use of technology and scientific knowledge. How best to use discoveries? What discoveries not to use? How to guide potentially dangerous research? On what basis ought society to allocate its resources in the face of global and local threats? Society lacks a convincing morality. People need wisdom to help guide them. This used to come through religion, but religion has become either irrelevant to secular modernity or it has tried to build other but doomed, backward-looking worlds parallel to it. To help make the world a better place for humans and nonhuman kin, I propose that theology—the system of understanding that emerges from religious wisdom—embrace modernity and guide secularity's latent spirituality. Developing a truly scientific method for itself offers theology a first step in this direction because science speaks with the voice of contemporary truth.

The second ingredient of my proposed method for theology is an analysis in chapter 5 of the scientific method, an explication for theology to follow. I draw on Ian Barbour's presentation of it. Much happened in the 1960s and 1970s to the understanding of the practice of science because of the revolution in the philosophy of science brought on in part by the work of Thomas Kuhn. It also left the understanding of science rather ambiguous because no one can easily define scientific objectivity. Science involves both the subjective and the objective, wrapped in a helix so intertwined that the two strands become inseparable. Barbour's portrayal of this compromise offers a balanced starting point, portraying science as comprised of metaphysical assumptions and research traditions, theories and models, and criteria for the evaluation of theories.

Chapter 6—the core of the book—uses the above resources to present a detailed response to secularity's challenge. I contend that theology can also comprise the same three elements as in Barbour's picture of science. When it does this in the manner I suggest, I call it "key-theology."

The *theos* part of the word "theology" is the most fundamental theological assumption and the one that, to a large extent, defines theology as a discipline as distinct from, say, biology or sociology. The discipline of theology centers on an idea of God (whatever that word might mean); a God idea centrally organizes and dominates any theology, the notion on which all other ideas depend and with which they fall in line. This equally applies to key-theology.

Key-theology knows about God as science knows about the physical world. Science describes reality. It looks at all through its particular lens of its fundamental model, the physical. Key-theology similarly describes reality in that it attempts to explain it rationally both as a whole and in its content. Key-theology describes in the sense that the larger corpus of ideas arising from its fundamental metaphysical model "God" sees all through the lens of this model. Both science and key-theology describe reality through their respective lenses. By doing this, key-theology knows about God.

Key-theology aims to know about God; God is thus the *object* of key-theology. The *subject* matter for key-theology—what key-theologians study to discern the nature of God—is the phenomena of the world. These include reality, as a whole and as people experience it, potentially all phenomena and all experience. Key-theology, that is, includes the subject matter of all other disciplines.

Having chosen an initial God lens, the key-theologian develops further models from it for God and for the world, and then develops these into theories based on criteria. This whole process involves construction: working out the models and their implications and relations, deciding on positive and negative analogies, comparing them with other theologies, and applying them to points of interest.

Sources for key-theological models vary considerably because key-theology tries to encompass a wide swath of reality. Key-theologians look for models in phenomenology, history, hermeneutics, philosophy, politics, biology, social studies, and physics. Religious dogma, scripture, and experiences also offer models and elements for key-theology, but only potential models, for they—like all other proposals—need evaluation before acceptance or rejection.

Once key-theologians create a theory, they need to evaluate it. Barbour considers the list of criteria for scientific theories and then applies them to religious beliefs:

> Any system of thought [should desire] *simplicity* . . . (e.g., minimum number of independent assumptions and conceptual categories); but it . . . seldom [becomes] a major consideration in either science or religion. *Coherence* involves both internal consistency (the absence of contradictions) and systematic interrelatedness (the presence of connections and implications between statements). But *supporting evidence* . . . [offers] the most important criterion. Religious beliefs must give a faithful rendition of the areas of experience taken . . . [as] especially significant: religious and moral experience and key historical events. But they must also adequately interpret other events in [people's] lives as active selves. Hence [the list includes] *extensibility* of application (fruitfulness) . . . as

an additional criterion. Finally, *comprehensiveness* in the coherent ordering of diverse types of experience within a systematic metaphysics is desirable, though . . . secondary to other criteria.[7]

A key-theology, however, makes factual assertions beyond personal
or communal, private or subjective, lived experience. By not adhering
to an instrumentalism, key-theologians need more than usefulness as a
criterion; key-theology contains several types of factual statements besides the obvious ones pertaining to history and social and personal experience. A key-theology can make cognitive descriptive claims for any
part of its subject matter, which covers human experience and history,
and the physical, biological, and social worlds in all their aspects. In
fact, some aspect of the universe and human experience of it anchors
any key-theological statement. Each of these facets falls within the domain of some discipline of knowledge, and so key-theology's statements impinge on the subject areas of other disciplines. Each such statement needs evaluating within those disciplines.

Science and key-theology can share the same method and describe
reality according to their respective assumption or lens. Science and
key-theology share truth.

In chapter 7 my proposal interacts with such modern writers on the
subject of theological method as Philip Clayton, Alister McGrath,
Nancey Murphy, Peacocke, and Wentzel van Huyssteen. All these major current voices in the area draw upon a version of contemporary philosophy of science. However, if they then develop their theologies, they
make significant and nonempirical leaps from which they can develop
the theology with which they started. Their work is thus apologetical.
To be genuinely open to what key-theologians can learn about God requires not making such leaps. It requires opening all beliefs to empirical examination and opening up to learn from what science and other
experience can teach.

How then might key-theologians do theology, the science of God,
with the above methodological proposal? Drawing on happiness as a
starting point, chapter 8 starts to develop an example of a theology that
uses this method.

Social psychological and neurochemical research report on what increases a person's happiness in the long term. Because scientific research suggests how the universe, including human beings, operates and

comes to be, science can—and does—suggest how people might increase their happiness. These strategies have evolved into each person. This is an aspect of God at work. Happiness strategies, therefore, say something about how people might live in tune with the work of God. That is, such scientific results inform the understanding of the human spiritual nature and thus of God in relation to human beings.

Many drives compete within each person, however. To gain greater happiness is not the only one. Choices allow people to balance happiness with its competitors (such as justice), and each person can choose how to achieve that balance. Human self-awareness enables this decision, drawing from memories about what previous decisions led to and from cultural wisdom about what others' decisions suggest. The "best" way to act emerges from a constant process of discovery: a discovery of who the person is in relation to each of the inclinations that compete within, and a discovery of what each inclination means for him or her.

Decision making between inclinations is significant *spiritually* because people employ their free will to choose and achieve a balance between them. Free will (a unique human ability but one that is continuous with the capabilities of other animals) equals, in more traditional terms, self-awareness at the core of God. Spirituality (traditionally, God's way) asks self-awareness to develop the person as best the individual can. To be spiritual means to take account of all the aspects of the self and to decide from among them what is best. To be spiritual means to ask what a balance between the inclinations and attributes means, and then to seek it. In particular, if people want spiritual happiness, they should answer what comprises the balance of happiness with the other demands on them (what is more important for them to choose)—including the fact that they seek justice—and try to achieve it.

Happiness is only one human quality that leads to key-theological insight through scientific research. Such investigations could launch all of key-theology. In ways like the above, key-theology can and ought to adopt the scientific method and use the results of scientific research. When they primarily research the nature of what it is to be a human being and a person, scientists are, in fact, modern-day key-theologians practicing *Science of God*.

The usual stories modern Western culture teaches about the world and human beings involve the evolution of the universe from the big bang to humans as biological beings. These accounts brand as primary both matter and the science that seeks to explain it. People also need, however, a story that makes human experience primary. I show in this last chapter that to accept the inseparable intertwining of the spiritual and the physical can help elevate the human to sit alongside matter. Evolution becomes as much spiritual as biological or physical. Scientific research can generate knowledge of God and people's spiritual selves. The universe that science explains leaves behind the image of cold and mechanical matter; matter involves endless depths and mystery. It ties intimately with human subjectivity by producing it. Matter is spiritual.

Science of God outlines views on the method of theology and critiques the current science-theology dialogue. I pose the challenge of science to theology's method, and offer and apply an original answer, a way truer to the scientific and spiritual yearnings of practitioners. In so doing, I hope to forward discussions in science and theology, theological method, and systematic theology.

NOTES

1. Polkinghorne 2001.
2. See Sharpe 1984.
3. Kaufman 1975.
4. Kaufman 1975. See Sharpe 1979.
5. Nielsen 1973a: 275.
6. Nielsen 1973a: 275.
7. Barbour 1974: 143.

Chapter One

God the Mystery:
The Rising Question on Method

The State of Arkansas passed a law late in 1981 requiring that schools devote equal time to creation science as to evolutionary science. According to this law, theories claiming to have established scientifically the emergence of the universe and life—especially of humans—according to a literal interpretation of the biblical book of Genesis must have as much exposure in Arkansas schools as does the biological theory of evolution. The State of Georgia Department of Education in 2003 expunged the word "evolution" from its school curricula. The official U.S. battle over evolution has continued much the same since the original Scopes trial in 1925.

The American Civil Liberties Union challenged the Arkansas law at a month-long "Scopes II" trial at Little Rock. Judge William Overton ruled the law violates the separation of church and state and so breaches the Constitution of the United States.

The debates and the decision in the Arkansas case made headlines in many corners of the world. It was surprising how much interest, heat, and threat the case raised, and how many scientific periodicals carried extensive coverage. The threat continues to generate attention. One day, perhaps, this attention may so fire the scholarly and public imagination that everyone will want to look into the success of creation science and its parent, Christian fundamentalism.

A person does not have to be from the conservative let alone a fundamentalist camp to see that the conservative side offers lessons, especially in what it highlights about authority and the needs of society. A

11

person can applaud creation science's observations, adoption of the scientific method, and several of its motivations—while also deploring its erroneous use of science. It seeks to answer real wants, but selectively warps perhaps the most powerful tools society offers. Fundamentalism shows how not to answer societal needs

WHAT IS THEOLOGY?

The plaintiffs in the Arkansas trial first provided the court with a general discussion on religion, the sources of the Old Testament, and the growth of fundamentalism in the United States. It then described the character of religious claims in comparison with other claims such as those of philosophy and science. The court heard that science uses experience to test hypotheses that it may relinquish if the empirical cards stack against them. Evolutionary theory satisfies this criterion; creation science does not and so is not a genuine science.[1] Legislating that it is a science, comments the plaintiffs' witness Michael Ruse, attempts "to force a crude form of biblical literalism into school biology classes."[2]

Ruse rightfully opposes creation science as a "perversion of learning."[3] He goes further and calls it as a "travesty of thought."[4] Whether that is accurate or not, the question centers on the nature of creation science. What is creation science if not a science? It probably is a theology. The question then becomes, What is a theology? This chapter briefly outlines several qualities of theology—its nature and purpose—and the rest of the book elaborates on them. The book's interest lies in the relationship between theology and science, focusing especially on theology's use of the method of science—of which creation science offers an extreme and wrongheaded example.

Adherents of a religion assume beliefs about such things as God and the supernatural, which dogma, sacred scriptures, and other special documents inform. Adherents also live religiously in some way: "living . . . in the light of . . . belief in God," writes Max Charlesworth, "praying, worshipping, performing rituals, or witnessing."[5] They speak a language for this religious life, a language built from that of common use. Theology reflects on these religious activities and the language used for them, constructs theories about them, and tries to explain them based on the beliefs. Anselm of Canterbury thus depicts theology as "faith seeking understanding"; a theologian attempts rationally, coherently, faithfully, and systematically to express and spell out the religion's beliefs (or the beliefs of what the theologian considers an important group of people) in order to understand the religious life. The task of theologians moves from the beliefs through to the activities and back again. Its language emerges from and merges into the other two languages.

Creation science is theological because it builds from fundamentalist beliefs to mold, underpin, and explain the religious life of evangelical Christians. It reaches further than this, however. Because it believes it applies to all of society, not just to the fundamentalists, it also tries to mold science.

Theologians may look to their beliefs to explain other things than religious activities or to express attitudes (or other subjective functions of religious language). They may also wish to apply them to specific areas within or outside this religious context, such as biblical exegesis, social concerns, liberation from political oppression—as well as natural science. When they do, they still base their work on and develop a set of beliefs.

Two twists complicate this picture where it seems theology works from and toward the ideas and practices of believers:

- Theologians can also play leader roles for religious beliefs, language, and life, by suggesting matters beyond the accepted beliefs. Theologians can in this way lead believers into that new area. John Robinson achieved this in the 1960s and 1970s by proposing a nontraditional understanding of God in his book *Honest to God*.[6] Creationism does this too for fundamentalists by explaining how the geology, biology, and cosmology discovered by the sciences fit with a literal interpretation of Genesis.
- Theologians may also consider it important to spell out or be faithful to a set of beliefs other than those they associate with a religious tradition. Fundamentalism usually aligns itself ardently with patriotism and capitalism. Schubert Ogden, to cite another example, thinks theology should primarily be meaningful and truthful to what he identifies as the experiences at the heart of human existence.[7]

In both twists in their roles, theologians try to make their work faithful to a set of beliefs they consider essential to the tradition to or from which they speak. A theologian thus attempts rationally, coherently, faithfully, and systematically to express and spell out a set of beliefs including, primarily, beliefs considered religious.

THEOLOGY'S AUTHORITY AND SUBJECT

Theologians may venture beyond the limits of their traditions. How far can they go without falling off those edges? Theologians have to decide whether they accept their or any other tradition's beliefs about God, the world, and human beings. Where does theological authority lie?

The chief question that urges an Arkansas-like fundamentalist-modernist controversy centers on authority. Is science right, or is fundamentalist Christianity right? Secular culture squares off with fundamentalist Christian subculture for the prize of being correct. Ought the natural universe or ought someone's literal interpretation of the Bible arbitrate the truth?

Fundamentalism calls on the strength and power of existing authorities in its climb to its own strength and power. One is a particular type of interpretation (a literalist one) of the Bible. This did not exist in ancient times. Rather, writes Karen Armstrong, fundamentalists are

> ardent modernists. By attempting to return to "fundamentals," they [fall] in line with other intellectual and scientific currents . . . addicted to scientific rationalism. . . . Doctrines [become] not theological speculations, but facts. . . . Fundamentalists [try] . . . to create a new way of being religious in an age that [values] the *logos* of science above all else.[8]

Fundamentalism, therefore, seeks its authority from two places:

- *The Bible*. Fundamentalism relies on a certain interpretation of the Bible (though literalist interpretations may vary). This means the authority lies with those people who created that interpretation or with those who claim the validity of that interpretation. Proudly Protestant fundamentalism derives from the same humanism that facilitated the rise of modern science, stressing each individual's access and responsibility to a given authority.
- *Science*. Creation science approaches the world looking for the facts similarly to how natural science approaches the world (only with dif-

ferent criteria as to what facts it will accept). Fundamentalism probably hopes the power it gains by thus fraternizing with science will rub
off on it and lead to a wider acceptance of its moral and religious
claims. It relies on the prestige and truth-status that science holds in
Western society.

Fundamentalism also rejects such sciences as biological evolution. It
thus wants the prestige and truth-status of a science while at the same
time repudiating some of the findings and data of science—an ingen-
ious political maneuver. Fundamentalism contradicts itself for the sake
of asserting power. It cannot do this if it wants thinking moderns to take
what it says seriously.

If a theology wishes to claim a likeness to science and wants people
to take it seriously, it must accept the findings of science in all realms,
including geology, biology, and cosmology. If a theology wishes to call
itself a science, it must enter into discussions and accept observations
that may lead to the undermining of cherished beliefs. Absolute certainty
will go. Authority will leave the institution, tradition, book, or charismatic person and will reside, as it does with science, in external reality.
All theologies have a foundational authority they call upon; if a theology
wishes to call itself a science, it must remove the authority from the subjectivities of people, books, traditions, and institutions, and place it in the
world of observation and intersubject experience. This approach acknowledges the influence of people, traditions, institutions, books, and
subjective experience on every science and on theology. But it denies
that one or more of these influences finally arbitrate the truth. After all,
even considering the most subjective of these influences—subjective
experience—many people have similar experiences (including what they
might term spiritual encounters) and these experiences are not so purely
subjective that no one else has them. Authority lies in external reality.

THEOLOGY AS DESCRIPTION

A theology that calls itself a science must accept observations of the
world and intersubject experience. Much of this book expands on this
statement. An important issue that helps raise the discussion concerns
the descriptive nature of theology.

Charlesworth poses two forms of the problem for theological language.[9] The first he calls a first approximation, and it leads to the second, which concerns whether or not theology is descriptive. For the first, take, as an example, the theological phrase, "God makes things out of nothing." The word "God" refers to an object not wholly within the human world of experience, a technical word that might translate into such familiar and mundane words as, "a supreme personal being on whom the world depends for its existence and value."[10] The remaining words, "makes things out of nothing," are also ordinary words. Making something out of nothing, however, lies outside human experience of making things; people always make something out of something else. To lump these words together into this phrase places a strain on them to the extent that the word "makes" becomes unintelligible. Perhaps, someone might respond, this phrase opens a special use of the word "makes," applicable only to God. This, however, only emphasizes the meaningless combination of the words. It so qualifies the word "makes" that the meaning first used and then depended on ceases. Charlesworth writes that, in general,

> when a religious believer expresses his [or her] beliefs he [or she apparently speaks] . . . about very peculiar objects, states of affairs, events, and processes that are nonmaterial, nonspatiotemporal, not empirically observable, and not subject to limitation or imperfection. . . . Yet . . . the believer can speak of these religious objects [only in] a language . . . devised to deal with the material, spatiotemporal, observable, and limited objects of . . . ordinary mundane experience. . . . The difficulty [arises because] . . . these ordinary mundane words, when used of the extraordinary supramundane objects of religious belief, appear . . . so outrageously stretched and strained and subject to so many qualifications that they lose all intelligible meaning.[11]

Theology uses the language of ordinary experience to speak of extraordinary objects. Theologians have the habit of so qualifying this language, however, that it loses its meaning.

Charlesworth poses the second approximation to theological language's problem in terms of theology's descriptive versus its nondescriptive nature. The first problem outlined above assumes theological language must describe in some sense for it to have meaning—describe, that is, supernatural facts rather than ordinary, natural, and empirical facts. Language can do other things besides describe: it can, for instance, prescribe or emote. Charlesworth writes,

> "The door is open" (proposition) [has meaning] . . . in that it . . . [provides] a true or false description of what is the case; but "Shut the door!" (command) is not true or false, and neither is "Would you open the door?" (request), or "Is the door open?" (question). There is no state of affairs to which these latter locutions correspond, or of which they are true; yet they are (or can be) used quite meaningfully.[12]

Perhaps theological language primarily expresses attitudes and approves or disapproves of particular ways of living. Perhaps theological language is primarily nondescriptive (or subjectivist or expressivist). Such a role pays a price, however: the question of the truth or falsity of a statement no longer applies, but only whether it appropriately or inappropriately applies to the situation. "The question, 'Is the door open?' is not false," Charlesworth points out, "but inappropriate if, say, the questioner is in a forest."[13] Further, to specify the appropriateness or inappropriateness of the conditions requires statements that depend on facts. Charlesworth summarizes the problem of theological language with the following:

> If [theological] locutions are descriptive in function, they will enjoy the . . . advantage of being true or false. . . . But the price of this is that they will then be subject to the difficulties . . . exposed before, namely, how are [theologians] to specify the extraordinary or supramundane facts or state of affairs they purport to describe. On the other hand, if [theologians] take [theological] locutions to be nondescriptive in function, seeing them, say, as emotive expressions or as quasi-moral expressions of attitude, then [they] escape these latter difficulties, for if it is not the function of [theological] locutions to describe certain peculiar facts, [critics] cannot meaningfully ask for any proof or demonstration of these facts. Once again, however, as the price [theologians] pay for this logical advantage is that [theological] locutions are no longer true or false, [they] then must face the difficulty of how [they] are to justify them as appropriate or inappropriate without having recourse to true or false propositions about facts.[14]

Descriptive versus nondescriptive language does not pose a new problem for theology and philosophy; it rises, as Charlesworth outlines, throughout the history of Western philosophy.[15] It runs through Plato, the Neo-Platonists, Thomas Aquinas, and forward. It became especially important for Immanuel Kant, who saw religious language primarily as moral (what he called practical) in its intent, independent of the facts of the world. In the nineteenth century, many thought science preempted an account of theological language as descriptive. A number of streams appeared from there, each attacking the descriptivist approach. The existentialist school following Søren Kierkegaard (Jean-Paul Sartre, Gabriel Marcel, and so on) held that theological statements make sense only in the subjective realm distinct from objective facts, which science describes. The analytic tradition, including the outspoken logical positivists (Rudolf Carnap, A. J. Ayer, Antony Flew, and so on), held that theological discourse deals with values, not facts, and is meaningless because it does not fulfill the conditions for meaningful descriptive language.[16] The Wittgensteinian wing of this positivist tradition (Richard Braithwaite, R. M. Hare, Donald Hudson, Norman Malcolm, D. Z. Phillips, Paul van Buren, Peter Winch, and so on) also considers that theology deals with the subjective and not the factual, but is meaningful because of its nondescriptive nature, expressing attitudes or creating an irreducible and peculiar "language game."

This book rejects the nondescriptive approach and attempts to build a descriptive method that avoids the difficulties Charlesworth points out for such approaches.

THE DEMISE OF NONDESCRIPTIVE THEOLOGY

The evolution-Genesis debate repeatedly draws public attention. One reaction, laughing and not weeping at a Scopes II trial, says no critical questions arise there; theology concerns only the inner experience of the subjective self and not the geological and biological world. Such laughter turns hollow. The logical positivists, despite their extreme position, to some measure correctly critique theology: subjectivist theological discourse does deal with values, not facts, and thus is meaningless, failing to fulfill the conditions for meaningful descriptive language. This change climaxed during the 1960s. The death of God occurred; nondescriptive theology, namely existentialist neo-orthodoxy, died as a truthful theological force.

To redefine the meaning of the word "God" in purely subjective and existential terms leaves it as "only a subliminal courage to go on with the business of living."[17] Walter Thorson continues: the "God-in-the-depths becomes a rather shapeless and fluid blob" because it is indistinguishable from a person's fluctuating psychological experience.[18] Existentialism accepted positivism's cleavage of the world into theology versus science and, in retreating to the subjective realm of being, took with it and drained the life from God and God's objectivity. Classical theism strangled itself, concludes Joe Barnhart, falsified in its loose elaborative talk.[19]

Thorson considers both extreme objective positivism and extreme subjective existentialism "absurd distortions of reality. They . . . [attempt] either to avoid the risk, or to evade the responsibility of authority, which is implicit in knowing the truth."[20] He adds that Christianity's interest lays in a God of objective events, a God of authority. God acts in the world out there as well as in the world inside the person. Theology about a God of objective events allows evaluation of its truthfulness. Thorson writes it is his "experience that scientific colleagues find an orthodox religious faith interesting and meaningful even if they do not themselves in the least believe it to be true, precisely because it is possible for it to be proved wrong, at least in principle. Religious beliefs [that one can in no way disprove or vindicate] have little or no meaning for them."[21] Philosophers call this openness to having an idea proved wrong the "principle of falsification."

The realization that theology ought to concern itself with a God of objective events marks the watershed in near-recent theology. The image of God must show God obviously involved in the world, otherwise the god is not God, the god is not relevant to the problems and successes of society and of individuals, and the god is not adequate to tradition.[22] (Not that adequacy to tradition must decisively judge a theology.) On this side of the watershed lie theologies of liberation and theologies of ecology; both subscribe to a God at work in the objective world of history, society, and nature. The issue beneath these theologies and what remains unresolved concerns theological method in general: how are theologians to do theology on this side of the watershed? How ought they to evaluate suggestions for God's interactions with the objective world?

Theology as a description of God at work in the world makes factual claims (for instance about God acting in history) that do not reduce to an inner mysticism, a psychology, or a sociology. These theological assertions lie open to confirmation or infirmation through such avenues as historical research. Barnhart encourages the creation of rival conjectures in theology, each open to the testing ground of internal contradiction or confirmation-infirmation under observation of reality (including history), "the buzz-saw of falsification," as he calls it.[23] Theologians now face the challenge, he continues, "to venture out further, to speak more, to risk elaboration, to dare to engage in explication and clarification."[24] They must leave all a priori approaches behind—including the dogma of the tradition (though this may provide conjectures)—and now must face risk: "the risk of eventually becoming a refuted conjecture," or perhaps, less tragically, of only helping to gestate a more compelling successor.[25]

LIFE AS A POINT OF THEOLOGY

Theology attempts rationally, coherently, faithfully, and systematically to express and spell out a set of beliefs including, primarily, beliefs considered religious. How to do this for the secular-scientific world is more than a matter of how to develop confirmable or infirmable theory that describes objective reality. It also concerns living.

Why are creationists creationists if not to satisfy intellectual curiosity about the origin of life and the universe? Something more than holding a set of science-like ideas motivates them. Robert Jastrow points out that the big bang theory in cosmology is just about the same as the biblical view of the universe's origin because both suppose it began sharply and suddenly at a definite point in time.[26] Jastrow remains, however, an agnostic: "I keep coming close to the edge of faith, but I never quite make it over."[27] Edwin Olson thinks "theistic conviction does not automatically follow when a person becomes aware that scientific knowledge has its limitations."[28] The extra piece beyond intellectual curiosity and knowledge opens the door to becoming a believer.

Olson recognizes three aspects of this extra piece, three reasons for creationism's success:

- It arises from "zeal issuing in hard work."[29]
- It offers a fresh product for which a broad market clearly exists. For years, many Christians have felt suspicious of science because they think it tries to undermine their faith and its simplicity. Creation sci-

ence suggests they can hold to that naive biblical faith while at the same time subscribing fully to science. And,

- It speaks to what is happening in Western culture. Olson writes:

> One need not be a very perceptive observer of current [Western] society to discern the erosion of Christian behavioral standards. The opposition to Christian mores has moved from insidious to blatant, forcing a defensive posture on those who would style their lives according to biblical principles.[30]

Fundamentalism continues its success, and it grows more assured and aggressive. Tim LaHaye and Jerry Jenkins's apocalyptic novel, *Glorious Appearing*, came out in 2004 and concluded the Left Behind series, the best-selling adult books in the United States at the time. It portrays Jesus' second coming. Jesus returns to earth through the clouds riding mounted on a white horse, his eyes set with a "conviction like a flame of fire." He comes to judge and to punish. He speaks and the bodies of unbelievers in their millions eviscerate. "Men and women soldiers seemed to explode where they stood," the authors explain. "It was as if the very words of the Lord had superheated their blood, causing it to burst through their veins and skin. . . . Even as they struggled, their own flesh dissolved, their eyes melted, and their tongues disintegrated."[31] The book portrays Jesus as a masculine warrior vanguarding conservative Christians' assault on the secular society around them. They fight a war of culture, battles from the older issues over abortion, women's rights, and prayer in public schools, to more latterly over the Pledge of Allegiance and gay marriage.

Society has run amok behaviorally and ethically, fundamentalism proclaims, apparently bent on destroying itself. People all suffer as a result. Fundamentalists ascribe this to the godlessness of the world. They feel, therefore, they must disown society as it currently exists and stand against it. "They tend to think there are absolute truths, things that are unyielding for all time," says John Kenneth White.[32] "If abortion is wrong," comments Steven Thomma, "it is wrong for everyone. They see the world in morally absolute terms and want their values universally applied."[33] Their agenda is not, as one might at first suspect, the satisfaction of intellectual curiosity or even the conversion of people to Christianity; they want to transform society to how they envision it should be.

Fundamentalism and its progeny creationism firmly respond to society's problems, and so behind them stands widespread and vigorous support. It offers an impressive and probably the most successful religious response at present to society's problems.

It is also an inadequate, wrongheaded, and ill-fated response. Ruse describes the testimony of "the real scientists" at the Arkansas court hearing:[34]

> Francisco Ayala spoke on genetics, Harold Morowitz on the second law of thermodynamics, Stephen Gould on the fossil record, and Brent Dalrymple . . . gave an absolutely scintillating and lucid lecture on the dating of rocks . . . One could not listen to such experts without being aware of the strength and beauty of science, or of what a vile phenomenon scientific creationism really is, with its gross distortions of honest methodology. . . . One realized that good science in itself is to be cherished, along with the other noble products of the human mind. To have been in that court room when Ayala talked of his fruit flies or when Gould talked of his fossils was to have sensed vividly that it is those who would deny evolution who are anti-God, not those who affirm it. If God exists, he cannot possibly want [people] to turn [their] backs on reason and sense, ostrich-like burrowing [their] heads in the comforting but arid sands of Genesis.[35]

"In its isolation and inflexibility," writes Olson, creationism does "more harm than good."[36] With its exclusion of the Bible from debate and its attempt to fabricate a scientific medium, creation science offers "a poor strategy for a truly Christian impact on the world."[37]

Yet, fundamentalism addresses important things. Observers and thinkers should be aware of the problems and needs—social and religious—it tries to solve and fulfill. They should learn from its success. They should note its methods. Then they should devise better ways to solve and fulfill the same problems and needs. These better ways would hopefully lead to new religious movements that fulfill their proper social roles.

CONCLUSION

So rose and continues to rise the challenge of how to do theology today. Tradition versus modernity, biblical literalism versus science: who should direct society? Letting go of liberalism with its emphases on historical and personal transformation and social action, to crack creationism: how might theologians proceed? The death of neo-orthodoxy and existentialism as the primary modes of theology, and doing away with fundamentalism by meeting it on its own turf—these offer major opportunities.

Such a popularly credible and powerful approach to religion has yet to rise. How might scholars develop the beliefs and language of these religions-to-be so they adequately fill the same needs that fundamentalism answers and, at the same time, embrace, underpin, and help guide science and secular life? How to do theology forms part of this challenge. To devise a scientific way for doing theology, descriptive of reality outside of human beings and yet also helping to meet the pressing concerns of people's lives, this forms the agenda.

The critique of creationism leads to questions about the nature of theology, its subject matter, and authority. The religious and theological end is to explore God—first by honestly asking what God is—not to obey religious leaders. True security and assuredness lie in openness to life, not in following people. Theology ought to offer a vision of a full life lived under the true authority, that of objective reality. Society requires an exploring theology whose gaze encompasses everything and to which it subjects itself. Theology, that is, needs to follow a scientific method, and think of its language as descriptive and responsible to the world outside the human.

NOTES

1. See also Root-Bernstein 1981.
2. Ruse 1982: 317.
3. Ruse 1982: 319.
4. Ruse 1982: 317.
5. Charlesworth 1974: 3–4. See Kaufman 1975: chap. 1; MacCormac 1976: chap. 2.
6. Robinson 1964.
7. Ogden 1966; 1972a; 1972b.
8. Armstrong 2000: 178–79.
9. Charlesworth 1974: 4–11.
10. Charlesworth 1974: 5.
11. Charlesworth 1974: 5–6.
12. Charlesworth 1974: 8.

13. Charlesworth 1974: 9.
14. Charlesworth 1974: 10.
15. Charlesworth 1974: 11–14.
16. See, for example, Klein 1974.
17. Thorson 1968: 39. For summaries of critiques of the nondescriptive approach, see Pratt 1970: 37–45; Trigg 1973: chap. 4.
18. Thorson 1968: 36.
19. Barnhart 1976.
20. Thorson 1968: 28.
21. Thorson 1968: 39.
22. Cupitt 1981; Diamond 1975; Fawcett 1970: 88; Gilkey 1963; Pannenberg 1976: 327–28; Wiebe 1976: 40.
23. Barnhart 1976: 7–8.
24. Barnhart 1976: 8.
25. Barnhart 1976: 9.
26. Jastrow 1978. See also Morrow 1979.
27. Olson 1982: 28.
28. Olson 1982: 27–29.
29. Olson 1982: 29.
30. Olson 1982: 30.
31. Quoted in Kirkpatrick 2004: 1.
32. Quoted in Thomma 2004: 7A.
33. Thomma 2004: 7A.
34. Ruse 1982: 319.
35. Ruse 1982: 319.
36. Olson 1982: 30.
37. Olson 1982: 28.

Chapter Two

God the Outcast: Model Making

Science and modernity challenge theology methodologically: does authority lie in science or does it lie in tradition? If it lies in science, or partly in science, how might it allow room for the wisdom and experience that tradition encapsulates and requires?

For theology, this challenge to method leads to three interrelated questions:

1. What is the philosophical nature of theological language?
2. How does the idea "God" relate to the answer to (1)?
3. What method should theology employ given the answers to (1) and (2)?

Gordon Kaufman tries to answer these questions.

LEAVING HOME

Kaufman was born into a Mennonite household in Pennsylvania on April 1, 1920. His upbringing was in accord with his denomination's teachings. Though he excelled as a student, allowing his mind to soar, he did not escape his childhood influences. Rather, he grew from that base while incorporating what he still sees as its central points. He completed his formal education at Yale University as a Ph.D. student under H. Richard Niebuhr, a neo-orthodox theologian who had lived the religious fervor and opportunity of Karl Barth, first under the constrictions of Nazi Germany and then amid the openness of the United States. Niebuhr held to the belief that God is totally beyond everything: nothing physical, mental, or otherwise can approach God (an extrapolation and abstraction from the old cosmology in which God physically transcends the world and everything in it—a more extreme transcendence than what people normally observe). Yet Niebuhr also felt the need to see the work of God in the world in which he lived, especially in history. Niebuhr's influence on Kaufman seems considerable. Does authority lie with tradition (God totally beyond everything) or with life in the modern world? This tension pervades Kaufman's writings up until and beyond the period in which he wrote *An Essay on Theological Method*.[1]

After an initial teaching post at Pomona College near Los Angeles, Kaufman took up an appointment at Vanderbilt University, and from there he moved to Harvard Divinity School. He developed a reputation as a magnificent teacher with an inspirational vision, a keen intellect, a caring understanding and encouragement, and an ability to embed in students the movement of history. All these show in his *Essay*. His intellectual development appears to have involved the growth of his childhood Mennonite roots into a neo-orthodox systematic theology,[2] pruned back to its rudiments with a concomitant discarding of many details, and then redeveloped into a more socially accountable type of theology.

Kaufman's ideas continue to grow from the stage of his *Essay* in that he further explores the adequacy of theological models at promoting the drive toward humanization: justice, freedom, and equality. He also suggests recognizing the existence of an extrahuman force in the cosmos. This he calls "God" and says it works toward humans' humanization under the guise of "serendipity."[3] All the way through, however, rides the same understanding of the God-world relationship, namely, that, despite how people picture God, God in God's self lies totally beyond everything.

Kaufman draws a distinction in a 1972 book that helps further introduce his position.[4] He suggests there exists a real God totally beyond human understanding and control, and there also exists an available God, namely people's understanding of God, which they construct. No one can know anything about any connection that might exist between the real God and the available God. A skeptic might ask about the point of a real God. Why should a person start to consider a God who, for all intents and purposes, lies totally disconnected from humans and who makes no contact? To take the other extreme, if all that God is is what people think God is, what stops taking anything for God? Kaufman does answer the second question: if the Christian God is of interest, then Christian tradition provides guidelines for constructing a God image. The skeptic may continue and ask whether these guidelines indeed represent the most salient aspects of Christian belief. The debate may thus continue, and thus the issues Kaufman addresses open up.

KAUFMAN'S THEOLOGICAL METHOD

Kaufman's *Essay* attempts to describe the method by which a self-critical theologian might work.[5] Theology, for Kaufman, is a public activity of general significance that attempts to understand a people's faith and religious life. Trying to understand how a people's religious symbols function, theology criticizes, reinterprets, and reconstructs them and thus helps them to achieve their purposes more adequately.[6] Theology is a human endeavor.

The central idea of theology, the term that ties together all other theological ideas, is "God." All language uses, including those of the Church and theology, build on those of ordinary language, and so ordinary language becomes theological when the word "God" presides over it. Thus, suggests Kaufman, theology must start with the idea "God" and its use in ordinary language.[7] It can no longer base its thinking on some authoritatively given dogma or experience or revelation of God neatly tied up in a book.

How does ordinary language use the word "God"? Writes Kaufman: "The word 'God' appears to designate the last or ultimate point of reference to which all action, consciousness, and reflection can lead."[8] Ordinary language depicts God as the limit that nothing reaches. No one can experience and so connect with God because everything people experience is relative and God is absolute. Ordinary language does not merely claim humans can *never know everything* about God—as one person can never know everything about another person or, for that matter, as a person can never know everything about him or herself—but insists humans can *know nothing at all* about God. This forms the logical or formal function of the word.[9] Such an ultimate reference point is indispensable (though Western culture uses other unifying words as well, for instance, "matter") because it unifies the plurality of life.

Theology, according to Kaufman, constructs as opposed to describes. No one can perceive God as an object to describe because God lies beyond all the objects humans can perceive. Theologians can only assemble pictures of God. The same thing happens with the word "world." No one can experience and describe the world as an object, and so humans can only construct images of the world. Theologians must construct "world" and "God" but, Kaufman adds, they should do this subject to the words enabling humanization to happen in its fullness.[10] Kaufman continues this theme in the epilogue to his *Essay* by exploring the question of truth for theologies. He suggests theologians only have "pragmatic and humanistic" criteria for assessing theological claims:

> A theological construct may be regarded as true—in the only sense of "true" properly applicable here—if it in fact leads to a fruitful life, in the broadest and fullest and most comprehensive sense possible. [Theologians] can never jump out of [their] concept of the world, or of God, in order to see if the "real world" and the "real God" correspond to those concepts; [theologians] have no independent source of information about them which can provide a check on [their] ideas. The only [applicable] test . . . is to see how satisfactorily these ideas do the intellectual and cultural work for which they have been constructed.[11]

Kaufman proceeds to outline "three moments of theological construction," the order in which, he thinks, theologizing should proceed:[12]

1. The first step builds an idea of world, the whole (another important idea) of reality, using metaphors and models to depict the world as people feel it really is and yet something an idea "God" might limit.
2. The theologian's second step fills out the formal understanding of God (God as ultimate limit) with other models. Initially describing the relationship between God and world, this stage limits the already constructed idea of world. The idea of God must also have a "humanized and humanizing quality," something the initial idea "world" lacks.[13] Kaufman outlines five major considerations for developing an idea of God:

(a) the formal requirements of the relationship between the first and second movements of theological construction (God limiting the world);

(b) the human significance of the models used (their "religious power and moral implications");[14]

(c) the logical considerations of consistency and coherence;

(d) aesthetic concerns; and

(e) the "interests, problems and needs" of the situation within which the theologian works.[15]

3. The third step reformulates the idea "world" to make it fit intelligibly with the newly derived idea of God, producing a "theological world."

Two topics arising from Kaufman's *Essay* need exploring: the way he chooses his starting point for theology, and the content of his starting point. These considerations lead to revising his suggestions for how to do theology.

THE THEOLOGICAL STARTING POINT

Kaufman bases his theological method on his assumption of God's absolute otherness. This needs investigating from a number of vantage points, starting with how he selects his starting point for theology.

Revelation, Dogma, and Religious Experience

Kaufman suggests starting theology with the word "God." Theology cannot start with what some people consider the revelation God gave to them (though it may conclude with this and may admit this as more important) or the dogmas of what some consider God's Church, for all these presuppose the idea "God." Neither can theology start with religious experience, Kaufman adds, for language undergirds and molds all experience; to start with religious experience presupposes ideas whose meanings and uses need scrutinizing beforehand. Experience— especially new experience—acts, rather, as the last court of appeal or testing ground for theology, since the meaning of ideas comes to the fore in the way they shape and interpret experience. Theology must start, Kaufman insists, with the word "God."[16]

However, someone might interject, discussion on the nature of God for those who want to start with revelation, dogma, or experience does not necessarily go round in circles—confirming or writing large their ideas of God—because they can find their notions lacking and in need of revision. They could suggest, moreover, that their "God" ideas, though they inherited them from culture and language, derive historically from revelation or experiences of God. They merely use and assume ideas whose use and meaning previous generations gleaned from their own religious experience or revelation.

Regardless of such possibilities, Kaufman suggests that to begin with revelation or religious experience or dogma presupposes the idea "God" and, therefore, theologians should start theology by seeking to understand "God." Kaufman further suggests theology start particularly with the way ordinary language uses "God." The meaning of a word derives from its usual use. Kaufman assumes this philosophical position, but that is not all he believes. He also accepts a rational approach to doing theology, even to considering questions of method. These examples illustrate that Kaufman makes assumptions at a level similar to those of people whose starting points compete with his.

Everyone begins with assumptions. Kaufman's may make more sense for the current scientific age because they seem more secular than those of a person who starts with revelation or religious experience or Church dogma. However, proponents of this relative judgment craft their position from what they assume.

Choosing the Meaning of "God"

Suppose the idea "God" does found theology and that ordinary language does provide the word's use (Western Christian theologians seek to develop their own word "God"; how other cultures and traditions use their equivalent terms is not of interest at this point). Kaufman then suggests the content of this normal use: the word "God," he says, functions as a limiting word, unifying all experience by acting as its ground and unapproachable point of reference.[17] This meaning lies, he thinks, at the center of the modern Western use of the word "God."

Kaufman previously tried other ways to justify this as an intelligible starting point and core meaning for "God." One employs the concrete experiences of being limited—especially people's inner selves as personal and hidden realities—as an analogy he generalizes into "God."[18] Michael McLain, Kai Nielsen, and Don Wiebe criticize this because they think Kaufman includes an unintelligible dualism in his notion of self and that this automatically leads to his idea of God as the ultimate limit.[19] In the later *Essay*, Kaufman tries yet another angle to justify the idea of God as the ultimate limit, namely that of ordinary language use. In an even more recent paper, he just says God's absolute otherness is fundamental to Christian use, without justifying and defending this requirement for future understandings.[20]

Why should someone accept that ordinary language assumes Kaufman's suggested use of "God"? Why should a person accept this one as opposed to another, say, God as the "Supreme Being, Creator, and Ruler of [the] Universe"?[21] Alternatively, perhaps the word "God" points out that all will be well in the end, that the loving and caring forces impinging on humans are stronger than the hurting and hating forces. By what criteria did Kaufman make his choice? Perhaps he has a special insight. Alternatively, perhaps he asked millions of people what they think the word "God" means or how they use the word, and then averaged out the replies.

Furthermore, why should Kaufman select a logical function (God as the ultimate limit)—and a seemingly empty one at that—as opposed to a material function (God as hope, for instance), as if only the former exists or has precedence in ordinary language? Functions do not appear so special that he needs to reject all meanings.

It is insufficient for Kaufman just to say "the ultimate limit" constitutes the ordinary use of the word "God." He needs further criteria and analysis for selecting some use or meaning for ordinary "God" language. Perhaps he really selects it for historical reasons (Barthian correction against nineteenth-century liberalism), or because he finds it the basic use of the word in his experience and development as a theologian. Perhaps finding a core meaning is too difficult. Whatever his real reasons, waving the magic wand "ordinary language use" will not necessarily produce his desired golden carriage.

Anyway, it may not help if Kaufman were to specify how he selects the basic use or meaning of the word "God" from usual discourse because one common way may not exist. Some people think of God as life itself, while others see God as a being outside space and time. Different people may mean and use the word "God" in different ways, yet all related as family resemblances along the lines Ludwig Wittgenstein suggests for the word "game."[22] No ideas or uses need be in common to all instances of the word "God."

Suppose further that one usual use or meaning of the word "God" is "life." God as life does not offer an absolute limit, is not beyond everything, because it does not limit life. Not all usual uses may presuppose "God" as the ultimate limit.

Kaufman might object that life is not the God he means but some other god (as with the gods of other religions and ideologies) and that he really wants to refer to the God of the Western Christian tradition. He has guidelines for deciding what idea of God he considers relevant or adequate. These guidelines mean he has another basis for theology. If the criteria for the other "God"-deciding basis have to do with tradition or the Bible (defining, say, hubris and idolatry),[23] then the contents of revelation and tradition become part of theology's starting point. Kaufman's starting point for theology involves more than the ordinary use of "God" because he has to decide which ordinary use he will use.

Does "God" Unify Life?

Kaufman suggests people's lives need a unifier, that they must have one, and that mainly the idea "God" has functioned this way. This is why the word "God" in ordinary language acts as the ultimate limit. Because theologians seek to do theology for modern Westerners and so discuss their present use of language, it seems appropriate to ask if an idea exists that does unify the lives of the majority of modern Westerners and, if so, whether this idea is "God." Perhaps people do need such a unifier; but do most people have one?

If they do have a life unifier, the majority of modern Westerners do not have the same one, but rather often use "me," or money, or matter, or death, and not "God." Those people who feel religious enough to use the word "God" in a nonprofane and deeply meaningful way often find their lives in different sections, disunited: the secular portion of life and the religious.[24] Neither do all people consider it good or necessary to unify life.[25] Despite Kaufman's desire, the word "God" does not function "most frequently" as "the reality in which all life and meaning is grounded."[26]

Even if "God" did unify people's lives, that does not mean the word "God" functions for them as an ultimate limit. Kaufman suggests "matter" could act as the foundation for everything,[27] but this does not limit all in the way he suggests "God" ought to. A unifier does not necessarily limit everything.

Room for Change

Suppose theologians do accept this logical function of the word "God" as the basis for theology, something they derive from the use of the word in ordinary language. What room then exists for change (especially change that theology instigates and guides) in the use and meaning of the word? Alternatively, does change take place in the more material aspects of the word, ones that theology adds at the later constructive stages?

Further, logic is relative; quantum mechanical logic differs from Euclidean logic, for example. "God" as the logical procedure of limiting everything is thus also relative. Kaufman's prescriptive starting point does not necessarily form an absolute that stands for all time; it is as relative as the other positions he seeks to surpass. To prescribe such a thing as eternally basic to theology may just ensure the theology's replacement later on.

Kaufman may feel that, with this logical function, he isolates something unquestionable and essential about the idea of God.[28] Hopefully not. Hopefully, the theologian can creatively suggest new meanings and uses even for the foundational use of the word and especially for its ordinary use. Theologians may need to suggest new uses and meanings that go beyond any usual use. Moreover, if the word "God" does not function universally as a unifier—as it perhaps used to—maybe the time has come to grow into new uses of the word, ones that allow for unification, and perhaps ones that do not require "God" as the ultimate limit. Does Kaufman's scheme allow for this? Or does he forever tie theology to his perception of the word "God"?

The Starting Point to the Rest of the Scheme

The remainder of Kaufman's discussion on theological method—his metatheology that one might hope would be independent of theological stance—depends on the idea of "God" as ultimate limit. For instance, he sees the bulk of his method—his "three moments of theological construction"—as the building of two notions: an idea "world" that "God" radically limits, and an idea "God" that can act as a radical limit. His meaning of the phrase "theology as construction" is not merely the obvious "theology as a process of creating models and metaphors," or theology as a "human and public activity."[29] To cite another example, he says theology cannot describe because God lies beyond all and is not a perceivable, describable object; theology, therefore, only constructs, and the court of appeal for "God" constructions finally rests on the sense that they make of life and the sort of life they encourage. Kaufman's theological method depends on his understanding of God.

Perhaps it should not come as a surprise that Kaufman's understanding of how to do theology rests on his theological assumptions, trimmed down to the naked bones. Perhaps it should not come as a surprise in the case of any theologian that her or his understanding of how to do theology rests on her or his theological assumptions. Theologians probably cannot escape making some such commitments, especially on a core word like "God," and their respective theological methodologies depend on these. Thus, if theologians feel, as many probably do, that what Kaufman takes as essential for the word "God" is in fact true, they may well like to follow Kaufman's prescription for theological method. Some may doubt Kaufman's assumption and so not want to pursue this approach. A question that remains, therefore, concerns the basis for deciding on such commitments; theologians need to choose the "best" relative idea for their basic theological assumption and starting point. How to understand "best" offers the greatest challenge.

KAUFMAN'S UNDERSTANDING OF GOD

Kaufman's theological starting point faces problems beyond the way he tries to find it; the idea he chooses itself raises several questions.

Limiting the Limit

Kaufman suggests the word "God" functions to limit all ideas. Presumably, this use of the word would also act to limit itself; what does it mean to say the idea "God" limits the notion that "the idea 'God' limits all ideas"? This equates to criticism of Barth's insistence on God being beyond all human knowledge, and yet this itself constitutes knowledge of God. Kaufman does recognize this logical incoherence in the idea of God's radical transcendence (after Georg Hegel and others), but continues to promote it.[30] Is it appropriate to accept something logically incoherent?

This rule governing the function or use of the word "God" (God as the ultimate limit) differs radically, in Kaufman's mind, from the word's meaning and content. He uses this distinction to avoid working through the incoherence because it requires, he thinks, a gulf between material ideas and formal ideas, restrictions on the material not applying to the formal. Is this excuse acceptable?

Kaufman unclearly differentiates the terms "material" and "formal." He says the formal God notion he isolates does not really say "*what* God is at all; rather it provides . . . a rule that [theologians] are advised to use in trying to think of [God]." He elaborates on this:

> In the search for God [humans] must always press on, never resting content with what [they] have discovered or expressed. . . . Whenever [people] suppose that God has become directly available to [them] or is in some way (even intellectually) disposable by [them], [they] can be certain it is . . . not God.[31]

This formal notion appears in other places, however, as more a content of the word than a rule by which theologians ought to treat all notions of God: "The word 'God' appears to designate the last or ultimate *point* of reference to which all action, consciousness and reflection can lead."[32] Kaufman has not fully separated the formal from the material.

The distinction between the material and formal aspects of the word "God" lacks warrant and the two may overlap. Thus, the formal or logical procedure of God as the ultimate limit faces the criticism of the material aspects of the idea "God." This, as seen above, creates confusion if not incoherence.

Perhaps this points to the inadequacy of the limiting process and it needs removing or replacing. Hugh Jones suggests, rather than making the formal statement that God is ultimately "a mysterious and unknowable X," that theologians might more correctly say they have "no tools for this task" of knowing about God.[33] Jones does not go far enough, as the rest of this book will elaborate: everything humans perceive is ultimately mysterious and unknowable, but people do have tools for knowing something about every one of them, including God.

The Real and Available God

Prior to his *Essay*, several of Kaufman's papers and one of his books, *God the Problem*, posed the issue concerning God in a pair of terms he coins, the "real" God, and the "available" God.[34] The available God comprises what people know of God, and the real God is in principle unknowable because this God must limit even ideas of God.[35]

This suggestion of Kaufman's draws a deal of criticism:

- Thomas Idinopulos asks how the real, hidden God relates to the available and acting God. "How do [people] know that the God [they] find in [their] experience is the real God who acts, and not a false God of [their] own construction?"[36]
- Paul Sponheim suggests Kaufman does isolate a connection between the real and the available God, because, for instance, the distinction between them depends on a covert appeal to the real God. He suggests this connection needs developing.[37]
- Alvin Porteous thinks Kaufman sees the relationship between the real God and the available God as a postulate of faith that people can verify only by how well it promotes humanization.[38] No objective way exists to determine the relationship.[39]
- Jones caps it all by saying Kaufman's distinction is "not only 'highly dialectical . . .'; it is downright confusing."[40]

Kaufman's attempt to conceive of God as an ultimate limit through the ideas of the real and available God therefore falters.

Theological Language as Not Descriptive

Kaufman's theological starting point faces a third collection of problems. If theological language does not describe, if the available God does not relate to the real God, how can theologians talk about truth in a theological context? To say that one theological idea is more truthful than is another surely equates, at least in some people's minds, to considering it a more accurate description of divine reality. Kaufman attempts to face the question of the home of truth with a specific understanding of the reality of God.

Kaufman's position could build up this way. People often use language in an objective manner; if they use a noun or an adjective, they usually assume the referent (whether a quality, physical object, or psychological state) has objective existence. They use language accordingly. This appears justified with such words as chair and hair, even if people do not perceive all they might perceive about a chair or a hair. It becomes questionable when referring to a person: does a personality have an objective existence? This problem becomes more apparent with talk of God because, Kaufman reflects, many uses of such words lack a referent. People nevertheless use language as if a personality and God have objective existence. Because they readily use some language referentially ("a glass in the cupboard," "I speak to Leslie"), people feel surprise when, on reflection, they realize they may not directly perceive any referents to some religious statements ("Our Father in Heaven," "I pray to God"). The use of language produces the feeling that a real, objectively existing God exists somewhere and somehow. The question of the real God, then, rises as an automatic response to language use.

That response, however, is wrong according to Kaufman. "Real," when referring to God, means something else than what normally is meant. In Kaufman's opinion, talk about God refers to religious ways of life. Theologians ought to find the proper meaning of the word in the sociological and psychological spheres. To talk of God as the most real of all things therefore means the "God" way of living defines and constitutes true-life reality for the believer.[41]

The word "world" (which includes the idea of "whole") works in a similar way, writes Kaufman. The world supposedly has an objective existence, but humans cannot perceive it. Is it infinite or finite in extent? Did it have a beginning in time?[42] A person cannot properly ask these questions, Kaufman suggests (along the lines of Immanuel Kant), let alone answer them. Theologians ought not to consider the world an object of perception. Modern physical cosmology, however, does ask and answer such matters: gravity and the paths light takes define the edges of space, and the beginning of the world occurred with the cosmic explosion as in the big bang theories. Despite Kaufman's hesitation, humans can and do gain knowledge of the "whole" from inside the world. Anyway, one could ask whether people experience anything—not only the world—as a whole, or do they only experience parts or aspects of it? The answer is they experience both the whole and the parts, and the parts relate to the whole. Humans thus do know the world as an object despite its inclusion of the idea "whole."

Effects on Believers

Kaufman's approach sees God language as functional and not descriptive. The chief inadequacy of this approach perhaps lies, as the introduction pointed out, in its injustice to the idea of God's involvement in the world. God is not God if God is not involved in the world moment by moment. Thus, Schubert Ogden thinks theologians ought to respect the believers' belief in an objectively existing God.[43] The God they think they know—their available God—is, for them, really real, has objective existence, is the real God. They know this from their belief in or experience of God's actions in the world. Not that a theology must include everything a pew sitter believes. Rather, if anything lies at the core of the idea "God," it is that God is real, meaning God acts in the world. A theology must uphold this for it to operate adequately.

Moreover, if people took to heart the complete inadequacy or incorrectness of what they know of God, they may feel less inclined to comply with the moral code associated with God. Perhaps this explains why, with people less and less believing in the traditional "God" as a forceful reality, proportionally fewer people nowadays hold to the traditional Christian morality this God stands for and that founds mainstream churches. If theologies aim to uphold a certain morality, the image of God they provide probably ought to depict God as real. (Though, as later discussions will point out, morality need not require religion or belief in a god.)

Prescribing a Description

Theologians no longer claim God literally sits on a throne in the heavens or causes wind to blow. These changes in the understanding of God describe a historical development in theology. How much of past God talk was wrong? Current theological anarchy seems especially due to the fall in the objectivity of such symbols as "God" and the thaw in that firm base for theology.[44] What can theologians rightly say now of God? Kaufman refuses to recognize any God language as objective truth or to acknowledge that "God" refers to an objective reality. Following a description of theological change, he prescribes that the God people conceive of cannot be the real God, that God totally outstrips all God ideas. Kaufman takes a description of the theological process by which theological ideas have proved inadequate and makes it a prescription for theology. It becomes the starting point for Kaufman and not something he observes along the way.

Proclaimed persuasively without proper historical context, Kaufman's prescription can also too easily place absolute authority in the hands of those who claim to know God's will.

This descriptive to prescriptive move by Kaufman follows a more widespread tendency. Earl MacCormac, for instance, requests scholars no longer take all their (metaphorical) theories as literal truth—in his terminology, as myths—because this hinders the consideration of new hypotheses. He thinks scholars can take certain of them, however, as literal truth: namely, those theories that have passed into ordinary language, have thorough empirical support, and have lost all their tentativeness.[45] Unlike Kaufman, MacCormac does not transform his description into a blanket prescription.

To recognize the inadequacies of taking theological language as objective need not mean prescribing no God language as objective. An intermediate path exists, one that acknowledges objective theological language as inadequate, but asserts the greater adequacy of some objective language over others. Theologians can admit the inadequacy of their descriptions without going to the extreme of denying the possibility of any description.

ANOTHER WAY OF KNOWING FOR THEOLOGY

Kaufman's solution to the demise and inadequacies of past theological objectiveness attempts to preserve God's transcendence unsullied by the secular world's critique and its compromised ideals and gray values. His theology overreacts overcautiously to feeling proved wrong once again. On the other hand, like the schemes he rejects, his also falls short. Perhaps Kaufman does not offer the only solution, or, in fact, even an adequate solution. Perhaps God does not absolutely transcend everything.

This problem for theology parallels the one that philosophy of science faces and to which MacCormac's proposal refers. Scholars used to believe scientific theories accurately describe the actual nature of external reality. Extreme counterpositions state that scientific theories define reality and no independent objective criteria or standards exist to adjudicate the accuracy of theories; science does not describe objective reality but, rather, only elaborates systems of ideas. Kaufman reflects this subjectivist swing.

Against these extreme positions, mediating moves point to the existence of an objective reality that theories in some way describe. Humans can in part analyze and describe this objective world scientifically; the world to some measure stands independent of theories and allows for communication and judgment between them. Yet people cannot—and never will—totally delineate the world. This philosophical position thus also acknowledges the role of subjectivity in scientific knowledge. Sometimes called "critical realism," it says science is to an extent objective and to an extent subjective. Science describes reality, but the description partly involves the describer. The degrees of objectivity and subjectivity remain unknown and open to debate.[46]

Theology used to think it simply describes God, albeit incompletely. In reaction to such simplicity, Kaufman prescribes the God conceived of cannot in any way be the real God. God infinitely outstrips "God" ideas. The same in fact applies to any person or any facet of the world because ideas of each referent have changed and it outstrips notions of it. People ought to believe they can both describe it—claiming objectivity for the description—and acknowledge the subjectivity. Theologians should do the same in theology. In particular, theology needs to regain against Kaufman a more objective and descriptive approach to God language as philosophy of science has done for language about physical reality. Theology could then say "God" acts as the ultimate reference point without also the need to say God lies beyond description.

The problem Kaufman highlights is an aspect of the relationship between experiences and linguistic ideas, between what people feel as real and what they know. Kaufman justifiably suggests experience depends on language; it does not exist in the raw ready for humans to put into words. People do not come in contact with the real God but rather, says Kaufman, if they do encounter God, they do so with the available God. Yet an independent reality exists that molds experiences and leads to the search for new language or forms of expression for them. The available God depends on the real God. The relationship between language and experience does not follow totally one way or the other, totally objective or totally subjective. The relationship is very complex and scholars have no clear and adequate overall model for it.

CONCLUSION

Kaufman's theological method suggests theologians start by construct-ing a model for the world and then, second, a model for God in which God utterly qualifies the world. Kaufman's third step reconstructs the "world" model so qualified. He thus reacts to the empiricist challenge introduced in the previous chapter by safeguarding theology and the real God with a chasm between "God" and "world." This makes theol-ogy nonfactual in relation to the real God. Rather, for Kaufman, theol-ogy ought to judge its "God" ideas on their ability to encourage the hu-manization of the world.

The sense of the absolute transcendence of God—not a regular type of transcendence where God somehow exceeds the universe, but an ab-solute one where humans can know nothing at all of God—pushes God completely out of reach. It creates an incoherent dualism. Not only does it constitute an inherent contradiction (to know that no one can know anything of God is, in fact, to know something of God), but it also wipes away the immediacy and relevance and spirituality of God—which well-functioning religion and moral direction for people's everyday and broader cultural lives require. Kaufman's method for finding a starting point for theology, plus his starting point or basic theistic idea itself, both seem to falter.

Kaufman started his theological journey in the neo-orthodox school with its traditional beliefs, a sense of the utmost transcendence of God, and the separation of theology from science. When he wrote his *Essay*, he had rejected much of the first but retained the others, the second espe-cially shining through. He bravely faces telling and cutting objections to theological language and the weakening and confusing torrent of theo-logical claims. However, theology needs a different solution than his to this confrontation; this problem needs resolving without thinking, as he does, that the real God lies utterly beyond all language and description. True, theologians have yet adequately to understand the relationship be-tween God and the universe, but they need not give up on it. Perhaps they can maintain the belief in the objective existence of a perceivable God and yet answer the problems that cause Kaufman to abandon this approach. Whatever it does, theology must hold ideas of God fully responsible to the life people experience and to the world in which they experience it. That offers the chief challenge behind developing this *Science of God*.

This consideration of Kaufman's *Essay* results in the following matters that the next chapters on theological methods need to bear in mind and elaborate:

1. The constructive nature of theology; theology creates and evaluates models and metaphors.
2. The hub symbol "God" forms the starting point for theology; theology begins by examining and constructing the idea "God."
3. Criteria exist for assessing theologies including the basic notion chosen for "God."
4. A tension exists between theology's subjective nature and its objectively regarding something called "God," between the possibility of its describing God and the impossibility of its describing God. It falls into neither extreme.

These points emerge from the discussion of three questions for theological method that the beginning of this chapter raised:

1. What is the philosophical nature of theological language?
2. How does the idea "God" relate to the answer to (1)?
3. What method should theology employ given the answers to (1) and (2)?

In response:

- Theological language describes the same way scientific language describes; this answers question (1).
- It does this using the idea "God," which it assumes has a referent; this answers (2).
- Theology constructs theories subject to certain criteria—theology should follow a method closely analogous to science's—in part answers (3).

How can theology be descriptive in a scientific way? The next chapter looks at possible answers to this, showing where they falter and where they shine.

NOTES

1. Kaufman 1975: xii.
2. Kaufman 1968.
3. Kaufman 1976: 101–4. See also Idinopulos 1972: 721; Kaufman 1993.
4. Kaufman 1972.
5. Kaufman 1975. The reactions to it below first appeared as Sharpe 1979.
6. Kaufman 1975: x–xi, 1–8.
7. Kaufman 1975: 8–11.
8. Kaufman 1975: 11.
9. Kaufman 1975: 11–15.
10. Kaufman 1975: 19–38.
11. Kaufman 1975: 72.
12. Kaufman 1975: 41–64.
13. Kaufman 1975: 52.
14. Kaufman 1975: 55.
15. Kaufman 1975: 55.
16. Kaufman 1975: 1–8.
17. Kaufman 1975: 11–15.
18. See the various articles in Kaufman 1972.
19. McLain 1969; Nielsen 1973c: 73–84; Wiebe 1974a. Kaufman 1972: xiii–xviii replies to McLain, and in a measure agrees.
20. Kaufman 1978.
21. *Concise Oxford Dictionary.*
22. Wittgenstein 1968: 31e–32e.
23. Kaufman 1975: 48.
24. See Cupitt 1975; 1976: chap. 8.
25. Miller 1974.
26. Kaufman 1975: 14.
27. Kaufman 1975: 13.
28. Campbell 1974: 3–4.
29. See Kaufman 1975: x; 1976: 90.
30. Kaufman 1972: 16.
31. Kaufman 1975: 49.
32. Kaufman 1975: 11; emphasis added.
33. Jones 1978: 94; see Kaufman 1972: 150.
34. Kaufman 1972.
35. Kaufman 1972: 86. See also p. 113.
36. Idinopulos 1972.
37. Sponheim 1975.

38. See Kaufman 1975: epilogue; 1976.
39. Porteous 1973.
40. Jones 1978: 95. See also Griffin 1973: 555–58; Runzo 1975: 686–87.
41. Kaufman 1975: 55–56.
42. Kaufman 1975: 22.
43. Ogden 1966: 38–43.
44. Kaufman 1975: 35–37.
45. MacCormac 1976.
46. See Barbour 1974: chap. 6; Cushing, Delaney, and Gutting 1984; Peacocke 1984.

Chapter Three

God Removed:
Challenges from an Extreme

The logical positivists (perhaps the best known in this context being Antony Flew) slapped the empiricist gauntlet in the face of theology. Since the early 1960s, Kai Nielsen has championed persistently and imaginatively a milder but related crusade against religion and its theology, attempting not only to draw up the rules of battle, but also to spar with many heroes of the theological cause.

The challenge to theology is this: a theistic assertion cannot have factual significance or meaning unless someone can stipulate what would make the assertion probably true and probably false, what would experientially confirm or infirm the assertion. While weaker than the extreme logical-positivist demand (which talked about the need for truth rather than meaning), Nielsen's still slices with a lengthy edge. It requires of theologians that they not talk empty air, not use words posing as statements of experiential fact—words perhaps full of subjective meaning and significance but void of anything factually confirmable or infirmable. The theologies of such people as Karl Barth, Rudolf Bultmann, and Paul Tillich grate away in the back of his mind.

The challenge is thus one of a secular-scientific society to a belief system whose norms of meaning and truth vary from it. Nielsen is not a historical relic from the recent past. His ideas tie with the "death of God" response of the 1960s that claimed the prevailing theologies had no experiencible referent. Nielsen's concerns also reflect the challenge to religion that lead to the explosion of charismatic, Pentecostal, and fundamentalist movements: experientially vivid or apparently factually founded, these forces claim confirmable or infirmable verities. Their armies claim undeniable certainties. They are, unfortunately, wrong. Nielsen's challenge is vitally important to theology for it inextricably to live and proclaim within contemporary society. To communicate adequately to the secular-scientific world, theology must adopt modernity's standards of meaning and truth rather than spit in its face.

Being empirical lies at the heart of science. While room exists to debate what "empirical" means or the philosophical assumptions it entails, a theological method must be empirical if it wishes to be scientific and to communicate adequately. This book therefore concerns empiricism's challenge to theology and theology's attempts to meet and deal with it. This chapter develops a collection of empirical questions to ask of proposals for theological method in the light of science.

Empiricism for religious language covers a large area crisscrossed by an incoherent collection of networks of debates, too complex to categorize simply. Enter Nielsen, handily, as a guide. His championing the empiricist challenge to theology raises a large number of questions that theology ought to heed if it wishes to develop an empirical method; his prolific publications probably cover every skeptical attack in the debate. To study Nielsen's writings and those of his protagonists also charts the wide variety of island-like theological positions in their reaction to, and fate before, the whirlwind of secular critique. His guidance may ensure a comprehensive coverage.

Nielsen feels strongly about church and religion, going right to the jugular with his sleeves rolled up and fingering through the surgical gloves of philosophical analysis. This chapter's selecting him as its guide places confidence in an ardent atheist determined to do his damnedest against religious language in as wide a range of questions as possible; if this book's methodological proposal can satisfactorily answer him, it successfully submits its ideas to one of the most critical attacks that anyone might mount against it. What he says contains some truth.

This chapter thus surveys Nielsen's attacks on theology and thereby lists the relevant questions he might ask of a theological method. It uses his statements of others' positions, rather than their own, because it aims to draw out his argument so as better to confront it. Structurally, it comprises outlines of his view of and challenge to religious language, responses that attack the way he poses the challenge, and efforts to answer the challenge either by redefining religious language with a hope to avoid it or by confronting it with a direct answer. Max Charlesworth divides approaches to the secular critique into two camps, depending on their philosophical attitude to religious language: whether they are descriptive or nondescriptive. The discussion below will use this tool. Nielsen insists religious language must be descriptive to remain true to its claim of factual significance; he finds, however, that it does not succeed.

NIELSEN'S CHALLENGE

The process of secularization produces gradual social and ideational change. Empiricism, as part of this, becomes more and more embedded into Western culture, aspects of it feeling very persuasive. Reflective and critical common sense has incorporated it; "it enters," Nielsen writes, "into the underlying, sometimes unwitting, assumptions of more and more people."[1] Its challenge to theology originated well before the contemporary empiricists.[2] One of them, Flew, finally broke open the door and released it, as a mature bull, into the china shop of religious language (plus theological language and philosophy of religion).[3] Nielsen seizes Flew's challenge and rides it, cape billowing, into the debate.[4] He writes:

> Imagine two past friends, a believer and a skeptic, standing together aboard ship on a starry night. The believer remarks to his friend, "How can you really deny that God made all this?" The skeptic replies that awe-inspiring and vast as it is, he cannot see the hand of God in it. "From a human point of view," the skeptic continues, "perfections as well as imperfections and order as well as disorder exist in nature, but [no one has] reason to say that God created or ordained it all." Whatever the believer points to as evidence for God's creative activity, the skeptic interprets naturalistically. On closer observation they seem to use different terminology to describe the same phenomena. Finally, an observer of this discussion begins to wonder if anything more than a purely verbal and attitudinal difference separate the believer and his skeptical friend.[5]

Skeptics and believers use different words to describe the same things. Is the difference between them only in their attitudes and choice of words?

If so, Nielsen concludes, the believers' claims lack "factual and cosmological significance" and become merely talk "about natural phenomena in a high-toned manner."[6] Such clauses as "Time can flow back-
wards," and "People can feel unconscious pain," cannot elicit a "yea or
nay" because no one can know whether or not the supposed statements
are true or false, because no one can understand what the speaker of the
clauses wants to assert. To understand such clauses as statements requires understanding what would minimally support or contradict their
falsity or their truth.[7] The same holds for religious language.

Nielsen thus suggests that the most pressing problem for religious
language is to understand how statements like "God exists," "God has
a plan for the universe," "God grounds human existence," or "God
loves humanity and designed the world" may have factual meaning.
Theistic sentences such as these appear to form factual assertions, "vast
cosmological assertions," and believers use them as such.[8] An assertion,
however, must have something that could count for its truth or falsity.
Do these theistic statements thereby operate as assertions? This forms
the nub of the debate. A religious claim, a would-be assertion, needs a
potential empirical anchor to distinguish between the conditions that
might justify it and those that might not.[9] Nielsen rewrites Flew's challenge as the following:

> Believers regard certain of their very central religious claims—claims
> upon which the rest depend—as factual statements; but if they actually
> are factual, then [it must be possible] . . . to describe two states both of
> which have distinct empirical content, one of which actually obtains when
> the religious statement is true, the other when it is false. . . . [In other
> words], if a certain empirically determinable condition obtains, the state-
> ment is true, if another such condition obtains, it is false. If [it is not pos-
> sible to] conceive of any such conditions, then the putative factual reli-
> gious statement in question is neither true nor false. Flew challenges the
> believer to state these conditions of confirmation or disconfirmation.[10]

The same holds for nonbelievers. "If you think of yourself as an atheist or as an agnostic try this experiment on yourself: what conceivable
turn of observable events, if only you [could] . . . observe them, would
make you say you" got it wrong or probably got it wrong when you de-
nied or doubted a God does or probably does exist?[11] Nonbelievers
probably cannot answer the question; neither can believers when asked

about evidence for God's existence. "God exists" and "God does not exist" both fit the same evidence. Even worse, they both fit all conceivable experiences.[12] This robs both God claims and their denials of factual meaning. To deny nothing factually asserts nothing factually. (This example also raises the question of the line Nielsen draws between theism and atheism. What would count as an appropriate use of the word "God" and what would not? Would Nielsen's case work against any or all of the uses of "God" that traditional believers would reject?)[13]

Nielsen and Flew's challenge differs from that of the strict logical positivists and empiricists, though it formally arises from their philosophical context.[14] Unlike logical positivism, it does not assert conclusive confirmation or infirmation as the primary requirement, and therefore does not automatically preclude the right of certain words, such as the metaphysical and religious, to remain in language. Nielsen, in fact, shuns the arbitrariness he feels in this approach.[15] He thinks the criterion of factual meaningfulness and intelligibility, as in Flew's challenge, more aptly applies to sentences that purport to be factual. Thus he asks "what it would be like for [a theological] assertion to be true or probably true and what it would be like for the assertion to be false or probably false."[16]

Several pairs of terms appear in the various stipulations of Nielsen's criterion. Gary Colwell outlines and then summarizes them by saying that, in Nielsen's eyes, a theistic assertion becomes factually meaningful only if it is possible, at least in principle, to

1. show what its truth or probable truth, and its falsity or probable falsity would entail, or
2. see that it opens itself to experiential confirmation or disconfirmation, or
3. confirm or infirm it, or
4. state what would happen if it were true, or
5. specify empirical conditions that count for and some that count against its truth, or
6. verify or falsify it in a weak sense.[17]

Nielsen appears to prefer the wording of (3), that a theistic assertion makes a factual statement if in principle a person can confirm or infirm it.

Nielsen's criterion of meaningfulness relates closely to the requirement that chapter 1 provides: "To devise a scientific way for doing theology, descriptive of reality outside of human beings and yet also helping to meet the pressing concerns of people's lives, this forms the agenda." Factual meaningfulness equates to large measure with relevance for a secular person.

Theological assertions fail the test for factual meaning, Nielson decides. Consider the statement, "God works out God's purposes through history and nature." Theists make it compatible with anything, everything, or nothing that has happened or could happen in history and nature; they do not allow anything to count against their basic religious claims because they make them fit any state of affairs.[18] Theological claims, therefore, do not qualify as assertions. Theologians should thus not claim them to be matters of fact, as they spuriously do. Only a verbal and an attitudinal difference distinguishes a sophisticated believer and a skeptic, Nielsen concludes, like the person from the United States calling an elevator what someone from England terms a lift.[19]

Nielsen does not question the truthfulness of theism, the evidence for or against a theistic assertion. Rather, his interest lies in the logically prior question of whether theistic assertions have factual meaning, intelligibility, coherence—whether they make sense as proposed statements. If they do not have factual meaning, the questioner cannot try to find out if they are true or not, even if they fulfill some other function in language. Nielsen thus finds fault with the thoughts of Paul Ziff; for Ziff, the theology of the theist is intelligible but wrong because the idea of God's omnipotence conflicts with physics, whereas for Nielsen it is not even intelligible.[20]

Nielsen raised a storm in the 1960s and 1970s by publishing innumerable articles, papers, and books attacking theologies. He especially singled out liberal positions that adhere to a semblance of tradition or else try to justify themselves in the face of the empiricist challenge. Much of his argument and polemic he aimed at undermining theistic responses. The "whole religious weltanschauung," according to his "whopping thesis," builds "a house of cards" because its cornerstone beliefs "are unintelligible, incoherent, irrational, or false"; religious people who recognize this behave "very irrational[ly] . . . something [they] ought not to do."[21] He believes people do not need religion: "no moral or human need, let alone necessity . . . [requires] a nonevasive and informed person . . . to have religious commitments of any kind."[22] All thinking people should become humanists.[23]

Nevertheless, Nielsen attracted the attention of a multitude of theologians. Their engaging him testifies that his motivation as a dogmatic atheist fails to obviate his argument.

NIELSEN'S ASSUMPTIONS ABOUT RELIGIOUS LANGUAGE

Nielsen starts from the logic of Flew's challenge, but he also carries with him a number of explicit assumptions concerning his targets and the nature of religious language.

Which Religion and Which Theism

First, his interest lies in the chief religions of his culture: Judaism, Christianity, and Islam. "It is not that I believe that these religious forms of life are superior to other religious forms of life," he writes, "for in general I do not. I impose these limitations upon myself simply because these are the religious forms of life that engage" modern Westerners and call forth rejection or commitment.[24] The questions to ask concerning religion, and any rejection of or commitment to a religion, start with this trio of religions, and usually end with them as well.

Within these religions, the approaches Nielsen most easily dismisses he terms "anthropomorphic," "supernaturalist," and "Neanderthal," those that picture God as "a kind of mysterious cosmic superman who orders things one way rather than another."[25] He raises two points against them. The first concerns their origin, people having fashioned them "projectively to fit [their] cultural preoccupations." Why do

the Eskimos see Sedena, a female God, who lives in the sea and not on the land and who controls the storms, the weather, and the sea mammals, while the Israelites with a very different family structure and very different problems see Yahweh, a God of the desert and a ferocious male God who protects the Israelites from alien peoples? The Alaskan Eskimos by contrast have their risks in the winter sea mammal hunting; here they meet some of the crucial crises of their lives.[26]

Cultures tailor their "anthropomorphic deities . . . projectively to meet the anxieties and emotional needs of their members." They do not first see or somehow apprehend Sedena or Yahweh and then make certain claims. Rather, they project "certain needs onto the universe and then" make "up stories about these deifications."[27]

The chief problem with belief in anthropomorphic deities, according to Nielsen, boils down to the lack of good evidence for any of them. "Who has seen or in any way apprehended [under controlled conditions] Sedena, Yahweh, Zeus, Wotan, or Fricka?" No one. To believe in an anthropomorphic god, therefore, equates to "bald superstition" like belief in fairies or Santa Claus.[28] In particular, the idea of God as an "incredibly powerful physical being . . . is manifestly absurd and false," even idolatrous.[29]

With this statement, Nielsen rails a little against anthropomorphic believers. He probably now regrets that he did not devote more time and energy to them, given the resurgence of old-time anthropomorphic religion in the United States both among those he calls "plain folks" and among more complex folks as well.[30]

He rails a lot more against belief in the replacements for these anthropomorphic gods. Now, God exists "neither up there, down there, [nor] out there in any literal sense." Humans cannot "see or even apprehend" this reality God. God transcends "the whole cosmos" and creates and sustains it. However, God "still somehow [is] a person, an individual—though an infinite individual"—whom no one can identify, a "non-spatio-temporal" being "in no spatio-temporal" relationship "with the world."[31] This replacement theology, observes Nielsen, is the jargon of Tillich (with touches of Bultmann and Barth): "God . . . somehow [comprises] either the mysterious ground of being and meaning or some necessary existent upon which everything depends."[32] Nielsen focuses his energy on this "God." Barth and neo-orthodox theology vigorously repudiate an anthropomorphic God—by thinking of God as totally other—but still pursue a theology in which God retains such anthropomorphic qualities as love and purpose. Tillich's images abstract this "God" even further.

Anthropomorphic beliefs arise as projections, writes Nielsen as quoted above, "tailor-made . . . to meet the anxieties and emotional needs of their members."[33] Nielsen similarly posits a psychological genesis for all God talk: "belief in the Divine, etc., results from the projections of [people's] own feelings of awe, fear, duty, or Highest Goodness onto the universe." To become an adequate non-anthropomorphic object for the religious attitude of dependency, finitude and so on (so that people do not tailor-make God "for the human arrival"), the word "God" must refer "to something 'out of . . . experience' and 'beyond human comprehension.' "[34] God language also expresses and evokes such feelings and attitudes as worship and the negation of despair. To satisfy these personal needs and to create awareness of God's involvement, the word "God" must refer to something simultaneously within people as well as wholly other.

Related to this theory about the genesis of religion is one of a sociological nature. Faced with "human suffering, degradation, and exploitation," religion develops

> eschatological hopes for a new time and a new [humanity] grounded in a radical transformation of [humankind] and social relations such that, when [people] have shuffled off these mortal coils, [they] will in Heaven at last have a society based not on [human] inhumanity . . . but on love, in which a genuine classlessness, and in that sense equality, will have been obtained, where there will no longer be any master or slave, and there will be genuine human flourishing.[35]

Nielsen thinks that, via the ideological distortion of religion, believers project genuine human hopes for emancipation "into some peculiar never-never land called Heaven."[36]

Ideological Sentences

In a number of his earlier papers, Nielsen spells out his theory of religious language, how he thinks it best to understand the functioning of God talk especially once believers move away from anthropomorphic deities. He finds that their beliefs resemble some other uses of language. In particular, God sentences function like what he calls "ideological sentences" (abbreviated to "I-sentences").[37] These offer "pseudo-factual" statements:[38] people state them in such a way that they appear like hypotheses or statements of fact, with the grammatical form of indicative sentences, whereas they really express values. They really are "distinguished normative statements,"[39] which function mainly to recommend a way of life or to try to change people's attitudes. They appear surreptitiously as factual statements because this helps increase their motivational power as value judgments; like laws of nature, they seem mysterious and crucial.[40]

Nielsen wishes to take note of seven peculiarities of I-sentences:

1. no one can confirm or infirm the statements that I-sentences make;
2. users of properly functioning I-sentences do not recognize them as such;
3. I-sentences express the hidden commitments of their users;
4. users of I-sentences resist translation of them into non-I-sentences that express values or preferences;
5. I-sentences say more, according to their users, than they would if merely motivational or value judgments; more than normative, they feel objective in a mysterious sense (in turn suggesting their factual nature);
6. the "mysterious objective nature" of I-sentences enables their users to claim for them an absolute status; and
7. to display the ideological nature of a sentence requires examining its use or function, not its grammatical structure.[41]

It seems to Nielsen that, structurally, God sentences act like I-sentences:

- it appears superficially that their users employ them to make assertions (statements of purported fact such as "God made the world");
- they do not overtly say something evaluative;
- when used seriously, they convey fundamental commitments; and
- their users do not think of them as merely evaluative or normative.[42]

I-sentences and theistic sentences differ, however.[43] A person can argue for and support the normative aspect of I-sentences without appealing to ideology, but cannot intelligibly utter theistic sentences without accompanying them with assertions. This arises because Christian utterances express commitment to a person on top of their moral norms. "God sentences . . . are necessarily associated with stories (parables, myths)," Nielsen writes, but, unlike assertions, no one can falsify "God sentences (e.g., 'God is Divine,' or 'God made the world,' or 'God is in Christ')." Parables help people understand what they mean when they use God sentences, but they still do not fully know what they mean when they say such things as "God governs the world."[44]

If believers became aware of the real function of God talk, Nielsen avows, they would reject it because it lacks sufficient meaning.[45]

Meaningfulness

The fact-like assertions of theology raise the problem for Nielsen. For example, the doctrine of God's providence says God's loving sovereignty and guidance ultimately directs the universe. This "no longer means for sophisticated believers that some supernatural reality, some creative source of all reality other than itself, . . . [directs] the scene so that [people] can discover in the way things go the loving 'hand of God.'"[46] So, how does God relate to the universe if not in anthropomorphic terms? Modern theists answer with a nonanswer. As soon as they think of God as a "Pure Spirit," they have no idea what they would need to experience to undergo a vision of God, and thus they do not

> understand what it means to say "God raised the quick and the dead" or "God [made] . . . the heavens and the earth." "God" becomes an empty word to fill the blank before "_____ raised the quick and the dead," "_____ made the world," and the like.[47]

"The realm of the supernatural remains unrecognizable," Nielsen concludes; no conceivable course of events, no number of natural disasters or moral calamities would call God's reality and providence into question.[48] Belief becomes indistinguishable from atheism because both are compatible with anything that anyone can conceivably experience. The word "God" thus becomes factually meaningless.

What are the alternatives? To imagine undergoing an encounter with or a vision or experience of God probably requires, Nielsen suggests, so anthropomorphizing God "that God becomes something with a kind of gigantic body."[49] Only then could a rough idea form of what God's existence or nonexistence would entail.[50] Nielsen, of course, has ruled out belief in such a God as idolatrous or blasphemous.

Secularization thus attacks religion twice under Nielsen and apparently covers all cases: first, it renders the older theology—the "Big

Daddy-in-the-Sky" type—mythical and useless for a believer in the modern world and, second, it fails the alternative theology on grounds of factual meaningfulness.[51]

Nielsen places considerable weight on the need for factual meaningfulness of religious utterances. He does acknowledge their linguistic meaningfulness, even in nonanthropomorphic contexts. People do know, for instance, how to use the word "God" in their language and they can identify deviant from nondeviant contexts. Thus Nielsen contrasts, "a God exists," with, "a Trig exists," and cites as deviant, "Jack God Jill down the hill to fetch a pail of Jesus." To say, "God brews good coffee," with serious intent utters something literally meaningless and misunderstands God talk. Moreover, a sentence such as, "God created the world" allows drawing inferences such as, "the world [is not] uncreated, the world just did not happen to come into being, and the world did not exist before God."[52] Such God sentences are to some extent understandable; they have linguistic meaning in certain contexts even to atheists and agnostics. This is not enough, however, because the phrase, "nothing noughts itself," also passes the criterion of linguistic meaningfulness. Hence, Nielsen concludes, the need for factual meaningfulness.

QUESTIONING NIELSEN'S CHALLENGE

Nielsen summarizes his challenges to nonanthropomorphic theism with the following:

1. No one can identify God, yet to make a genuine assertion that uses the word "God" or a similar expression, the speaker or writer must identify God. Only then can they understand what they talk about and so know that they have indeed asserted something genuine. But, of course, they "have no idea how to identify God."
2. Personal predicates—for instance "protects," "punishes," "forgives"— appear essential for God talk. Yet a religious milieu attenuates their meaning so much it seems to empty them "of all intelligible meaning." Speakers do not understand what they assert or what they deny when they say "God protects God's children."
3. While such utterances as "God exists" and "God protects God's children" purport to offer factual assertions—in other words, true or

false ones—no one can even in principle confirm or infirm them. No one can describe anything somebody might experience that would count for or against them.[53]

Point (1) reaches the core of Nielsen's challenge: "non-religious, straightforwardly empirical, factual statements" must potentially, at least in principle, confirm or infirm "religious propositions purporting to make factual assertions."[54] Several commentators refer to this as the most adequate statement of the challenge, including Colwell as mentioned above and Kenneth Konyndyk, whose work will come up below. It offers a good benchmark to use.

This chapter so far has presented Nielsen's understanding of religious or theological language and his case against it. A wide range of responses has risen to Nielsen and he has entered into dialogue with some of them.[55] The discussion will now look at and, where possible, try to address some of them. They fall roughly into two categories: attempts to undermine the foundations of his challenge, and attacks on and dialogue with him over particular understandings of religious language. This section will deal with the former type of writing, looking at questions the literature raises about his challenge itself.

Holes in the Challenge

Nielsen's challenge unveils a principle of factual meaningfulness in its nakedness and consequently has seen many attacks, both technical and simple, over its tenability.[56] The several this section touches on—some easily responded to and others not—offer a sampling.

Nielsen requires that nonreligious, straightforwardly empirical, factual statements infirm or confirm theological propositions. Stuart Brown disagrees: *to make a genuine truth claim from metaphorical religious language need not require reexpressing it without metaphor*.[57] Nielsen's insistence does appear correct in that believers often make theistic assertions they consider literal and not merely metaphorical; theologians may wish to claim the metaphorical nature of the language, but believers do not operate this way linguistically. Forgetting about believers and concentrating on theologians, could they express religious language completely as metaphor and have it be true and factual? Nielsen argues that any factual truth claim must be in principle confirmable or infirmable.[58] Further, theological systems at some stage must link with the empirical and leave the purely metaphorical. If God makes any difference in the world, God does something people can look at empirically. The theologian may wish to interpret this metaphorically, but at its root lays a potential fact.

Another, perhaps related, point asks *why theologians cannot justify religious language with religious language* rather than with, as in Nielsen's challenge, factual, nonreligious statements. Without insisting on the mutual independence of the religious and the empirical modes of discourse, why should the factual and empirical judge all others?[59] An answer to this lies in the secular nature of contemporary society and its elevation of the scientific method to the arbiter of truth. As said above, theology must face this directly, accepting (while commenting on) the modern worldview rather than hiding in a religious or linguistic ghetto of the past.

A relatively straightforward critique comes from Paul Clifford: Nielsen's challenge is incorrect because it says *counterevidence may infirm a proposition, but no amount of positive and supporting evidence may ever confirm it.*[60] Nielsen, however, does not seek to infirm or confirm a proposition; he merely insists on the openness of factually meaningful statements to this.

John King-Farlow shrugs off of a challenge such as Nielsen's with an assessment based on the notion of causality: what with the turmoil that quantum mechanics brings into science's understanding of causality and particularly into physics', *why should anyone use traditional empiricism as a causal reasoning for the existence or nonexistence of the existence of a nonspatial entity?*[61] In response:

- Nielsen's challenge does not concern the existence or nonexistence of God, but the factual meaningfulness of God talk.
- The rebuke about applying traditional ideas of causality (referring to the possibility of infirming or confirming a statement) may still apply. What form of causality or logic ought then to apply? Any form? Might quantum mechanical logic pertain to regular life? At this point, nothing comes forward as an obvious contender for theology apart from the logic used everyday.
- Nielsen would say he does not apply traditional empiricism, but common expectations for factual meaningfulness. He believes he

uses the intelligibility criterion normally used when deciding whether a statement is factual. His challenge thus makes the implicit practice explicit.[62]

George Mavrodes also criticizes the relevance and force of Nielsen's challenge to theology by attempting to show it lacks logical substance.[63] Nielsen's challenge entails an impossible task, he says, not just for theology, but when applied to any discipline; it requires *deciding on "the meaningfulness of a disputed statement by determining the truth of another statement" that cannot be understood until the meaning of the disputed statement is understood.* The truth of the second statement needs establishing before it is possible to understand the first one.[64] Like Clifford, Mavrodes seems to have misinterpreted Nielsen's challenge; it does not seek to determine the truth of "another statement," but of the possibility of truth for the "disputed statement."

The relationship between truthfulness and meaningfulness inevitably arises with the questioning of Nielsen's challenge. As already seen, Nielsen distinguishes the two and says people can find religious language linguistically meaningful even if not factually meaningful or coherent. This answers another criticism of Nielsen's challenge, that *it attempts to render perfectly meaningful everyday discourse unmeaningful.*[65] Nielsen is not a logical positivist.

Nielsen confronts the attempts of Norman Malcolm to undermine arguments for religious skepticism.[66] One of Malcolm's points *distinguishes between belief that God exists and belief in God*, the former raising problems and the latter not. It is unrealistic to assume, Malcolm writes, that grounds exist "for believing in the existence of God" and that this belief requires "a distinction between causes of the belief and grounds or evidence for its truth."[67] Nielsen's reply attempts to show that Malcolm fails to show how this distinction offers another phrase for the possibility of belief in God without first believing God exists, or that the latter can raise problems absent in the former.

Konyndyk considers various interpretations of Nielsen's challenge, and concludes: *"All of Nielsen's formulations of [it] are intolerably obscure and some are simply wrong."* Thus, he adds, the challenge still awaits vindication and no reason compels the acceptance of "one of the crucial premises in Nielsen's argument for skepticism about theistic claims."[68] He also notes that even A. J. Ayer recognizes the failure of

Nielsen's criteria "to provide a test for factual significance" that applies
"to sentences without . . . knowing in advance . . . they have truth
value."[69] Note the phrase, "without . . . knowing in advance . . . they
[theological propositions] have truth value." Nielsen must know before
applying his criterion to a theological proposition that it actually is (or
actually is not) true. On the other hand, Nielsen would admit to his proposal's ideological bias.[70] He talks about the lack of normative neutral-
ity in philosophy and he knows that he holds preconceived conclusions.
Motivations, including politics, underlie his dogmatism.[71] People cannot avoid ideological bias on matters of life meaning: ways of life already form fundamental ideological positions.

One may wish to agree with Konyndyk's or any of the other critiques
of Nielsen's challenge. One can do this, however, without denying the
force of the challenge in general to theology, or the power Nielsen's insight affords. Whether Nielsen and his colleagues can state an unassail-
able principle or not, the force of their challenge still confronts theists:
it lies in the clout of the secular march, demanding the inseparability of
truth and reality from the here and now. Nielsen performs a great service for theology by making that general challenge explicit and thus allowing theists to charge, horns down, at a small red cloth fluttering in
front of them. They tend to forget, then, the less visible darts in their
back and the starvation that make the conditions for religion uncom-
fortable. Konyndyk and other heroes may catch various red cloths in
their horns and tear them to shreds, but plenty more await where they
come from and the anger and frustration will not abate. Perhaps the
toreador-bovine image allows extension to its end: though at first apparently the weaker in the arena, the flag waver will eventually butcher
the mercilessly teased and overpowered bull.

The Wrong Challenge

The naturalistic and humanistic philosopher, Ziff, sits on the same side
of this debate as Nielsen. However, he also engages Nielsen about the
way to attack religion and repudiates Nielsen's criterion for factual
meaningfulness.

Ziff starts by assuming people use the word "God" as if "God" were
a name (a position Nielsen unwillingly accepts for convenience). The
set of conditions associated with a name determines the understanding

of its referent, and whether or not someone or something satisfies the conditions determines whether or not the referent exists. To find the phrase "God exists" intelligible, continues Ziff, requires finding the set of consistent conditions, with each of them intelligible. Ziff imagines a popular, plain person's idea of God and from it compiles a list of conditions associated with the word. He then divides the list into troublesome and trouble-free conditions, the latter category comprising those understood and found intelligible (at least to some degree).[72]

Nielsen launches into Ziff's distinction between the troublesome and trouble-free conditions associated with the word "God."[73] For example: "Native and/or fluent speakers of all ideological convictions" agree about how correctly to apply the word "loving" in a secular context. In a Jewish or Christian religious context, however, "loving" becomes "a disputed engendered term."[74] Paul Edwards explains why: Loving is an activity a person does, and a person requires a body. To use intelligibly the word "loving" of God, therefore, requires in the mind's background an image of God with, in some mysterious way, a body. But, of course, God cannot have a body according to the theologies in question and no one understands "a loving but bodiless being."[75] Thus, to speak of a bodiless being acting in a loving way raises, contrary to Ziff, severe problems. "Some feel," writes Nielsen, "they can make nothing of [this] religious use [of the word 'loving'] at all."[76] Ziff's trouble-free conditions turn out, Nielsen concludes, as troublesome as the troublesome ones because people still do not understand how to use the word "God" intelligibly.

A central ploy by Ziff in upholding the intelligibility of the plain person's idea of "God exists" involves a repudiation of Nielsen's criterion for factual meaningfulness. Nielsen remains unconvinced that Ziff has made a thorough case for the intelligibility of God talk even on his own terms, and even if just focusing on Ziff's trouble-free conditions.[77] To assume some other criterion without due justification does not sidestep the problems that Nielsen's challenge raises.

Robert Hoffman and Jack Glickman also exchange with Nielsen over Ziff's criteria of intelligibility, but Nielsen shows how his considerations are unavoidable when reflecting on God talk. Neither need this impose empiricist dogma.[78] The use of "God" as if God has a body, Nielsen tells us, persists as a discredited relict from an age in which people thought God had one, and it mistakenly leads to belief in the intelligibility of God talk.[79] Even many religious people feel perplexed by the idea of a bodiless being who can act. Theologians ought therefore to ask for the truth conditions for such discourse. If they find such conditions, they might avoid speaking nonsense and ensure that at least some people understand what the religious words mean. The critics also want more justification for the criterion of factual meaningfulness. Given the alleged fact-stating pretensions of many theological utterances, it seems appropriate to employ the criterion normally used for deciding whether a statement really is factual. Nielsen says he does this, that his challenge makes explicit the implicit, normal practice.[80] (This telling position of Nielsen goes to the crux of the problem: ought the theologian to accept as authoritative the practice in contemporary secular experience or the practice in religious tradition?)

Sydney Hook, another skeptic, enters this fray. He claims the central question is whether adequate evidence exists to back the claim that God—as conceived by "developed" theism (Thomas Aquinas, Blaise Pascal, Martin Luther, . . .)—exists rather than whether the idea of God is factually meaningful. Nielsen attempts to show the ineffectiveness of Hook's argument against a sophisticated theist; it requires, as do the alternatives, the resolution of the question of meaning—confirmable or infirmable in principle—coherence, intelligibility.[81]

As the white knight jousting for supremacy, Nielsen gallops under the banner of his challenge, attempting to dismount any of his fellows, including Ziff and Hook, who ride under a variant flag. He appears successful.

Challenging Whom?

Two further and interrelated criticisms that Colwell raises concern the type of theism Nielsen addresses.[82] Their appearing on the scene so late in the action (1981) may reflect the growth, especially in the United States, of the self-confident, staunchly evangelical wing of Christendom. Some (for instance, Mavrodes and Konyndyk) emerge through the Reformed tradition, which as well can staunchly aspire to scholarship.

Nielsen assumes he analyzes "sophisticated theism," suggests Colwell. Other forms of theism exist, he writes, that offer far more adequate versions of Christianity.[83] He points in particular to the anthropomorphic types, which are not necessarily false or mythical, and which attract sophisticated, nonfundamentalist adherents. Further, a theology need not be fully anthropomorphic or devoid of anthropomorphism in its model for God, but can include elements of both; to factor out all anthropomorphic elements and leave God totally transcendent "runs counter to what the Bible suggests, what church history suggests, and what the beliefs of vast numbers of Christians today suggest."[84] Nielsen's view of his opponents fails to recognize the "empirical strength" of religion, Colwell concludes, and can never dislodge its foundations.[85]

Colwell chides Nielsen for failing to note the traditional, conservative types of theism, but other writers—for instance, James Livingston—criticize Nielsen because they think he aims at only traditional and nonmodern ideas.[86] Similarly, King-Farlow seems to think Nielsen comments on biblical theism.[87] Writers of many ilks squirm and react uncomfortably to Nielsen and so equate the object of Nielsen's challenge with their theological opponents; they feel their own positions threatened and thus redirect his force onto someone else. His challenge in fact targets all theologies—apart from the fully anthropomorphic—because they all to some extent spiritualize God talk.

Nielsen's skepticism does at times appear to confuse the types of theism it addresses. Take, as an example, two 1974 articles in which he asks whether the term "God" possesses a highly theoretical yet objective reality. In one article, he aims his challenge at the idea of a metaphysical God who, as an infinite individual, transcends the universe, but who possesses no physical properties.[88] This God picture is Tillich's. In the other article, he aims his challenge at the idea of the nonanthropomorphic God of the mainstream or near-the-mainstream believer in which God by definition completely transcends the universe, but whose image contrasts with certain new ideas of God.[89] These new ideas do not develop the word "God" from its use in or near the mainstream religious tradition, but introduce new definitions and are naturalistic in that they take "God" purely as a theoretical construct, a moral myth, or a symbol for ultimate concerns. This last new use is Tillich's; in fact, Nielsen refers to an article of his in which he specifically discusses Tillich's theology.[90] Is Nielsen confused? In the first context, he says his challenge addresses Tillich's idea of God. In the second, he appears to say it does not address Tillich's idea. In fact, he does both.

Colwell's chiding of Nielsen for ignoring traditional, conservative types of theism nevertheless offers an important lesson: Nielsen must make clear what type of theism he challenges. In fairness to him, though, his challenge derives from the religious context in which he wrote, namely mostly in the late 1950s through to the early 1970s. His challenge aims at Tillich's popular theology of those times, deriving from Bultmann's nonanthropomorphic emphasis and from Barth's demand for God's total transcendence. Nielsen did not target the more conservative theological, religious, and social climate of the years following that, which probably were (as were Nielsen's) reactions and countervailing swings to the milieu of the 1960s. Whether his critique applies to these later years asks another question.

Evangelical (and other conservative) theologies do not slip out of Nielsen's knot unscathed, even if Colwell may wish to give that impression. This occurs for two reasons. The first arises because evangelical theism is not fully anthropomorphic; it also contains Platonic elements—perhaps reflecting its roots in the theology of the Epistle writer Paul—and, when it thus pictures God as a spiritual being, it opens up Nielsen's challenge of factual vacuity. The second opportunity for Nielsen arises when evangelicals elaborate those elements of their theology that may have factual import (evil in the world, for instance) with supernatural categories (mere mortals can in no way understand the eternal and divine purposes of God). If evangelicals' theology displays a proposition open to confirmation or infirmation, they should offer it to this adjudication.

The second challenge to evangelical theism comes from Nielsen's reasons for rejecting anthropomorphic versions of Christianity, as outlined above. He finds them inadequate for life in the modern world. While he does not develop this theme—his major opponents falling into the "sophisticated" variety—it could offer a major challenge to a conservative or evangelical Christianity.[91]

On the other hand, evangelicals believe God acts in specific ways and at specific times in this world. They thus allow the empirical into theology and with this could answer Nielsen's challenge. Later chapters will develop this possibility without the evangelical context.

NONDESCRIPTIVE RESPONSES TO NIELSEN

The first part of this chapter looked at the challenge Flew raises to theology and that Nielsen reraises, Nielsen's own assumptions and account of religious language, and several questions others ask of the challenge. The rest of this visit with Nielsen's writings will examine others' responses to his challenge and his evaluations of their attempts. This will provide an overview of many philosophical positions taken over the nature of religious language. It will also afford a preview of the traps to avoid if wishing to meet Nielsen's challenge, and an introduction to possible opportunities if wishing to pursue the slant on theological method that his challenge represents.

The responses fall into two categories, the division into which at times is inadequate but most of the time is useful. This section focuses on responses that use a nondescriptive approach to religious language, a sidestepping or a denying the validity of Nielsen's challenge by, for instance, erecting an altogether separate domain for religion that has naught to do with the materially factual or scientific. The second broad approach focuses on descriptive approaches. It attempts to engage Nielsen's challenge by, for instance, showing how potentially to confirm or infirm religious language as it stands.

Religious Language as Attitudes to Life

People in general and the common garden variety of religious believer refer in their religious language to metaphysical realities. In comparison, one nondescriptive response to Nielsen's challenge reduces the reference of religious language to basic commitments and ways of life. Nielsen particularly has in mind the work of the nondescriptive theologians R. B. Braithwaite and R. M. Hare (and less explicitly T. R. Miles and Paul van Buren). These two "sincere Christians," writes Nielsen, try "to preserve what they take [as] . . . essential to Christianity . . . in the face of what they regard as devastating logical objections to traditional cosmological views of the world."[92] They also attempt to be solidly empiricist.

The Braithwaite approach says religious assertions primarily "announce allegiance to a set of moral principles."[93] These basic value orientations or decisions require an ultimate commitment; the word "God" expresses "that for which the speaker is willing to live and die."[94] Though religious sentences may look in this perspective like moral ones, the two types differ in that the former refer "to a story as well as to a cluster of intentions."[95] Further, Christian religious claims differ from those of other religions because they tell the story of Christian doctrine.

The point of introducing Braithwaite's position is to see how it fares against Nielsen's challenge. It appears to do well. It avoids subjecting religious ideas to the possibility of confirmation or infirmation because it says that value commitments "can be neither true nor false."[96]

Hare presents a more developed version of Braithwaite's stance. For Hare, writes Nielsen, "something important" lives in the faith of "simple believers" and "he wants to strengthen that belief by freeing it from its philosophical muddles." He aims to do this with a demythologized version of the Christian faith "rooted in the empiricist view of the world."[97] He is also aware of the dangers of demythologization and the attempts at restructuring theology that fall to Nielsen's challenge by the death of a thousand qualifications.

Hare starts by saying Christianity need not require belief in the supernatural. The most important ideas in religion are not those that take the form of factual assertions, but those that require belief, acceptance, and action. Not that this reduces religious belief to living out certain moral principles: religion does not reduce "to morality, even in an extended sense." Rather, Hare sees a Christian as living in accord with a specific way of life: a "total attitude to life" that involves people's "wants, aspirations and ideals" beyond their "moral attitudes."[98] Religion must also include beliefs—embedded in such statements as "God exists"—"that what these ideals prescribe or proclaim will someday" come to fruition and save "moral endeavor from futility."[99]

Ilham Dilman advocates a similar position: "Believers . . . have beliefs, which provide them," Nielsen quotes, "'with a perspective on life, a fixed framework for their judgments and decisions,' while nonbelievers neither do nor can have such conceptions."[100] What is this perspective? Nielsen paraphrases Dilman:

> To have a genuine sense of transcendence (this religious transcendence) is to come to understand and to take to heart the incontrovertible fact that this universe . . . "is absolutely devoid of finality," while at the same time feeling thankful for this world and feeling a sense of gratitude for one's life and for the world, no matter what one's conditions or what happens.[101]

To emphasize this point further, Dilman repudiates metaphysical attempts to understand God's transcendence: theologians ought not to construe God "as a being beyond the objects with which [people] are familiarly acquainted."[102] Rather, Dilman suggests, they ought to understand God's transcendence in terms of love and selflessness.

Nielsen rails against Dilman's, Hare's, and Braithwaite's "attitudinal" positions. Believers use "God sentences, such as in the act of praying or in statements about God's creative and sustaining activity in regard to the world" to make what they think of as true or false statements, and they use the word "God" as a proper name that more or less denotes something.[103] Thus, religious language does not reduce to only normative functions and attitudes to life, and these attitudinal positions do not accurately portray how religious believers use religious language. (Though it includes these normative functions and attitudes and though perhaps it could change to become only them.)[104] Braithwaite also recognizes that he eviscerates "religion of the claim to that objective content . . . essential to give it point."[105] In conclusion, Nielsen writes, attitudinal positions offer a "low redefinition" of religious language, "just as to define an M.D. as someone who can administer first aid is a low redefinition."[106] This idea of God has become "so minimal," he adds, that it results in "no conception of God at all." It has turned into a "Godless Christianity."[107]

Hare agrees that religion needs objective content, and so offers the possibility that God orders the world in certain ways. He opens to empirical testing claims about what constitutes this ordering. But testing in a weak sense, Hare says, because secondary elaboration also protects such beliefs against countering instances, and empirical investigation cannot fully establish them. People need faith to accept fully a religious framework of meaning. Nielsen remains unconvinced that Hare meets the objections of the orthodox Christian: Hare still leaves out, "and has no way to accommodate . . . what is most crucial to the Christian or Jew, namely, belief in God."[108]

Nielsen finds another flaw in the attitudinal positions (which he also applies to the approaches of John Macquarrie and D. Z. Phillips).[109] "A Marxist humanist . . . —say a man like Régis Debray or Isaac Deutscher—who was thoroughly and even iconoclastically atheist, could well discover the significance in the revolutionary struggle to create for the toiling and exploited masses a new quality of life and a new image of [humanity]."[110] Atheists, agnostics, secular humanists, and even religious people who do not believe in God (Buddhists, for example) may have moral values and a wider significance for existence.[111]

Thus, belief in God does not equate to having a meaningful life and moral ideals. Redefining religion in Braithwaite et al.'s "low" manner, concludes Nielsen, converts the nonreligious "into the religious by stipulative fiat."[112] Believers and unbelievers do differ and the difference boils down to certain intellectual matters essential to having faith: "the Christian believes in [the objective existence of] God and the atheist rejects such a belief."[113]

Moreover, religious lifestyles (for Christians, a commitment to the morality and way of life of Christianity) and attitudes (that nothing can harm them and that all will be well no matter what), lack a point or rationale without belief in God's existence.[114] The logic of such beliefs exceeds just denying-with-hope the futility of the religious way of life. The beliefs make claims about what actually exists, and what actually exists needs to justify them.

Religious belief goes beyond the believer having an "affective disposition and moral orientation."[115]

Fideism: An Unassailable Domain for Religion

Chapter 2 introduced Gordon Kaufman and his book, *An Essay on Theological Method*. Nielsen engages Kaufman's earlier 1957 paper, "Philosophy of Religion and Christian Theology," as an example of what he calls "fideism."[116]

The idea of revelation must assume people have in principle absolutely no access to it, Kaufman argues, God giving it unpredictably; "only God can make [it] known to [human beings]."[117] Therefore, the Christian theologian must "refuse to give the canons of human reason primacy over the commitments of Christian faith."[118] This leads to a more extreme type of the nondescriptive approach than the attitudinal one because it radically separates the religious from other ways of life.

What constitutes revelation? John Hick suggests people come to know the nature of God from Jesus as the Christ, who mediates God to humans, providing the details for beliefs about God with his life, teachings, and death.[119] Other people have different understandings of what comprises revelation. Only through parables can people gain knowledge of God, says I. M. Crombie; not taken literally, the images of parables guide toward an incomprehensible reality beyond human experience.[120] Some Christians see revelation in biblical parables, some in the person of Jesus Christ, some in church dogma and tradition, and others in certain normative texts.[121]

With these different understandings of what constitutes Christian revelation, let alone the understandings from other religions, how does a true revelation differ from a false one? This is impossible to answer from the outside. Kaufman claims that, by its essence, revelation must self-confirm or self-validate. A person can only determine or express the marks for recognizing revelation as true revelation from within it.[122] Therefore, to become a believer requires accepting in faith the truth of the revelation. A system of thought and life then forms, and nothing more fundamental links it with other systems of thought and life.[123] "All that recipients of the alleged revelation can reasonably do," Nielsen continues, "is confess their faith, proclaim the truth, and in an analytical fashion block misunderstandings of what constitutes a revelation."[124] And for those outside? Neither philosophy nor theology can "assert with finality the error of the other and the truth of itself."[125]

The position that Kaufman adopts in his paper is an example of what Nielsen calls "fideism": only believers—not all and sundry—can experience or judge the truth of a religious assertion. Fideism falls into the nondescriptive positions because it requires the acceptance of the meaningfulness and the truth of religious claims regardless of factual support, avoiding the public confirm-infirm criterion as primary for factual meaning.

Wittgensteinian Fideism

Nielsen associates a stronger and more developed type of fideism with several followers of Ludwig Wittgenstein (though Wittgenstein did not necessarily hold to it), and names it after him. One of Nielsen's lists names as examples such thinkers as J. M. Cameron, Stanley Cavell, Robert Coburn, Peter Geach, G. E. Hughes, Malcolm, and Peter Winch.[126] Other scholars augment this list, including Brown, Dilman, Paul Holmer, Phillips, and John Wisdom.[127] As with Kaufman's fideism of revelation, Wittgensteinian fideism emphasizes the self-contained nature of faith in matters of meaning and truth, its ideas adequately understood only from within itself. It differs from Kaufman's by emphasizing and developing the idea of faith and its associated form of life.

Frank Dilley thinks Wittgensteinian fideism arises from a combination of two things. First, "a philosophical movement associated with the later writings of Wittgenstein," which claims the basic acceptability of language "as it stands" and each language game having its "own standards of intelligibility and rationality." Second, "a theological movement associated with the writings of Søren Kierkegaard and . . . Barth," who both believe that revelation alone provides religious truth.[128] Kaufman's paper on revelation and his book on theological method similarly insist, as seen above, that God totally and absolutely transcends. Combining this with Wittgenstein's ideas applied to religion as a form of life pushes the latter to the extreme and forms polarities.

Nielsen lists a "cluster of dark sayings" that, when accepted, tend to generate such a position.[129] They produce four steps:

1. Forms of language equate with forms of life. The forms of life proffer the given.[130]
2. Each mode of discourse equates with a distinctive form of life, each with a logic of its own—its "own specific criteria of rationality/irrationality, intelligibility/unintelligibility, and reality/unreality"—and each acceptable as it stands.[131]
3. Thus, the rationality, intelligence, and reality of forms of life become "systematically ambiguous," which means that "no Archimedean point [exists] in terms of which [a person] can relevantly criticize whole modes of discourse or, what comes to the same thing, ways of life."[132] This emancipates religious language "from any connection with science or rationality,"[133] and the philosopher cannot "evaluate or criticize language or the forms of life."[134]
4. It also means that the philosopher's task becomes neutrally to display, describe, and clarify "the workings, the style of functioning, of religious discourse . . . to the extent necessary to break philosophical perplexity" about how they operate.[135]

A religion is a unique form of life with its own distinctive criteria of coherence, rationality, or intelligibility, and only a person within its mode of discourse can understand or criticize it.[136]

Religion Not a Whole and Coherent Form of Life

Nielsen's case against Kaufman's revelatory fideism starts by questioning the possibility of verifying the legitimacy of a putative revelation.[137]

Nothing could count toward proving something as a genuine revelation because then human methods justify it and this contradicts its internal logic; no one can predict it and it must stand in judgment on all human activities. Revelation is totally divine. Further, Nielsen reminds his readers, nearly a thousand faiths compete for the allegiance of humanity, and most of them claim uniqueness and conflict with the others over their revelations. What reason do the members of a confessional group have for thinking they offer "the real article, or that any of the alleged revelations is the real article?"[138] Even if accepting one as true because an authority says so and that authority is trustworthy, who judges between the authorities? Only ethnocentric hubris would allow taking one of the revelations as the real thing.[139]

Revelation does not lead to an obviously justifiable form of life divorced from other forms of life.

Nielsen raises several points against Wittgensteinian fideism.[140] The first questions the assumption that religion creates not only a form of life, but a whole and coherent form of life and discourse—a long-established fait accompli—where God talk forms "a coherent order just as it is":[141]

- "All times and at all places," Nielsen writes, have had "skeptics and scoffers, people who, though perfectly familiar with the religious language game played in their culture, would not play it . . . because they found it incoherent."[142]
- So many people find religion incoherent that it cannot be adequately performing its distinctive tasks.
- Many other religions besides, say, Christianity, grow within modern Western culture.

Whether religion forms a coherent and whole form of life still needs settling. Perhaps, to help decide the issue, the idea of a form of life needs further development.[143]

Dilman attempts this, as seen above, by developing the idea of a religious form of life with beliefs that provide adherents "with a perspective on life, a fixed framework for their judgments and decisions."[144] Nielsen's criticism says that, while Dilman aims to portray the way religious believers use their religious language, his picture of this wrongly reduces and inadequately represents it. Yet, Nielsen adds, Dilman's position is typical among Wittgensteinian fideists in their attempts to insulate God talk from other forms of discourse and yet provide a coherent account of its use.[145]

A Form of Life: Truth from Fulfillment of Needs

Diogenes Allen's book, *The Reasonableness of Faith*, also develops ideas on how religion might function as a form of life.[146] His argument starts with the requirement that, in the words of Nielsen, "no reasons [must] count decisively against the truth of . . . religious beliefs." Then, second, "the fulfillment of [believers'] needs—which can lead [them] to respond with faith and to retain [their] faith—can be a reasonable ground or basis for [them] to adhere to religious belief and to assert [the beliefs] as true."[147] What needs might this fulfill? Nielsen writes:

> One comes to fear the judgment of God, hope that one may escape death *and* "live as [a child] in the fellowship of God," and one comes to yearn for a righteousness and a purity of heart which . . . is beyond [human] powers of attainment but which, with God's grace, [believers] trust [they] shall attain "in the Kingdom that shall come." . . . [In other words, one comes] to have a need for a certain kind of judgment on [one's life], a certain kind of immortality and a certain kind of moral purity and these are all distinctive religious needs.[148]

In Allen's logic, writes Nielsen, all these words represent "distinctive religious needs and can arise only with the hearing of the 'word of God.'"[149] Religious believing creates the needs. Then the believing meets the needs. Third, the satisfaction of the needs also proves the truth of Christianity.

Nielsen fires away at what he considers several weak points in this position. First, Allen says fulfillment of needs provides a ground for belief provided no reasons count decisively against the religious beliefs. Nielsen points out, however, that Allen "has done nothing to show what would or would not count as a decisive reason against a religious truth-claim."[150]

Nielsen's second line of attack concerns the needs Allen enumerates:

- A number of other sources than the act of religious believing can fill these needs.[151]
- Neither the truth nor "even the probable truth of the religious truth claims . . . [satisfies the] need, but only the belief—no matter how ill-founded—that they are true."[152]

Central in Allen's case lies the role of religious experience in fulfilling the needs and verifying the theological claims. This affords Nielsen's third offensive, similar to what chapter 2 depicted. Some theologians say, writes Nielsen, that, when people experience God, they "experience (or perhaps experience to the full) [their] finitude, . . . have feelings of dependency, awe, wonder, dread, or . . . feel a oneness and a love and a sense of security, no matter what happens." However, Nielsen explains, such experiences are human and psychological and are open purely to a secular reading. Why, he asks, should theology "multiply conceptions beyond need and say these understandable human experiences are also experiences of God and that [it can best explain them] as experiences of God or as attesting to the reality of God or as showing that somehow" the person experiencing these experiences stands "in the presence of God?"[153] Nielsen could ask of Allen, as he does of John Wilson, "What possible or conceivable experiences would count for the 'theistic hypothesis' and count against the 'naturalistic hypothesis?'"[154] If the theologian cannot answer this satisfactorily, and because the scholar "ought not to multiply concepts beyond necessity, '[God exists]' is a hypothesis" better done without.[155] This does not dispute the psychological reality of religious experiences; rather, it questions that people experience in them something called "God." If they do not constitute experiences of God, they may not fulfill the religious needs and verify the theological claims. (Thus Nielsen also disagrees with Illyd Trethowan, whose case for theism says it derives from experiences of God that lack a naturalistic explanation.)[156]

Allen not only employs religious experience to warrant his case for the meaningfulness of religious language. He also claims religious experiences authenticate themselves and thus the believer can know, if actually having had them, "that they must [constitute] experiences of God." According to Nielsen, however, the only plausible self-authenticating experiences come from psychological realities "such as the fact that I am in pain, am tired, or that I now intend to have a drink before I go to bed." This does not happen with nonpsychological experiences. "I may be perfectly confident that I am seeing an exit sign at the end of the hall and still be mistaken or I may be quite confident that what I hear is the surf breaking and still be quite mistaken." No religious experience can guarantee that in it people experience God.[157]

Nielsen undermines Allen's efforts to establish the meaningfulness of religion's truth claims with a new criterion of truthfulness, namely the fulfilling of needs by belief in the claims. The tests for a religion do not only lie in its psychological and sociological adequacy, but as well or more importantly in empirical adequacy as factually meaningful.[158]

Intelligibility within Religious Forms of Life

The above arguments counter the existence of religious forms of life, independent and complete. Now Nielsen faces the second aspect of Wittgensteinian fideism, which also defines the fideist position in general: each form of life possesses "its own criteria and each sets its own norms of intelligibility, reality, and rationality."[159]

Nielsen proceeds to the issue of meaning, the core of his rebuff: understanding, he says, must precede faith. To believe, for instance, that a putative revelation constitutes a genuine revelation requires understanding its contents and what the idea "revelation" means. This returns to Nielsen's challenge and entails distinguishing in principle between circumstances indicating the truth of the revelation and those that would count for its falsity.

- People cannot accept something if they cannot understand it, because they do not know what it is they are to accept.
- Ambiguity inheres in the meaning of revelation's religious utterances and this needs overcoming. "They really refer to one's father," the Freudian might aver. "No, to something supernatural, transcendent, spiritual," the theologian might reply.[160] This trinity of theological words falls precisely into the type not understood and whose intelligibility the theologian ought to seek.
- How does a person recognize something as a revelation when encountering it? This means beforehand having some idea of what it would be like to have such a disclosure.[161]
- Even to think and talk about revelation, people "must have some human criteria" for it and its appreciation.[162]

Nielsen thinks people in general do not understand the word "revelation" and its contents.

Several attempts fail to circumvent Nielsen's insisting on factual meaning:

- *People should accept revelation from Jesus on faith because Jesus is God.* Nielsen responds: A person cannot accept Jesus as God's revelation or "Jesus the Christ" unless she or he understands what the word "God" means.[163]
- *People should accept revelation now in faith or trust, with an eye to God's vindicating it later on.* Nielsen responds: Whether God will vindicate or has vindicated what people are to believe, they still must understand it "at least in some minimal sense," or logically they cannot disbelieve or believe.[164]
- *People should accept revelation from Jesus in faith because they trust Jesus and he would not mislead them.* Take the example of revelation in biblical parables. Christians supposedly trust in the faithfulness of these images because Jesus authorized them and Christians trust Jesus. Nielsen responds: To trust that Jesus (or any other religious authority) is not misleading through a parable, people must understand what they mean when they say—literally and outside the parable— that God exists and behaves mercifully toward them. Otherwise, they cannot know whether Jesus misleads them or not.
- *What Jesus stated is true in the sense that people can verify in principle whether or not Jesus asserted it.* If Jesus stated something, for instance that God exists, a person can apply "true" to that sequence of sounds. Nielsen responds: In this case, take Jesus as the religious authority and so assume he behaved in ways that vouch for the truth of what he said. People must know what he must say and do, however— what constitutes his evidence for the truth of his utterances—for what he said to be more than sequences of sounds without truth or falsity. On the other hand, no one knows what would count for the truth or falsity of what Jesus said, because no one understands what he said. This creates a vicious circle.[165]
- *Theological statements about God are coherent—have factual meaning—though people know little or perhaps nothing of God, just as statements in physics are coherent* though they concern something about which people know very little and of which can make little sense. Thus suggests J. N. Findlay.[166] Lay people see all around them the dramatic fruits of modern physics—from watches

to radiation therapy—but the formulas that comprise the physics remain meaningless gibberish; people take them on faith or they trust the physicist correctly asserts something factual with them. Similarly, the "knight of faith" can play the "language game of ancient lineage" by having faith or trust that what the religious authority says has truth and meaning really does have truth and meaning, though it appears incoherent.[167] Nielsen responds: When people do know something in physics—though they do not fully know what the physics means—they do have some vehicle for a factual (verifiable or infirmable) assertion. The physicist especially has access to this. With God statements, people have no idea as to their factual meaning and the religious authority—"priests, theologians, some kind of holy men"—have no special access to intelligibility and ride "in exactly the same boat as the plain believer."[168] Theology and physics part company here.

- *Religious utterances make genuine truth claims, none of which says anything about the universe that empirical data need to establish.* Rather, "they call for devotion to God."[169] Thus thinks Allen and Allen provides as a truth claim that one way to regard the world is "as a creature."[170] Brian McClorry writes similarly: "On the meaningfulness of God talk, . . . reflection about the content of what" people experience, verify, and falsify counts less "than reflecting on the activity of experiencing, verifying, falsifying."[171] Nielsen responds: For such ideas to mean something as truth claims, some observable state of affairs must exist that would count for or against such a claim, or some such state must be conceivable. "Only if [people] understood what it would be like for the world to be God's creature could [they] know what it would be like to see the world as God's creature."[172] It gets nowhere just to insist that religious utterances make genuine truth claims.

- *No one can express revelation.* Nielsen responds: To understand revelation, a person must be able to describe it at least in principle, because people cannot understand what they cannot even start to describe.[173] The utterly inexpressible lacks any intelligibility. If in principle no one (not even Jesus or any member of any church) can find meaning in the words, then no one knows what it is to have faith in what they say. If no one can provide a coherent account of what the words mean (a demonstration of their truth conditions), no one can render them intelligible to others.[174]

Intelligibility across Forms of Life

Nielsen says no to the existence of religious forms of life, independent and established, as Wittgensteinian fideism pictures them. He also says no to the second doctrine of fideism, that each form of life possesses "its own criteria and each sets its own norms of intelligibility, reality, and rationality."[175]

Then comes the third doctrine of fideism, following from the second: "forms of life taken as a whole" are not criticizable; "each mode of discourse is in order as it is."[176] Malcolm—in his wish to block Nielsen's point that, in principle, evidence must be available for or against God's existence—says this disregards the believer's "workaday religious instruction and practice."[177] He wishes, rather, to restrict the discourse to the religion's form of life. Is reality relative to a form of life? Does declaring religious talk legitimate only within its own order surrender claims to universal truth and thus accept conceptual relativism?[178]

No. Dilley shows Wittgensteinian fideism fails to account for how religious belief systems actually work—for instance by disregarding what they see as evidence for beliefs—because doing this requires reference to sources and criteria outside the faith.[179] Braithwaite also suggests that, while the decisions as to ways of life are personal, discussion occurs between the advocates of different ways of life—not a definitive establishing of any one set—on the basis of people's reflecting on everything they know. This opens up ways of life to reason. They therefore can be nonarbitrary and nonsubjective, yet personal.[180] Livingston similarly thinks fideism need not lead to subjectivism; the medium of a particular perspective may express truths that are more general.[181] Likewise, Malcolm agrees that a belief in the existence of God will change what the person expects to happen in the world, thus opening up the discourse to those out of the form of life. However, he adds, this does not provide sufficient grounds for deciding for or against God's existence. Nielsen thinks this point does not go far enough; the means whereby religious beliefs "get a grip" on the world—at least the means Malcolm suggests—do in fact support or undermine a belief in the existence of God.

Not only do Nielsen and others contend that relevant people and resources from outside the religious frame of reference can question theological assertions. History also argues for factual meaningfulness across forms of life: "religious views have varied relative to changes in scientific and metaphysical frameworks for interpreting ordinary events."[182] Modern people generally reject beliefs in fairies, magic, and witches.

The discourse of science and the discourse of religion participate in "the same overall conceptual structure," Nielsen concludes. Moreover, claims from either constantly use a lot of talk, neither scientific nor religious, from that conceptual structure, including "a number of [shared] key categories."[183] Within that overall universe of communication, people can and do judge as incoherent some religious assertions embedded in a religious form of life. An adequate account of actual religious talk therefore requires relating it to an objective type of language and a general, truth-evaluating system. It also means referring it to "extra-linguistic or context-independent conception[s] of reality" that lie in common under all modes of discourse and in relation to which people can judge forms of life.[184] Public testability, Nielsen's challenge, emerges within that shared and basic language. Philosophy can establish such general principles, despite what fideism says. Philosophy can work ideologically, articulating and defending a general outlook or appraising putative truth claims of, say, religion, as well as understanding how religious talk works.[185]

Conclusions

Fideism rests fundamental religious beliefs solely on faith, a leap into the dark.[186] Faith, according to fideism, requires accepting, say, theism as true, even potentially with a lack of evidence for its factual meaningfulness. Fideism says the religious mode of life authenticates itself fully: the meaning, coherence, and factual vindication of a religion can only come after the step of faith. Nielsen disagrees. True, to understand a religious idea a person needs to view it from within its tradition as would a participant; much of the use and meaning of religious words relates to the context that employs them. Fideism carries this too far, however. A person needs to understand the meaning of theism, Nielsen says, before adopting it on faith. Those in the group of faith do not corner factual meaningfulness, and the logics of discourses do not neatly compartmentalize.[187] Further, people do know the meaning and the proper use of the words and ideas of theism, or at least enough of them to allow communication between those in or out of the faith. Theists cannot hide inside a strongbox called faith to escape the fire of Nielsen's challenge. It has no lid.

Fideism denies the possibility of the factual nature of theology, a sacrifice too extreme and too far against the grain of theology and religion.

Only two paths remain open for fideism, Nielsen concludes. The first declares it sufficient for belief that people repeat "certain words [they] do not and cannot understand and [carry] or [attempt] to carry out certain principles of action that [they] trust will give a deep, though not clearly definable, point to [their] lives."[188] This fideism is senseless; believers will not feel happy with it.

The alternative rejects the extremes of fideism, clinging to the hope that religious utterances can have intelligible factual content. Dilley writes of the need to defend "religious belief systems . . . through the development of a comprehensive metaphysical theory grounded in religious experience, which theory is not only adequate to all the known facts but" also can claim superiority because it accepts Nielsen's challenge.[189] The above arguments slough off the various types of fideism. Perhaps the next task is to seek "a comprehensive metaphysical theory grounded in" experience (religious, scientific, and otherwise), that accounts for all known facts, and assumes Nielsen's challenge.

Tillich's Creative Terminology

Nielsen makes a point that above discussions raised but that needs remembering: traditional theists—including Barth, Kierkegaard, and Pascal—do not ask "What do theological ideas mean?" or "Are they factually meaningful or intelligible?" but, granting their intelligibility, "Why should [a person] agree to them when [they] cannot determine their truth or even their probability?" The present question asks what traditional theists took for granted: the logically prior matter that concerns whether or not religious utterances have factual meaning. "Can [a person] meaningfully assert or deny" a God exists?[190] The rightness of religious ideas or whether people should accept them comes later logically. The advance of secularism into the beliefs of current culture pushes the God question back, before that of truth or falsity, to the question of meaning.

Tillich aims to create a meaningful theology. His ideas play an important role in Nielsen's writings: as pointed out above, Nielsen primarily aims his challenge at the sophisticated religious language associated with Tillich.

Tillich wishes to create a niche independent of empirical fact; hence, he falls into the nondescriptive category. He molds for the niche, according to its contours, a new "God" in his attempt to recapture the crux of the Judeo-Christian experience of God. He thus differs from many of the nondescriptive theologians who also seek to carve out a niche for God talk independent of the world of factuality but in which they intend to resettle a traditional or near-traditional image of God. Tillich's God idea has become popular within theology and, Nielsen believes, fits the bill for mainstream or near-mainstream belief.[191]

Tillich talks about God as "ultimate concern." He does not take proximate ultimate concerns as his God idea, but rather the ultimate of ultimate concerns, utterly transcendent being itself, God. The difference compares to whether Jane Smith will become C.E.O. of the company versus what she feels her existence means when she faces death and her future nonexistence. Ultimate concern, the referent of religious symbolism, is not an object, a being among beings. Rather, it is being itself, a dimension of objects in an unexplained metaphorical sense. Because of that, religious symbols participate in the sacred and have a power, both of which people directly apprehend in religious experience. Humans herein taste the depth dimensions as feelings of holiness and know, thereby, the referent of "God," otherwise only abstractly analyzed in claims about religious symbols.[192]

Tillich's phrases are famous: "being itself," "the unconditioned transcendent," "being grasped by Being," "ultimate concern," and "the ground of being." Nielsen reacts with his own phrases: "a quasi-Platonic metaphysics," "a confusing interpretation of religious symbolism," "a loquacious obscurantist theology [that] stands in the way of a genuine understanding of religion," "loose and incoherent," and "conceptual chaos." Reiterating the conclusion by others (for instance, William Alston), Nielsen believes Tillich's account of religious language and symbolism is unintelligible.[193]

• The first of Nielsen's sorties resembles a criticism he makes of Allen's stand. According to Tillich's theology, people feel depth dimensions in religious experience. However, Nielsen, contends, "statements about feelings or . . . sentences expressing feelings," do not lead to "statements of a nonpsychological sort . . . , nor do such utterances by themselves constitute a sufficient reason for asserting the truth or the falsity of a nonpsychological statement."[194] I may feel guilty without being guilty; I feel or have a sense of the contingency of the universe, but this does not mean it is contingent. Neither does it help solve the problem of what counts for or against the contingency of the universe. Similarly, in a naturalistic way, feelings may teach something about human beings, but not about God. Nielsen therefore rhetorically asks the Tillichian theist to explain how naturalistic accounts (which Nielsen considers far simpler and, therefore, by Occam's razor, preferable to theistic explanations) inadequately account for the psychological states of religious experience.[195]

- The meaning of Tillich's phrases such as "ultimate concern" remains unclear at best. What makes a concern ultimate? How does Tillich know that ultimate concern ultimately concerns Being, that certain "experiences [are] experiences of the unconditioned transcendent"?[196] People do not already understand automatically the meaning of these opaque phrases or how to use them, because they are not in ordinary use. They need infusing with use and meaning, but Tillich's account of religious symbolism does not do this. Hence, no one can affirm or deny them. They remain meaningless.

- Tillich's ideas and theories attempt to explain or interpret experience. Some of his words, such as "Being," often function as names or referring expressions, as if a person could identify Being. They are not names, continues Nielsen; no one can experience them directly, or describe or designate their referents. Neither do they possess intelligible opposites; even the opposite of being, nothing, is not a name or referring expression.[197] (Thus Macquarrie makes a mistake when he says Nielsen takes being and being itself to stand for things, entities, or objects in the world.)[198]

- Tillich claims everyone has an ultimate concern. Nielsen suggests, however, that no one can know what it would be like *not* to possess an ultimate concern: the follower of Tillich must "explain in a straightforward manner under what conditions" it is incorrect to think a person "is ultimately concerned." Otherwise, Nielsen continues, the claim becomes a tautology, a pseudo-factual hypothesis, and an arbitrary and imperialistic tinkering with language. He calls it "linguistic gerrymandering."[199]

- Tillich says that everyone—even atheists—experiences an ultimate concern. He also must say, therefore, that everyone is religious or believes in God. Being religious, Nielsen retorts (with echoes of his responses to the attitudinal positions), differs from simply "a state of ultimate concern." Experiencing ultimate concern may form a necessary condition for religiosity, but it is insufficient; religiosity requires possessing, not any attitude or ultimate concern, but certain ones. Tillich's definition begs the old questions about belief versus unbelief, and as such spreads "sloppy thinking and evasiveness."[200]

In reply to Nielsen's questions about Tillich's theology, theologians may point to ineffability: far removed from the raising of analytic questions, being talk concerns the heart of human experience where the individual confronts the dread of nonbeing. Nielsen words this point sympathetically. Being talk, he says, can feel so paradoxical that it rightly eludes understanding. Some "concrete human experiences do lead to a confrontation with Being. And being itself" does involve "the Ineffable," namely that which lies beyond all ideas. In their "despair and estrangement," people come to an indescribable "but supremely Holy something" that they experience "in a compelling manner." In these "experiences of depth," people confront their existence and feel the unveiling of some reality. They find, however, that "words, symbols, and images" can at best only metaphorically and obliquely hint at these experiences. "To gain insight here" requires transcending "pedestrian literalness." It requires acknowledging the existence of some things no one can say or express literally.[201]

Religious language suggests indirectly and evokes within each person experiences and inexpressible truths such as Nielsen writes about here. No one can understand, however, an ineffable something; a person must use it in language for it to have meaning and this requires that people can express it. But no one can express something ineffable. In principle, ineffable things lack factual meaning. Ineffable experience cannot constitute theological knowledge.

Nielsen raises a number of other niggles that the thesis about ineffable experience prompts within him, some of which have come up before (and which augment what the above says about no one being able to experience revelation):[202]

• Metaphorical language, as Tillich claims religious discourse entails, must run parallel to literal statements with the same conceptual content; without literal God talk, metaphorical-symbolic-analogical God talk cannot exist.

- No one can talk of an encounter with Being or something similar that transcends the universe because, for people to encounter it, it must exist in the world.
- The thesis of ineffable experience rules out the existence of a religious community and communication between believers over the reality of theological matters. No one can even obliquely express the experience of an ineffable divinity.

The thesis of ineffable experience does not solve the problems Nielsen and his challenge raise with Tillich's language. Language is still on holiday, Nielsen would conclude.[203]

To create a language for religion, the theologian must make it clear and tie it to meaningful, actual experience. Nielsen would "like to see 'ultimate concerns' made a little more precise," and he "would like a little raw empiricism" about whom it afflicts and whom it does not. "No doubt Tillich has his finger on something important in any characterization of the human animal (it is still a long way to God) but, until his Germanic superstructure gets washed in the detergent of plain statement, [his ideas] . . . remain bespattered with a kind of Hegaloid mind." His "verbose grandiloquence" does not mean he is profound. One need not resort to the "mysterious and obscure" when talking about the "mysterious and obscure"; and to do so almost begs "for misinterpretation." To play "with words in Tillich's way" does avoid "the impediments to religious belief" but, "to live nonevasively," a person cannot "simply remain blank" while using his words. "Tillich does not put new wine into old bottles; he puts in grape soda and then labels it *Chateau Latour*."[204]

The religious reaction to secularization and a challenge such as Nielsen's typically sidestep and define a separate world or niche for religion in which God's absolute transcendence renders all worldly categories completely inadequate. The creative terminology of Tillich follows this pattern. It supplants (whereas most responses rejuvenate) traditional theological dogma to create a linguistic ghetto divorced from the ordinary language of the secular world. People feel safe within Tillich's jargon. But it is safe only because it beguiles. Nielsen challenges its factual meaningfulness—as he does all otherworld spiritualizations of theology—showing it forms a paper façade.[205] In the end, Tillich conjures with words to create a neat box of cards erected around the believer, but which remains irrelevant for the rest of the world.

DESCRIPTIVE RESPONSES TO NIELSEN

The above looked at responses to and victims of Nielsen's challenge, ones that seek to counter or sidestep it and so shed the traditional belief that religious language in some manner describes God. Into this fideism falls the nondescriptive category because it restricts the ascertaining of theological truthfulness to after the step of faith. Now the discussion will turn to the opposite type of positions, ones that engage the challenge and seek somehow to retain religious language as descriptive. Descriptive approaches open the truthfulness of religious statements to public examination of the facts of existence available in principle to anyone, regardless of whether they have taken a leap of faith.

This division into descriptive and nondescriptive, as pointed out before, oversimplifies theology. Not only is "descriptive" too broad a word, but religious language—even that of descriptive theologians— contains a lot that functions nondescriptively. It is not always clear whether a position falls more in the descriptive or in the nondescriptive category. Nevertheless, the division offers a way to organize responses to Nielsen's challenge based on their philosophical emphases.

Many descriptive theologies propose answers to Nielsen's challenge. Some sometimes feel overly engineered to meet it, but, nevertheless, they do try.

God as a Logically Necessary Being

Several theologians—to Nielsen's mind including Charles Hartshorne, Malcolm, Alvin Plantinga, and Ziff—try to demonstrate or at least uphold the logical necessity of God's existence. This "persistent and tantalizing claim," perhaps a maxim, thinks it logically inconceivable that God not exist.[206]

Nielsen repudiates this, of course. He first follows the critique of others to show the self-contradictory nature of the phrase "logically necessary being."

He continues, in the shoes of Hick, by showing that biblical characters and religious believers do not usually see the existence of God as necessary in a logical way, but rather that they consider God's existence a given fact.[207] Hick would rather think of God as "an eternal, utterly unbounded, indestructible, immaterial reality," a reality that creates all other realities and that depends on nothing else, including for its creation.[208] He also considers this idea, which he says lies behind the notion of a necessary being, to have factual meaning.

Now Nielsen steps out of the footwear of Hick to question this idea of God. He uses the usual empiricist ploy, asking whether any state of affairs in the world would make a scrap of difference for or against the factual truthfulness of Hick's God idea. He concludes nothing could, and so it lacks meaning.

"God" as Analogies

The Thomist view of theological method, that theology creates its ideas of God as analogies to mundane ideas, resembles Kaufman's approach seen in chapter 2 above. Both use the method of making models and both assume an utter transcendence for God, the referent of the analogies. Thomists design their theory of analogy to bring out the factual meaningfulness of God talk. Kaufman, however, thinks it has none.

A Thomist who receives Nielsen's attention is F. C. Copleston.[209] Copleston thinks people ought to avoid anthropomorphizing God and yet retain the meaningfulness of God. To do this, speech "of a transcendent and infinite being—the object of a religiously adequate God talk—[must use] the terms predicated of this being . . . analogically."[210] Human experience provides the ingredients for such terms. Yet theologians cannot use them in the same way as with words for mundane experience. Their analogical use lies in using them similarly as for finite things, but dissimilarly as well. (Norris Clarke replies to Nielsen's response to Copelston by providing his own account of analogy in which the testability of metaphysical theology provides the basis for its meaning. The point resembles Macquarrie's observation that Nielsen, in his excessive literalness, misses the truthfulness of analogy.[211])

Copleston draws a distinction between the similar and the dissimilar aspects of such a theological analogy by pointing to the difference between the "subjective meaning" and the "objective meaning" of a God statement. The former comprises the meaning the term has for human minds, and the latter comprises the objective reality to which the term refers.[212] The subjective meaning tends to form an anthropomorphic God, imperfect because of that, while the objective meaning lacks anthropomorphism.

Nielsen raises three objections to Copleston's theory. First, he says, no one can know whether the subjective meaning adequately characterizes the objective reality the term purportedly signifies:

> Having no grasp of the "objective meaning," [a person] can have no idea at all of whether [his or her] attempts to purify [the] "subjective meaning" succeed or fail. Indeed, "purifying" actually has no use here, for [a person] cannot know what would count as "purifying" the meaning of a term unless [she or he] had some grasp of the standard of perfection aimed at.[213]

As a second point, Nielsen attempts to undermine the intelligibility of the analogical account. Do the God predications differ from their analogical worldly counterparts? If they have no properties or relations in common, they are completely dissimilar and not analogical. On the other hand, their having one or more properties or relation in common does not constitute an analogy. Both counts undercut the theory of analogy and render it inadequate to describe God talk.

To move toward a third point, suppose a similarity exists. This opens God talk to infirmation or confirmation. Take the statement "God is intelligent" as similar to talk about a human who demonstrates intelligence. Suppose "to be intelligent is to have property X." If God does manifest X, grounds exist for asserting God is intelligent. However, if God never manifests property X or "if God does something inconsistent with ascribing X to" God, then grounds exist for denying God is intelligent. Yet this, in Nielsen's eyes, only *appears* to answer the challenge. Copleston does not fulfill in practice the promise of his case because he does not break out of the network of religious statements to provide "straightforward factual statements" to use in confirming or infirming theological statements.[214] He offers no anchor in experience.

James Ross provides a more complicated account of analogy than Copleston's (actually Nielsen examines two accounts by Ross). Nielsen's scrutiny tears it asunder, many of its shortfalls similar to those in Copleston's.[215]

Problems arise when applying ideas from the human realm analogously to God, if at the same time assuming God is nonanthropomorphic, an infinite being beyond and transcending this world. The problems probably occur—as they do for Kaufman's proposed method—because of the absolute transcendence.

God as the Form of the World

Two attempts by Macquarrie to elucidate the meaning of the word "God" were encountered above: first, God talk as providing a context of meaning for human existence and, second, talk of God as being. A third way from Macquarrie claims God is the "form of the world."[216] This images God as a reality, but not a reality independent of and transcending the world.

Nielsen responds: no form of the world can exist without a world. Macquarrie thus makes God depend on the world. This contradicts the Christian tradition, Nielsen says, and maybe the religious spirit as well.[217] With it, people cannot feel gratitude to God for their existence, or awe before their creator.

Further, the "world," Nielsen suggests, cannot constitute a group or class. The former implies the existence of several universes, which Nielsen thinks is nonsense. The latter implies what Macquarrie rejects, namely, God as a necessary being, contrastable and distinct from the world, thus allowing the world to have defining characteristics.

Nielsen's chief criticism has arisen before: to think of God as the form of the world "simply substitutes an unfamiliar incoherency for a familiar one."[218] He asks:

> what is it to speak of the form of the world? . . . Is the world a kind of "big thing" or "gigantic process" that could have a form? Surely not. Is it a totality? Well, what kind of totality?[219]

The putative statement "the world has a form" is incoherent and lacks factual meaning because nothing counts for or against its truth; "those who utter it have no understanding of what they [claim. They simply use] . . . words in an irresponsible manner."[220]

God as Historical Fact

Colwell claims that Nielsen's book, *Contemporary Critiques of Religion*,

> continually questions the factual significance of assertions like "God exists" and "God loves [humankind]," but . . . makes little effort to consider the empirical basis for such assertions, either in the factual content of the term "God" (in [Nielsen's] sense of "factual") or in the factual moorings

for the transcendental elements of God talk. By any reasonable standards, the deity of Christ is absolutely fundamental to any religious system which wishes to call itself Christian.[221]

Colwell does not fixate on the theological meaning of Jesus as "Son of God"—he recognizes this leads to as many problems as the idea "God" alone—but he thinks the term "God" needs applying straightforwardly to Jesus. People did and do experience Jesus the Christ as divine:

> a referent for "God" in Christianity is given in experience . . . the experi-ence of the divine *is* part of experience. . . . [Thus] many of the theistic as-sertions of Christianity are factually significant precisely because they are in principle historically and experientially verifiable.[222]

To ask about the veracity of "God exists" requires consideration of Jesus as God. This makes a difference; for example, Nielsen usually lumps together the Christian, Jewish, and Muslim conceptions of God, but the Christhood of Jesus, Colwell points out, makes the Christian one quite distinct.[223]

Colwell continues by attempting to obstruct potential counterargu-ments. Logically, reconciling the three persons of the Trinity need not block the meaningfulness of "God." Neither should Nielsen waive away—as he thinks he can—a not-purely-anthropomorphic-yet-still-somewhat-anthropomorphic Christianity like Colwell's. Nor have scholars conclusively falsified the historicity of the Gospel accounts (including the viability of miracles); in fact, they find support.

Colwell reaches the nub of his problem with Nielsen when he dis-cusses the difference between his own Christian theology and the ut-terly nonanthropomorphic theology of Nielsen's sophisticated believ-ers. To take their stance rules out any manifestation of God in history, says Colwell, because they picture God as absolutely transcendent.[224] This absoluteness in principle cannot provide empirical warrant for their theologies' theistic claims and therefore they must fail Nielsen's challenge. Colwell has a point.

On the other hand, in fairness, Nielsen does consider the biblical tes-timonies for Jesus. For instance, he discusses such issues as witness ac-counts of the purported resurrection of Jesus. How much evidence would prove the divinity of Jesus? Does a resurrection imply the super-natural nature of Jesus? Does it equate Jesus with God?[225] Nielsen cannot see that biblical accounts of Jesus, even those in which Jesus states his divinity, lead to factually meaningful claims.

Colwell only naively appreciates Nielsen's work, drawing on the book and not Neilsen's papers. Nielsen addresses a broader theism than merely Tillich's jargon and with this, as said previously, he also critiques the nonanthropomorphic otherworldly elements of Colwell's theology. Further, the anthropomorphic elements of Colwell's position—while avoiding Nielsen's wrath over sophisticated theism—fall victim to Nielsen's skepticism of, and the general cultural ambivalence toward, anthropomorphic theism.

It does not suffice to say, because of the Bible or anything else, that theological claims about God have meaning because people did and do experience God.[226] As seen above, Nielsen asks what the word "God" means. He seeks the meaning of this pre-question, the answer to which molds the understanding of what people read in the Bible and what they experience.

God in the Afterlife

God in Hick's Afterlife

One of Nielsen's most well-known debates was with Hick on the subject of eschatological confirmation.[227] Hick believes in the factual meaningfulness of theistic claims: they entail confirmable or infirmable predictions. On the other hand, he does not believe people can ever infirm God's existence or confirm it in this life. He contends, rather, that a person could confirm it eschatologically, in the next life. Nielsen summarizes Hick's case with these words: people "can *conceive* what it would be like to have an after-life" and what it would take "in the 'resurrection world' of the next life" to verify God's existence. "The existence of God is," therefore, "a factual issue and 'the choice between theism and atheism is a real and not merely empty or verbal choice.' "[228]

Nielsen questions several points here. The first involves humans' continued existence after death—at least the continued existence of at least some people. Hick claims God "reconstitutes" or "recreates" a person in a "resurrection body" in "the resurrection world."[229] This idea must have factual meaning (it must constitute an empirical assertion) to support the case for eschatological confirmation of God's existence.

Nielsen fails to see that "resurrection body" and "resurrection world" have factual meaning:

> what is this "resurrection world"? What counts as a space that is "a different space" from physical space? Has any meaning or use been given to the words "non-physical space"? What [is one] supposed to be contrasting with physical space, that either has or fails to have "properties which are manifestly incompatible with its being a region of physical space"? What is it to have a property manifestly incompatible with being a region in physical space?[230]

Nielsen finds no answers.

Even if he could rehabilitate the two terms empirically, Hick's case requires yet a further step: he needs to conceive of after-death experiences that unambiguously point to the existence of a loving God. He suggests two situations that, when occurring in conjunction, might fit the bill. Nielsen summarizes them as,

1. an experience of God's purpose for humanity as Christian revelation has disclosed it, and
2. "an experience of communion with God" as God has self-revealed "in the person of Christ."[231]

Hick then says, according to Nielsen,

- the New Testament documents depict the content of (1). They also
- indicate (to the believer at least) that experiencing "divine purpose for human life" means enjoying "a certain valuable quality of personal life, the content of which" the character of Christ provides. This "quality" so experienced forms "the proper density of human nature and the source of [human] final self-fulfillment and happiness."[232]

Nielsen finds this attempt at confirmation circular because it assumes the meaningfulness of such words as "divine purpose" and "destiny": the appeal to divine purpose for humanity assumes knowledge of how to "verify that [people's] lives have such a purpose." People do not in fact know what would count for or against their lives having a purpose (destiny, telos, final fulfillment, or final end) like this. Their actions may have purpose and they may live purposefully but, writes Nielsen, they still might find the idea unintelligible.[233]

Hick also believes that Jesus Christ, the mediator between God and humanity, points to the existence of a loving God and so makes knowable the infinite, almighty, eternal creator. This idea confronts the same sort of problem as does divine purpose; people do not understand the meaning of "God" and therefore this idea of mediator also fails to make sense.

Even if "God" were intelligible, Nielsen would challenge the existence of eschatological evidence for God's existence. To have a postmortem experience of Jesus Christ in the resurrected life does not evince the existence of God because no one knows what sorts of experiences might, if experienced in the afterlife, count as such evidence.[234]

Nielsen concludes this discussion by attempting to undermine Hick's "last resort," namely that only theists will find verification of faith because only they will experience the relevant postmortem occurrences.[235] Nielsen argues as he did in the section above on fideism: theologians cannot found the meaning of God language solely from what people might experience when they adopt the faith.

Hick cannot, despite his desires, "speed ahead of language and, independently of the forms of language, grasp what is the case."[236] The existence of God does not become a meaningful claim because of conceivable experiences in the afterlife.

God in Penelhum's Afterlife

The second response that relies on the eschaton comes from Terence Penelhum. He offers many of the same arguments as Hick, though he tries to learn from the shortcomings of Hick's positions and go beyond them.

The structure of nonanthropomorphic God talk offers itself for confirmation or infirmation and thus has factual meaning, Penelhum claims. However, he adds, only observable events in the afterlife—not those in this world—arbitrate between theism and atheism. Theism and atheism

> have different all-inclusive worldviews and these . . . involve different eschatological expectations. "The Christians' total view of the world contains essentially a belief in the ultimate triumph of God's purposes in the

world, which will take the form, in part, of an afterlife for [people] who
will live in union with God. . . ." If such a state of affairs comes to obtain,
[experience] will have verified the statements that God loves [humanity]
and that God exists. If it does not obtain, [experience] will have discon-
firmed those claims.[237]

Nielsen slams down his reasons—now familiar—for dismissing this
attempt to render theism factually meaningful.[238] Does anyone, he asks,
understand anything about what experiences in the hereafter would
count toward the truth or falsity of a statement like, "Heaven will comprise a community of persons infused by grace and over whom Jesus
reigns as the Son of God"?[239]

Theistic answers to such questions as Nielsen's chase themselves
round in circles because they involve theistic ideas whose intelligibility
Nielsen questions in the first place. "Jesus as the Son of God" and
"grace" provide two examples from the above statement. Nielsen suggests that Penelhum paraphrases the statement, in his attempt to avoid
such criticisms, with the following:

> [Heaven will comprise] a community of persons . . . [with personalities as
> if God had infused them with] grace (in that they manifest love, guile-
> lessness, self-sacrifice, understanding, purity of heart); that Jesus will rule
> over this community as the Son of God would (in a manner manifesting
> these same personality-traits plus a uniquely high degree of knowledge,
> authority, forgiveness); and that the members of this predicted community
> think and behave as they do at least in part because they consider them-
> selves . . . infused by grace, . . . redeemed sinners, . . . children of one
> God whose Son has returned to rule over his kingdom.[240]

Someone who does not understand what would count for the truth or
falsity of the statement "heaven will comprise a community of persons
under the reign of the Son of God," will still not understand the factual
import of the above quote. If no one can understand talk about the son
of God, emphasizes Nielsen, no one can understand what it would be
like to live in a community governed as if he ruled it.[241] Such predictions cannot contain theistic expressions if Penelhum wants to achieve
factual meaningfulness.

Nielsen debated with Penelhum in the years following the release of
Nielsen's challenge. No situation that counts for or against God's existence—for example, "the sudden disappearance of all degenerative

diseases"—works unless people know at least roughly what the word "God" means. All attempts to provide coherence to the word use other words as equally a problem, whether they speak of "'maker of the universe,' 'ultimate transcendent reality,' 'infinite individual transcendent to the world,' 'foundation of the world,' [or] 'self-existent reality beyond the bounds of space and time.'" God talk lacks meaning, Nielsen concludes, most chiefly because religious people do not understand "what they . . . [talk] about when they speak of God, where [they use] 'God' . . . non-anthropomorphically." Some, though, kid "themselves into believing they do" and "chatter on as if they really" understand what they say.[242]

God in Crombie's Afterlife

In trying to make intelligible a claim like "God is merciful," Crombie, like Basil Mitchell, provides a description of conditions, including those of an afterlife, on the basis of which he might give up the claim.[243] None of the conditions, however, for him count decisively against any of the claims; in the end, they become matters of faith.[244]

Nielsen raises points seen above when he argues against Crombie's version of eschatological confirmation, including where both the claims and their denials fit equally as well with any evidence. Take, for example, the claim "God loves us." Crombie supposes this is false if eternally, utterly, and irredeemably pointless suffering exists. However, Nielsen argues, to know whether this occurs requires knowing what happens throughout eternity; no one can logically decide on the issue now. No one can say, moreover, what people would have to experience at any time—whether now or in the hereafter—so they can rightly assert the falsity of such questions.[245] The claim "is dramatic but far too vague."[246]

Suppose, as a second point, that individuals continue to live on after their deaths. Suppose they then notice others suffering torture, people whom they considered good on earth; and others honored and enjoying themselves, people whom they considered evil on earth. Would this make suffering pointless? Would this show God does not love humans? Not necessarily; the knight of faith could claim that, in God's eyes, the evildoers were in fact pure of heart, and the real sinners are those thought saintly on earth. What one person would see as the pointlessness of suffering, another need not.

Suppose instead that a theist and an atheist in the afterlife agree that pointless suffering does not occur. This still does not suffice to clinch the theist's argument. The protagonists can disagree over the question of God's existence with no circumstances counting for the theist's claims over the atheist's. The factual content of their statements does not differ when they approach the issue of God's existence in the afterlife, the same as happens in this life.

Irrespective of these points, does Crombie succeed in giving factual meaning to statements such as "God loves us"? Only provided "God exists" itself has factual meaning and people understand the meaning of the word "God." But people do not understand it, continues Nielsen, for this constitutes the original point at issue.

The potential existence of pointless suffering does not offer a ground for the factual nature of "God loves us." Crombie's schemes do not meet the challenge.[247]

God Here and Now

The idea of an afterlife induces the same criticisms Nielsen raises for the contents of postmortem experiences, namely, assuming theistic expressions to justify its existence. To make a case successfully for the reasonableness of an afterlife would probably mean facing few problems in creating one for theism—probably a parallel one; both break the secular worldview in a similar manner.[248]

Nielsen, of course, feels dubious about the coherence of the idea of life after death as well as the idea of God. However, he tries to show the incoherence of the various eschatological ways for confirming theism without his dubiousness about life after death figuring prominently in his responses. Theologians would be better to change direction and not seek to base the meaningfulness of theism on potential experiences in the hereafter. The need for religion occurs right here in this present society, and theologians should not relegate its justification to the never-never; this may make it feel irrelevant for people's lives. Life is not primarily about the afterlife. Eschatological theologians probably do not intend to imply this irrelevance, looking more to a theoretical situation in which theism may open itself to confirmation (and with Penelhum, also to infirmation). Their approach, on the other hand, might easily lead this way. Theologians ought to explore an empirical case for the factual coherence of a form of theism based, unlike Hick's, Penelhum's, and Crombie's, in the here and now.

God from Morality

Some theologians claim that, without belief in an objectively existing God, life has no point and morality no basis. Theological language must describe a real God or else values lose their objective base and moral principles end up relative.[249] Nielsen denies this.[250]

"God" Independent from "Good"

He questions the belief that God's absolute goodness promotes God's attitudes and actions, which for humans in turn serve as the basis for absolute moral standards. Jews and Christians may say "God is good," or "God is the highest good," but, Nielsen continues,

> "God" does not mean "good" any more than "puppies" mean "young," for to say "A good wife will try to understand her husband's aspirations" is most certainly not to say, what is nonsense anyway, "A God wife will try to understand her husband's aspirations." "Good" does not mean "God."[251]

The meanings of the two words, "good" and "God," are independent; theists hold moral criteria independently to believing in God.

Nielsen then asks why the theist believes in the goodness of God:[252]

- Because factual evidence reveals it? But for this, people must already know what constitutes goodness so they can decide on the goodness of God.
- Because people define God as good? But for this, suggests David Basinger, they need to "know that the being whose attitudes and actions [they] accept as an objective moral standard is God."[253]
- Because God says God is good? But for this, people need to know why they should believe God's moral claims.
- Because God commands people to behave in particular ways? But for this, they need to know why they should obey God.
- Because of God's omnipotence and omniscience? But for this, people need to know that the creator of the universe is not evil.

• Because of fear of punishment? But for this, people stoop to a less than admirable reason for obeying God.

Theists must define goodness for themselves, Nielsen concludes, independent of their belief in God, and then associate this goodness with God.

In fact, life does have meanings and values independent from belief in God. Writes Nielsen: "God does not exist, 'but the napalming of children is evil'" is not a contradiction.[254]

> And while for a believer the loss of faith may be a shocking, soul-searching loss, it still remains the case that human love, happiness, companionship, and understanding are of value even in a Godless world. Even in such a world, the torturing of children remains vile. Indeed, certain "world-renouncing" or "other-worldly" ideals, ideals Steppenwolfian personalities are inextricably committed to, become absurd with the "death of religion." But other ideals—ideals of human happiness, solidarity, and achievement—retain their point. The bliss of religious ecstasy is lost, but the joys of life, refined and nonrefined, are perfectly available in a Godless world. . . . Even in a world without God such actions can have a point.[255]

Nielsen distinguishes between purposes *of* or *to* life as opposed to purposes *in* life. For instance, "to cure the sick, to achieve racial equality and social justice, to achieve happiness and a fuller and more varied life for [people] and for those to whom [they relate], to achieve love and close human bonds and solidarity"—these can exist in a life without God. Any person "can reflectively form intentions and purposes and find satisfaction in so doing." Morality thus possesses a secular ground; the goodness or badness of something pertains to it independently of whether "an omnipotent, all-knowing being" commands or wills it.[256]

Not only purposes and morals, but moral absolutes also exist independent of belief in God. As examples Nielsen points to the statements, "happiness is good" and "people should treat other people fairly."[257] Most persons intuitively recognize and know these absolutes as true, Nielsen thinks; the sense of the absolutes' "psychological realism" provides the basis for this objectivity. They usually are also the most advantageous for those involved. A way of life need not necessarily constitute a relative, individual matter but, rather, a person can find one way more reasonable and justified over another.[258]

Nielsen believes an objective standpoint exists on which people can base moral judgments, independent of belief in the existence (or nonexistence) of God. A moral humanity does not require the reality of God.

God from Divinely Implanted Morality

Basinger thinks he can build an adequate case against Nielsen and provide morality with an objective basis originating from both the human and the divine spheres. He objects to the idea that the moral standards the theist uses to assess the goodness of God are "separate from and more fundamental than the divine moral code" the theist judges, and that each theist rationally formulates (or senses) the moral criteria independent of divine influence.[259] Basinger believes, rather, that God created all human beings with divine moral sensitivities. Further, people use this divine implantation to judge God's goodness.[260] He rallies support for his thesis: it derives from the Bible; "careful" theologians in the Christian tradition uphold it; it explains the cultural universality of "certain basic moral precepts"; and, fourth, an intellectually viable relativism (a possible consequence of Nielsen's position) becomes impractical.[261]

Many objections confront this divine implantation theory. As already seen, Nielsen contradicts Basinger's fourth point above: relativism need not follow from Nielsen's challenge. For Basinger's third point, perhaps a biological implantation theory such as George Edwin Pugh's from evolutionary psychology can explain the existence of universal moral precepts: a moral implantation need not be divine.[262]

Basinger willingly concedes quite a lot to Nielsen. Theists affirm the goodness and worship worthiness of God because, from their investigations, they find God's actions and attitudes consistent with their moral expectations. Basinger might take these concessions more seriously. Instead, he removes the empirical aura from his theory by having it automatically explain all moralities and potential counterexamples; not everyone need affirm "a general theistic moral code," he tells us, because humans have the freedom to conceive of or commit themselves to alternatives, nor need they recognize the implantation. He also writes: "To counter Nielsen, a 'divine implantation' theist need only affirm that [she or] he believes such universal implantations to be an objective fact." Basinger tries to masquerade, as a reasonable alternative, his dogmatism protected by fiat from counterevidence: the assertion, "the creator of the universe implanted his [*sic*] moral standard within us," makes "a factual statement" that investigators can only settle "on evidential grounds ([for example], on the basis of indirect empirical evidence)."[263]

The weakness of Basinger's case begins in his misunderstanding of Nielsen's intentions. He writes that Nielsen does not make

> any claim concerning the truth or falsity of the theist's belief concerning God's existence, attitudes, or actions. His contribution is only that the theist cannot consistently maintain that his [or her] moral decisions [derive from] an absolute, objective moral standard independent of [human beings], even if [they do] profess belief in a wholly good God.[264]

Nielsen of course does attempt to undermine all sophisticated claims for the meaningfulness (and hence truthfulness) of God's existence, as well as to knock away theism's prop that requires a God to uphold morality.

God from God-Dependent Values

A 1978 reply to Nielsen by Osmond Ramberan concentrates on believers' worship of God. He restates Nielsen's position with this: The religious quest searches for a being "worthy of worship." Humans decide with their own moral insight, however, whether any being warrants worship. This decision does not depend on the will of God. Further, "God," in "God warrants worship," usually means that the person who says "My God," or "My Lord and my God," uses "God" evaluatively and thus makes a moral judgment logically prior to God's will.[265]

In Ramberan's mind, Nielsen defines religion in terms of worship.[266] In Nielsen's mind, worship does not constitute the defining characteristic of religion; think of the great bulk of his writings on religion that concern belief in God. Nielsen debates whether the word "God" has meaning, a question prior to the appropriateness of God worship. This realization takes much of the wind out of Ramberan's sails.

Ramberan's version of Nielsen's position, leaving out the worship emphasis, becomes: A person does not just obey God's commands blindly because of their goodness; he or she has to decide independently about their goodness or badness. Ramberan then replies: People may decide to obey God not for moral reasons, but, say, from a sense of gratitude; they need not therefore obey God's commands only out of moral obligation or moral blameworthiness for failing to do so. Moreover, a loving God would not command something morally wrong because it would contradict God's loving nature. To value things independently of God's will does not therefore mean commitment to a value system independent of that will.[267] Nielsen's case for a moral base free of belief in God need not mean God does not exist.

Ramberan again reads Nielsen incorrectly; Nielsen in fact argues against morality requiring belief in God. Ramberan says a person can choose a value system independent of God's will, but that the system may depend on God's will. (This sounds like divine implantation again.) This presupposes the phrase "God's will" makes sense, and Ramberan thereby assumes what his own counterargument sets out to prove. The original theist argument against Nielsen's challenge charges that morality requires belief in God and, therefore, to have morality, "God" must have meaning. Nielsen shows morality can and does exist whether or not "God" has meaning.

Another inadequate reading of Nielsen says he thinks people only obey God from moral or prudential reasons. Ramberan replies that this does not offer an exhaustive distinction.[268] But Nielsen does not say this in the first place.

Some attempts by theists to counter Nielsen take a small segment of his writings—sometimes taking it incorrectly—and from it build an opponent with which to wrestle. Such antagonists usually enter the ring with straw replicas of Nielsen and thus easily, they think, immobilize a foe—who actually sits in the audience laughing and weeping.

God as Infinite Spirit

Crombie employs a number of independent arguments to uphold the factual meaningfulness of God language. Some of these have already arisen: analogical predication (similar to the reactions of Copleston and Ross), eschatological confirmation, the authority of Christ (under non-descriptive positions), and the questioning of Nielsen's challenge. At base, he holds that theological statements—whether those of theologians or plain believers—offer factual assertions confirmable or infirmable in principle.[269]

Another of his attempts, "God as infinite spirit," involves two aspects of what the word "God" supposedly refers to—"spirit" and "infinite." They, and Nielsen's reaction to them, lend themselves to separate accounts.

God as Pure Spirit

The idea of God as spirit derives, suggests Crombie, from the notion of a complement that "could fill in certain deficiencies in [human] experience or scientific theory-making."[270] These deficiencies have to do with humans' spiritual nature, not in a Cartesian dualistic sense, but as hoping, loving, dreaming beings—ideas not fully reducible to purely physical language, or independent of space and the physical world. People's experience as spirits and not mere physical objects causes them to feel alienated from the physical world.

Yet people feel their imperfect spirituality somehow originates from a perfect spirit. The positive content of the idea of God as spirit, suggests Crombie, simply comprises "the idea of something" that "might supply these deficiencies."[271] He wants to think of God as pure spirit.

This idea must necessarily remain vague: no one can know what theological statements concern because they have to do with mystery. The word "spirit" does not stand for or denote anything known, though it expresses something that human self-understanding—"only in so far as [humans] are spiritual"—gives an inkling. Part of their use is their elusiveness, attesting to a difference between God and other beings. The religious use of the word "spirit" thus deliberately deviates from its common use. Crombie hopes this legitimizes his abstracting the notion of pure spirit as a distinct kind of entity or being; the skeptic might, after all, ask why theologians should abstract spiritual experience, because they do not abstract the physical and speak, for instance, of pure digestions. Knowing about this mystery avoids the logical incoherence of theological statements and makes speech about God intelligible.

Nielsen remains unconvinced and does not see that this tie with feelings of deficiency provides factual meaning to the words "*pure* spirit." Does the phrase mean anything? Just as people have no idea or understanding of an engine distinguishable from the parts that constitute it, so, Nielsen suggests, they have no idea or understanding of a (pure) spirit distinguishable from a human being. "Does 'a pure spirit' have a use any more than [does] 'a pure digesting'?" Nielsen thinks not. "Spirit" and "spirituality" do not label or name any part or aspect of a human being that resembles, even in principle, "something separately identifiable from the behavior of an animate human being or other animal." No such part or aspect exists that can "serve as a model for an appropriate, though vague, understanding of what . . . 'pure spirit' or just 'a spirit'" might mean. Thus, theologians "have no inkling or indicia in experience which point to, no matter how opaquely, a pure spirit. . . . 'Pure spirit' parades as a referring expression, but unlike 'the spirit of [humanity]' or 'her spirit was down,'" no one can grasp what the theologian is talking about.[272]

God as an Infinite Being

That apparently undermines Crombie's conception of God as spirit. What of the adjective "infinite" in his expression, "God as infinite spirit"? Putting "spirit" to the side now, Nielsen turns to counter the word "infinite." Does an intelligible use exist for the phrase "an infinite being" beyond saying "not anything finite"?

People experience, according to Crombie, inklings about the finitude and contingency of things. They feel the created, dependent, and derivative nature of the universe. These inklings produce an intellectual dissatisfaction in them and so they conceive in contrast to these feelings an infinite and nonderivative being. God talk satisfies the intellectual problem. Theology thus refers, Crombie continues, "to the postulated, though unimaginable, absence of limitations or imperfections."[273]

Nielsen concedes that people do experience contingency and finitude. The superstitious idea "God" tries to explain them: persons can, if their "grip on reality is not so good, think of a superhuman but quite non-spatio-temporal being, who is not contingent, dependent, derivative, finite in the way [they] are." This "cosmic Popeye" projection in turn leads to the sense of contingency and finitude and offers the contrast necessary to make the ideas of contingency and finitude intelligible. Nielsen challenges this explanation as an emotional one "born of . . . natural infant helplessness and . . . early indoctrination."[274] Everyone should grow up and reject it.

The feelings of finitude arise, Nielsen suggests, from comparing the physical state of humans with something else physical: the seeming agelessness of the stars contrasted with a person's brief life span. It does not surprise him intellectually that the universe comprises an indefinite number of things that came into existence and shall go out of existence. For him, this explanation renders intelligible the contingency experiences.

Crombie's idea of God as an infinite spirit thus fails to make God talk intelligible to Nielsen.

God as Love

John Robinson rejects the reduction of theology to either humanism or supernaturalism. Rather, he thinks God talk affirms, Nielsen suggests, "the reality of . . . a mysterious Thou": a "Thou" that Robinson takes as "the ultimate truth about reality." Further, the Christian believer affirms purpose and love reside "at the heart of things . . . in the very grain of the universe," giving "meaning to even that which in itself" has no meaning.[275]

First, Nielsen responds, what could Robinson mean—given he drops supernaturalism—by "a mysterious Thou . . . the ultimate truth about reality?" People have no idea what would constitute their encountering or meeting, or failing to encounter or meet this Thou. Nothing counts for or against the assertion that something constitutes the ultimate truth about things. Robinson's "language is idling."[276]

Second, Nielsen asks, what does Robinson mean when he says love and purpose lie "at the heart of things"? Because humans love (and, perhaps derivatively, because some animals behave likewise), love "in the very grain of the universe" may mean humanistically that, generally, people love. However, Robinson probably means more than this. Does he mean some "kind, loving, understanding people [live their lives] with integrity and concern for their fellows and that . . . their views about how [to conduct] human relationships . . . will prevail," even if only in the very long run? He probably means more than this too. For sure, he does not mean God, as a supernatural yet loving agent or being, lies literally at the heart of the universe. So, what does he mean? People have, in fact, no idea what his sentences mean, even if they "have a powerful emotive ring." For Robinson's words to have factual meaning, a person must know—and no one does—how to find them "true or false or even probably true or probably false."[277]

God as the Source of Public Religious Experience

Wilson attempts to defend theistic claims empirically, taking "God exists" as a factual statement open in principle to decisive infirmation.[278] His attempt to demonstrate the *decisive* falsifiability of theistic statements harks back to an early logical positivism whose severity had ameliorated by the time of Nielsen's challenge. Nevertheless, in a weaker form that omits the "decisive" tone, his case still has relevance as a descriptive response to Nielsen.

People can confirm or infirm theistic statements by their experience or nonexperience of the supernatural, Wilson claims. Hence, theologians can try to show "theistic assertions satisfy the minimum necessary conditions for . . . an empirical assertion."[279] Wilson attempts to show religious experience points unambiguously to an objective supernatural reality, while also accepting such experience as open to different interpretations.

> The tests [for this] must involve something that [people] see; and . . . [for] theistic sentences . . . to have the requisite sort of meaning, [people must be able to] . . . predict that, if [they] do such-and-such, then [they] will have certain quite definite experiences. . . . Certain sincerely alleged religious experiences may turn out not to [demonstrate the truth] . . . if certain definite experiences do not occur.[280]

(Not everyone can adopt the tests because, to conduct them, the testers must have had the requisite experiences. Never mind; at least a limited public can confirm or infirm theistic claims based on the experiences. [This approach need not lead to fideism because the experience may not require faith.])

What are these tests? Take the statement "a God exists in heaven" and try to investigate it as one typically would for a fact-stating claim. Wilson's approach says people should describe particular activities that, if they performed them, might confirm the hypothesis. He finds no shortage of such activities: how to pray, read the Gospels, worship, or behave toward neighbors.

Do these religious experiences, however, necessarily lead to "a direct acquaintance with God"? Nielsen suggests that, while the experiences lead some people to God, other people "learn, or relearn, after just those operations, to talk about these same experiences in secular terms."[281]

> [A person] may in a quiet hour say: "My Lord and my God help me" and kneel and make the sign of the cross. [That person] may then experience a sense of relief or come to *feel* . . . [she or he is] not alone in a barren and cold universe. In short, [people] may feel to the full [their] "creatureliness."[282]

Researchers might talk about these experiences in secular terms and they might explain them this way as well. Nielsen asks — as he did with the theories of Kaufman, Allen, and Tillich — whether religious experiences constitute encounters with a supposed supernatural being or whether it might be better and simpler to interpret them as natural. Perhaps, as an acceptable mode of human experience, they relate to anxiety brought on by "early Oedipal conflicts."[283]

More generally, how might a person

> know whether these experiential results — these feelings — either point or fail to point to the reality of God or the supernatural? The naturalist and secularist assert that these feelings do not point to this reality, and the theist asserts they do; but what could possibly establish with even the slightest probability that what one said was false and what the other said was true?[284]

Wilson offers some remarks that, according to Nielsen, attempt to face this question.

- He compares religious experience to blindness, suggesting some people are "God blind." People blind from birth can gain some sense of color words, but cannot know, for instance, what constitutes "red" because they cannot visualize or experience it. Some people may similarly have God blindness: they "could carry out all the operations, . . . learn how to talk to and about God, but . . . have no idea of what" would constitute direct experience of the supernatural.[285]

   Nielsen disagrees with this analogy. To his mind, the two types of blindness differ distinctively. Visual blindness has universal tests, but there are no agreed-on tests for "God blindness"; furthermore, no one even knows "how to start setting up such tests."[286]
- Wilson also compares the expectation that nothing tests atheism with the expectation of tests for theism, suggesting nothing should assess it either.

   However, responds Nielsen, people do not regard atheistic statements as factual, despite the existence of methods to validate them, whereas theists do regard theistic statements as factual. The comparison, therefore, only further points to the failure of theism.

Thus, Wilson's position "only *seems* to carry" his readers "to the promised land," Nielsen concludes. In fact, appeal to religious experience appears to pose as many problems as do other theological ploys. "Wilson's well-meaning effort" to do religion empirically "winds up in a complete failure."[287]

God as in Physics

A previous section mentioned Ziff's experimental case for the intelligibility of the statement, "God exists," based on the incompatibility of God's omnipotence with physics.[288] Physics also entered the discussion of nondescriptive approaches, particularly the ideas of Findlay. He says theological statements about God have factual meaning though theologians know little or nothing about God, just as people take some statements in physics as coherent though they concern something about which ordinary folk know very little and of which they can make little sense.

Theists raise still other analogies with physics in their descriptive attempts to meet Nielsen's and related challenges.

God as Like Electrons

Are theistic assertions descriptive in the same way as are assertions in physics about such things as electrons? No one can observe electrons directly or verify the statement "electrons exist," meaning it does not translate "without remainder into an 'empiricist language.'"[289] Yet people assume electrons exist; "electrons exist" makes a factually meaningful statement. Might theologians similarly assume "God exists" offers a factually meaningful statement?

Nielsen eagerly plugs this reply by theists.[290] He points out that, logically, someone might some day observe such entities as photons or mesons. (This differs from the practical inability to observe them.) Nonanthropomorphic ideas of God within the Christian or Jewish religions create a quite different situation. "God (the metaphysical God) is an infinite individual who . . . [transcends] the universe and who, by definition, possesses no physical properties."[291] Logically, no one can observe God.

Theologians may claim as a way out that the electron and its stable mates are not entities or particles, but theoretical fictions. Similarly for God. In science, responds Nielsen,

> [people] no longer feel incumbent to ask if . . . such things as magnetic fields or superegos [exist]. Such concepts [offer] . . . pragmatically

useful constructs since they enable [scientists] to make predictions and
assessments of behavior with greater ease than if [they] did not have
such concepts, but [they] can [remain] . . . agnostic about whether . . .
such things [exist]. But the believer cannot [remain] . . . agnostic in this
way about God, and . . . cannot regard the concept of God *simply* as an
important construct or as a useful heuristic device . . . and still remain a
believer.[292]

A believer cannot opt for this definition of God, and so the analogy with
electrons falls again.

Perhaps the theologian might take a further step and say the infinite
God differs from such finite realities as electrons, but the difficulties in
observing God resemble those for observing electrons. This does not
add a helpful analogy to the issue, Nielsen says, because of the great-
ness of the disanalogy.

God Experiences as Like a Bubble Chamber

Some theologians admit the impossibility of directly seeing or encountering God; nonanthropomorphic theism denies that anyone can literally
encounter God. This theological approach may still affirm the possibility of indirect encounters. Hick, for instance, describes experiences of
bliss in the afterlife as indirect observations of God.

To justify that people can have indirect experiences of God, some theologians look to physics. Here, an experimenter cannot directly observe
such things as electrons, but may indirectly encounter them in their
paths through bubble chambers. Nielsen summarizes this approach:

> [People] speak of a magnetic field or a superego and [they] cannot see
> either, but . . . recognized procedures [exist] for verifying statements
> embodying such conceptions. They [form] . . . part of a whole network
> of conceptions, but within the appropriate scientific context . . . recog-
> nized procedures of verification [exist] for statements using such con-
> cepts. Why can [theologians] not properly say the same thing about Je-
> sus and Christianity?[293]

Nielsen objects to this parallel. Science provides a theoretical structure that says what would confirm its objective claims. Theology, on the
other hand, does not know what its evidence unambiguously points to;
to confirm its objective claims, theology has to know what would count

as an observation or experience of the thing to which indirect experience supposedly points. If theologians do not know what experiencing this thing entails, then they do not understand what having evidence (indirect or direct) for it entails. It makes no sense to say so-and-so exists and that no one can have any inkling of what experiencing it entails, but a person can experience something else that provides evidence for it. "The 'it' here cannot refer to anything" because no one can understand the thing to which the alleged evidence supposed points.[294] Further, says Nielsen, what logically people cannot detect directly, logically they cannot detect indirectly as well, because "'indirectly' can only qualify 'detect' if 'indirectly' has a non-vacuous contrast."[295]

God as a High-Level Theoretical Term

A statement such as "electrons exist" has factual meaning though physicists cannot point to electrons. "In the context of a whole physical theory," Nielsen writes, "certain experiences"—which physicists can formulate as observation sentences—count for or against the existence of electrons. These observations confirm or infirm the electrons' existence.[296] In the same way, theologians may test the existence of God as a part of a whole theoretical system, and hence ascertain whether God exists though they cannot observe God directly. It is possible, in other words, to take God statements as high-level theoretical terms in a system of theology. It is also possible to assume that the system as a whole, not individual assertions by themselves, stands before the court of empirical enquiry.[297] Finally, it is possible to suppose that, if someone finds evidence potentially disconfirming some high-level theological assertion, theologians will alter or add various subsidiary statements or hypotheses to protect it. The system as a whole fails if enough of these lower-level adjustments fail.

Nielsen provides several counters to this approach. First, he raises the point already made above, that the idea "God" does not evince the same logical status as does one of science's theoretical terms or constructs, such as an electron.

Note also that (another of Nielsen's points set out above) logically no one can confirm or infirm God statements indirectly—say via this system image for theology—if the direct case is unintelligible.

Third, Nielsen thinks the descriptors "system" and "the myth of the whole" do not apply to a religion as they do to physics or mathematics.[298]

Religions, he writes, are not "neat or even unneat hypotheticodeductive-predictive systems." Rather, they comprise "activities, essentially social activities . . . with rites and loosely related doctrinal claims." Why, therefore, "in such a loosely organized activity as religion," must tests apply to the whole system?[299]

Does the system or web image, however, describe a theology as opposed to a religion? Nielsen does not appear to address this. If theologians can use the system image, they may wish to remove talk of direct confirmation or infirmation of high-level God ideas and emphasize the lower-level empirical anchorage of the whole system. They could then potentially reject some peripheral parts of a theology and stick with any others they find crucial, finally throwing out the whole system if they find the discord too great. They could thus treat the God idea as open though resistant to change and thus analogous to a high-level theoretical hypothesis or ideas in physics such as a meson or a photon or, even more abstractly, like physical notions of cause and effect or the quantifiable physical world. They could, as in Nielsen's description of science, treat "God" as "a high-level hypothesis used to interpret . . . experience but capable of modification and eventual abandonment, if certain events take place. . . . If a certain factual claim distant from the experimental periphery has a great deal of experimental evidence counting against it," theologians finally should abandon it. "To count as scientific, a factual statement must function this way."[300] Theologians could thereby hold the idea "God" tentatively and do theology as a science.

The system idea needs careful execution, however. Often, the skeptic can accept some of the peripheral ideas but find the central core beliefs meaningless. "One can believe," Nielsen writes, "that Jesus was a deeply spiritual leader, that he was born in Nazareth, and that he preached . . . love and cured people in a mysterious way and still find the claim that 'Jesus is God incarnate' utterly incoherent."[301] (Many religious people would agree with the direction here, but perhaps not the tone.) This reverses the usual relationship between high- and low-level components of a system of ideas, where people more easily accept or reject the peripheral elements in the face of confirming or infirming evidence, not the core ones.

Nielsen reacts sharply to the possibility of altering the God idea or holding it tentatively: it radically misconstrues, he says, the functioning of religious sentences in Western language.[302] While theologians may want to think or give the impression they open their beliefs to someone proving them wrong, they will not allow this to happen. Christians, according to Nielsen, will not or cannot say, or say clearly, under what conditions they would abandon their faith. To hold theistic assertions as provisional and tentative contravenes the God of Christian theism: Christian belief requires that believers give decisive adherence to God.[303] Further, to empiricize theology removes its mystery.

Nor could theistic assertions function this way in the future, Nielsen claims, if they are to fulfill the distinctive jobs of religious utterances. This would attempt a rational reconstruction of religion and not an analysis of Christian belief as presently operating.

Nielsen's guns fire too loudly for him to hear what he fears: if theologians attempt an empirical theology, they accept his challenge. However, he, the ardent pusher of atheism, does not want this to happen. He wants people to abandon theism rather than reconstruct and modify it to something more adequate empirically. This fails to acknowledge that, historically, theology changes and probably will do so in the future. Theology may even morph to meet challenges such as the one he offers and yet still adhere decisively to God, a God always portrayed provisionally.

God as the Suprasensible Cause of All Events

Anthony Ralls's case for the intelligibility of God talk starts by saying no one can directly encounter God. Rather, he thinks, people can only encounter the activity or effects of God. They infer or perceive the existence of God as a suprasensible cause, as they might perceive a forest fire by seeing smoke billowing above the canopy. It is possible to perceive two types of such causes: as the origin of certain particular and distinctive events such as the parting of the Red Sea, and as the origin of everything that happens. The two ways relate in that becoming aware of the existence of the suprasensible cause of specific extraordinary events leads to an awareness of this being as the suprasensible cause of all events.[304]

Nielsen rolls out his objections:

1. People can in principle directly perceive a fire, but they cannot directly perceive God. The analogy Ralls employs to help his case, therefore, only obscures the issues.

2. To insist on a unique causal relationship between particular events and a suprasensible origin employs an idea with no established use and that raises at least the same problems as with the God idea. For instance, to say one thing causes another requires that people can observe independently the two types of events to see if they always appear in conjunction; but no one can directly (or indirectly) perceive God. Further, the same evidence exists for as against perceiving God in some particular occurrence, and thus this theory has no factual meaning.

3. The idea that everything perceived shows God exists, nothing capable of demonstrating the contrary, lacks factual or descriptive content. A factual word or phrase must offer a non-vacuous contrast and Ralls's God idea does not do this.

Again the nub of the problem appears to lie in God's extreme transcendence (God as suprasensible), which means no one can encounter God and God cannot "spatially [relate] to the universe." Any state of affairs is thus compatible with God's existence.[305] What about a modified version of Ralls's position where God is the cause of all events but without a "suprasensible" aspect? Does this answer Nielsen's most severe criticisms?

CONCLUSIONS

Nielsen shows that each descriptive approach, when pushed to its limits, wants to treat God sentences as factual assertions, but that each fails to show how they have factual meaning. Theists allow no amount of evidence to infirm or even possibly infirm their basic assertions. They "will and must always" reject "falsifying instances . . . as somehow inconclusive."[306] Descriptive theologians retreat into a nondescriptive fideist cave when hard pressed.

This chapter surveyed Nielsen's attacks on theology and thereby listed questions he asks of a theological method. It outlined his view of and challenge to religious language, and mentioned several responses to the way he poses the issue. It then reviewed efforts to answer him by redefining religious language and thus hopefully avoiding his challenge (the nondescriptive approach), or by accepting it (the descriptive approach).

Though the secular challenge does not apply in its original and extreme form of logical positivism, it still, under Nielsen, asks of religion the important meaning question. (Luckily, Nielsen raised his issues as and when he did. It probably would not happen with such dedication now, because fewer and fewer Westerners grow up as he did in a religious environment and then release themselves into the secular world.) The issue does not merely involve the inability to provide an adequate justification for "God exists," but of saying noncircularly what might factually constitute God, what would or would not count for the idea "God." Might "God" make any conceivable difference? The persistent growth and prevalence of the secular-scientific approach to life over the last centuries in the West makes this question both valid and critical.[307]

Nielsen's response to theology fails to satisfy theologians. He does not fully communicate his point to them because they feel it too extreme and because they think they can shield their foundational beliefs, particularly with an absolute transcendence for God. Their reactions, in turn, create or bring out a dualism and exacerbate the problem of factual meaningfulness. Unfortunately, invoking this "God" also renders their beliefs even more irrelevant to contemporary social issues and secular ways of thinking and living. Theologians cannot satisfy Nielsen's challenge and retain their dualistic theism. They cannot retain their theism and meet the needs of modern Western society.

Anthropomorphic charismatic-Pentecostal, creationist-fundamentalist, and liberation theologies do satisfy Nielsen's challenge inasmuch as they shun a sophisticated and otherworldly theism. However, they fail the other half of Nielsen's critique, the one against anthropomorphism. Under Nielsen, all descriptive and nondescriptive sophisticated theologies fail—of course they do; they have to, given his atheistic agenda.

Nielsen leaves theological method with a challenge, not to justify theology's existence, but to choose more factually meaningful theologies over others, or to develop them afresh.[308] This book concerns the creation of a descriptive and factually meaningful theology given the difficulties that Nielsen raises. A starting point might ask what theological approaches show the least failure under Nielsen's butchering. Where are Nielsen's arguments weakest? His most vulnerable critiques appear toward those nonanthropomorphic responses that maximize factual meaningfulness, those that minimize or remove reliance on a dualistic otherworldliness where God completely transcends the world. The theological reconstructivist should follow this clue. In opposition to a dogmatism and dualism such as with fideism and otherworldliness, an adequate theology must build on empiricism and monism (which sees reality as a unified whole). A contemporary and secular outlook must have both of them; theologians cannot do empiricism without monism. Post-Nielsen, can theologians resurrect from theology this sort of factually meaningful residue? What ought they to accept about God from tradition and what ought they not to accept? Perhaps no such candidates currently strut the theological stage.

Nielsen is an atheist fundamentalist who takes the core of religious beliefs or theology as fixed. He requires philosophers accept as a given the first-order religious language that "the various confessional groups" use; philosophers must aim, he says, to provide "a perspicuous representation" of their discourse.[309] What if theology changes? It has changed and will change, despite Nielsen not allowing this possibility. No one need accept received ideas. Rather, an answer to Nielsen could say, yes, sophisticated theology (neo-orthodoxy) and anthropomorphism do err, yet theologians can try to find other ways.

The above critiques and responses suggest starting to meet Nielsen's challenge by considering theology descriptive, yet not straightforwardly so. Theologians could think of a theology as a whole, as a web of beliefs, with some elements more central and others more peripheral and open to revision. Nondescriptive elements interweave with descriptive ones; some parts more directly face questions of factual meaningfulness than do others.

To work out such a science of God, theologians might assume God exists and then (thinking of Nielsen's challenge) ask what sort of God exists, which amounts to asking what sort of God-world relationships exist. Theologians might thereby reject or put on the table what tradition says about God. They might consider God as a high-level theoretical construct; perhaps define God as the cause of all events, as creator.

Might an elaboration of this have the potential to produce a theological complex in which "God exists" becomes factually meaningful? Is this "God" potentially real to most modern Westerners? Such an approach in the end may not fall into the Christian or Jewish or any other religions' corpus as history will chart them—though it may aim at inclusion with one of them—but that is the risk honesty takes.

NOTES

1. Nielsen 1981a: 147. See also his 1971a: 13–16.
2. For older critiques, see Nielsen 1971a: 1; 1973b.
3. Flew and Macintyre 1955. See Nielsen 1969a: 17–18; 1971a: 16–22, 25–30; 1973c: 1–5; 1975: 98f; Slater 1973.
4. For Nielsen's personal point of entry, see his 1974a; Yandell 1968b:19.
5. Nielsen 1973a: 275; paraphrased a little for style. See also Wisdom's parable of the gardener; Wisdom 1944; reprinted in Flew 1951: chap. 10; Wisdom 1953.
6. Nielsen 1973a: 275.
7. Nielsen 1969a: 17. See also his 1965a: 138; 1971b: 227–29; 1973a: 274; 1975: 98, 103–4.
8. Nielsen 1962a: 110–11.
9. Nielsen 1974b: 199.
10. Nielsen 1966a: 14, 16. See also his 1973a: 276; 1981a: 153.
11. Nielsen 1972a: 30.
12. Nielsen 1974c: 26.
13. Nielsen 1966b; 1970a; 1970b; 1972a; 1972b; 1973c: 3ff; Reese 1979.
14. See Diamond 1975.
15. Nielsen 1970c: 3–4. See also Hoffman 1970.
16. Nielsen 1971a: 39–40.
17. Colwell 1981: 325–26.
18. Clifford 1968: 339.
19. Nielsen 1972a. 30, 1974a. 18.
20. Nielsen 1961a: 270–71, 281; 1970c: 5.
21. Nielsen 1970c: 1.
22. Nielsen 1974a: 19. See also Hook 1975: 127; Nielsen 1965b: 10–17.
23. See Geach 1974; Nielsen 1958; 1966b; 1970b: 149ff; 1970d; 1971a: 135; 1972a; 1972b; 1973c: 100ff.
24. Nielsen 1969b: 34. See also his 1971a: 2.
25. Nielsen 1969b: 35. See also his 1971a: 3; Slater 1973.
26. Nielsen 1972a: 29.
27. Nielsen 1972a: 29.
28. Nielsen 1972a: 29.
29. Nielsen 1970c: 2.
30. Nielsen 1977a.
31. Nielsen 1972a: 28–29.
32. Nielsen 1969b: 35–36. See also his 1971a: 3–4.
33. Nielsen 1972a: 29.

34. Nielsen 1962a: 126–127. See also his 1958: 25–28; 1967a; 1970a: 29–31; 1974c: 27.

35. Nielsen 1981b: 26.

36. Nielsen 1981b: 26.

37. Nielsen 1962a: 119–25.

38. Nielsen 1966a: 14.

39. Nielsen 1962a: 118.

40. Nielsen 1965b: 3.

41. Nielsen 1962a: 118–19.

42. Nielsen 1962a: 127. See also pp. 127–30.

43. Nielsen 1962a: 118–31; 1965b: 3; 1966a: 14.

44. Nielsen 1962a: 125–26.

45. Nielsen 1970d: 100.

46. Nielsen 1969b: 34. See also his 1971a: 2.

47. Nielsen 1969a: 20.

48. Nielsen 1972a: 31.

49. Nielsen 1969a: 19–20.

50. Nielsen 1969b: 35.

51. Nielsen 1969b: 35.

52. Nielsen 1970b: 132–33; 1970c: 2–3. See also his 1965a: 137–39; 1970b: 145; 1971a: 10–11; 1975a: 102–3.

53. Nielsen 1979a: 1–2. See also his 1974a: 18; 1978a: 193–94.

54. Konyndyk 1977: 7; Nielsen 1971a: 56.

55. Diamond and Litzenburg 1975 surveys the replies.

56. Konyndyk 1977: 1–2, 6, 15–16; Mavrodes 1964: 187–89.

57. Brown 1974.

58. E.g., Nielsen 1970b: 145–47; 1975b.

59. Nielsen 1966a.

60. Clifford 1968: 340.

61. King-Farlow 1979.

62. Nielsen 1970c: 20.

63. Mavrodes 1964: 190–91. See also pp. 187–89.

64. Mavrodes 1964: 191; emphasis added.

65. Nielsen 1970b: 145.

66. Nielsen 1967b.

67. Quoted in Nielsen 1967b: 167.

68. Konyndyk 1977: 15; emphasis added. See also Geach 1974. (For positive responses to Nielsen's challenge by theists, see, e.g., McClorry 1975; Shute 1973. See also Greeves 1972.)

69. Konyndyk 1977: 15.

70. Nielsen 1970b: 150–51.

71. Konyndyk 1977: 16–17; Nielsen 1962a: 135–36; 1974a: 18; 1981b: 26; Trethowan 1966: 39; Yandell 1968b: 19.

72. Nielsen 1970c: 6–9.

73. Nielsen 1970c: 14–16.

74. Nielsen 1970c: 16.

75. Nielsen 1970c: 16.

76. Nielsen 1970c: 16.

77. Nielsen 1970c: 10–11.

78. Nielsen 1970c: 11–14. But see Hoffman's reply, 1970.

79. Nielsen 1970c: 18.

80. Nielsen 1970c: 20.

81. Nielsen 1968a; 1975c. But see Hook 1975 in reply.

82. Colwell 1981.

83. Colwell 1981: 333–39.

84. Colwell 1981: 335. But see Nielsen 1962a: 113–15, 126, 133; 1963a: 273.

85. Colwell 1981: 333.

86. Livingston 1973: 400.

87. King-Farlow 1979: 81.

88. Nielsen 1974d: 227.

89. Nielsen 1974b: 204–6.

90. Nielsen 1961a.

91. See, e.g., Sharpe 1984.

92. Nielsen 1981a: 148.

93. Nielsen 1981a: 150.

94. Nielsen 1962a: 111–12.

95. Nielsen 1981a: 150.

96. Nielsen 1962a: 111–12. But see Yandell 1968b.

97. Nielsen 1981a: 153, 155.

98. Nielsen 1981a: 159.

99. Quoted in Nielsen 1981a: 158. See also p. 159.

100. Nielsen 1980: 55.

101. Nielsen 1980: 53–54.

102. Nielsen 1980: 53.

103. Nielsen 1962a: 112–13. See also Dilman 1981; Nielsen 1980: 54–60; 1981c.

104. Nielsen 1968b; Yandell 1968a. See also Nielsen 1961b: 179–80.

105. Nielsen 1981a: 151.

106. Nielsen 1962a: 113. See also his 1962b: 248–49; 1965b: 2–3.

107. Nielsen 1981a: 161, 147, 159.

108. Nielsen 1981a: 161.

109. Nielsen 1969b: 40–47; 1970b: 111–12.
110. Nielsen 1981a: 161.
111. Nielsen 1970b: 124; Nielsen 1980: 55.
112. Nielsen 1981a: 166.
113. Nielsen 1980: 56.
114. Nielsen 1981a: 165.
115. Nielsen 1980: 56.
116. Kaufman 1957; 1975.
117. Kaufman 1957: 235, quoted in Nielsen 1970e: 9.
118. Nielsen 1970e: 10. See also his 1970e: 8; 1970f: 161–62.
119. Nielsen 1963a.
120. Nielsen 1962a.
121. Nielsen 1966a: 29–30.
122. Kaufman 1957: 237.
123. See also Nielsen 1963b.
124. Nielsen 1963b: 164.
125. Nielsen quotes Kaufman 1957: 242.
126. Nielsen 1967c: 191. See also Pratt 1970.
127. Livingston 1973: 402; Nielsen 1973e: 7; 1978a: 194; 1980: 49.
128. Dilley 1976: 44.
129. Nielsen 1967c: 192–93.
130. Nielsen 1967c: 192–93.
131. Nielsen 1967c: 192–93; emphasis removed.
132. Nielsen 1967c: 192–93.
133. Dilley 1976: 44–47.
134. Nielsen 1967c: 192.
135. Nielsen 1967c: 192–93. See also Dilley 1976: 44; Nielsen 1974e: 106–8; 1980: 49–50.
136. Niclscn 1974a: 19.
137. See also Trigg 1973.
138. Nielsen 1970e: 10–11.
139. See also Nielsen 1978b.
140. See Nielsen 1972c.
141. Nielsen 1967c: 197.
142. Nielsen 1967c: 196.
143. Nielsen 1967c: 197–98.
144. Quoted in Nielsen 1980: 55.
145. Nielsen 1980: 59.
146. Nielsen 1973f.
147. Quoted in Nielsen 1973f: 14.
148. Nielsen 1973f: 15.
149. Nielsen 1973f: 15.

150. Nielsen 1973f: 18–19; emphasis removed.
151. Nielsen 1973f: 16–17.
152. Nielsen 1973f: 20.
153. Nielsen 1981b: 23.
154. Nielsen 1962b: 252.
155. Nielsen 1962b: 251.
156. Trethowan 1966; Nielsen 1970b: 143–44, 155 n. 13, 14.
157. Nielsen 1981b: 23; emphasis removed.
158. Nielsen 1962a.
159. Nielsen 1967c: 192–93; emphasis removed.
160. Nielsen 1963b.
161. Nielsen 1963b: 166.
162. Nielsen 1963b: 168.
163. Nielsen 1963a: 277–78.
164. Nielsen 1963b: 167.
165. Nielsen 1963b: 170–72.
166. Nielsen 1963b: 165–69.
167. Nielsen 1963b: 166.
168. Nielsen 1963b: 167.
169. Allen, quoted in Nielsen 1973f: 24.
170. Allen, quoted in Nielsen 1973f: 25.
171. McClorry 1974: 81.
172. Nielsen 1973f: 28.
173. Nielsen 1963b: 166.
174. See also Nielsen 1963b: 170–72, 1965b: 4–6.
175. Nielsen 1967c: 192–93; emphasis removed.
176. Nielsen 1967c: 192–93; emphasis removed.
177. Quoted in Nielsen 1967b: 170.
178. Nielsen 1974a: 19.
179. Dilley 1976: 44–47.
180. Nielsen 1981a: 152.
181. Livingston 1973: 401–2.
182. Dilley 1976: 46.
183. Nielsen 1967c: 201.
184. Nielsen 1967c: 199.
185. Nielsen 1973e: 7, 10.
186. Nielsen 1963b. See also his 1963a: 280–81.
187. See also Nielsen 1969b: 49–52; 1974e: 108–12.
188. Nielsen 1963b: 173; emphasis removed.
189. Dilley 1976: 47.
190. Nielsen 1963b: 163.
191. Nielsen 1961a: 281.

192. Nielsen 1961a: 272–73.
193. Nielsen 1961a: 271–72; 1970b: 138–44; 1974a: 18.
194. Nielsen 1961a: 273.
195. Nielsen 1961a: 274–75.
196. Nielsen 1961a: 275.
197. Nielsen 1970b: 139–40.
198. Macquarrie 1970b: 158.
199. Nielsen 1961a: 277, 279; emphasis removed.
200. Nielsen 1961a: 277, 278. 280.
201. Nielsen 1970b: 141.
202. Nielsen 1970b.
203. Nielsen 1970b: 124–25. See Macquarrie 1970a: 112–14.
204. Nielsen 1961a: 280–81.
205. Nielsen 1962a: 123ff.
206. Nielsen 1974f; 1979b: 1.
207. Nielsen 1979b: esp. p. 1.
208. Nielsen 1974f: 266.
209. Nielsen 1976. See also his 1966a: 28.
210. Nielsen 1976: 33.
211. Clarke 1976; Macquarrie 1970b: 160.
212. Nielsen 1976: 38.
213. Nielsen 1976: 39.
214. Nielsen 1976: 41–42.
215. Nielsen 1976.
216. Macquarrie 1970a: 111–14.
217. Nielsen 1970g: 122.
218. Nielsen 1970g: 121.
219. Nielsen 1970g: 122; emphasis removed.
220. Nielsen 1970g: 123.
221. Colwell 1981: 331; referring to Nielsen 1971a.
222. Colwell 1981: 332.
223. Colwell 1981: 329–33.
224. Colwell 1981: 336.
225. Nielsen 1963a: 278
226. Colwell 1981: 332.
227. Livingston 1973: 400; Mavrodes 1964; Nielsen 1961a: 270–71; 1963a; 1965a; 1966a: 28, 30–32; 1974b: 207–8.
228. Nielsen 1963a: 272–73, quoting Hick.
229. Nielsen 1963a: 274–75.
230. Nielsen 1963a: 275.
231. Nielsen 1963a: 275, quoting Hick.
232. Nielsen 1963a: 275–76, quoting Hick,

233. Nielsen 1963a: 276–77, quoting Hick.

234. Nielsen 1963a: 278–80.

235. Nielsen 1963a: 280–81.

236. Nielsen 1963a: 273.

237. Nielsen 1978a: 196, quoting Penelhum.

238. Nielsen 1978a; 1979a; Penelhum 1971a; 1971b. See also King-Farlow 1979.

239. Nielsen 1978a: 196, quoting Penelhum; emphasis removed.

240. Nielsen 1978a: 197–98.

241. Nielsen 1978a: 198; emphasis removed.

242. Nielsen 1979a: 5–6; emphasis removed.

243. Nielsen 1962a: 113–14; 1978a: 204.

244. Nielsen 1966a: 32.

245. Nielsen 1965b: 3.

246. Nielsen 1962b: 260.

247. Nielsen 1962a: 113–17; 1965b: 2–3; 1966a: 30–32.

248. See also Yandell 1968b.

249. E.g., Trethowan 1966: 47–48.

250. Nielsen 1961b; 1962c; 1964a; 1964b; 1973d; 1974a: 19; 1974b: 215–16; 1981b: 23–24.

251. Nielsen 1974b: 215.

252. Basinger 1981: 233–35.

253. Basinger 1981: 234.

254. Nielsen 1974b: 215.

255. Nielsen 1974b: 215–16.

256. Nielsen 1974a: 19.

257. Basinger 1981: 233, with regard to Nielsen and Abelson 1967: 108; Nielsen 1973d: chap. 3; 1977b: 33–34.

258. Nielsen 1960. But see Taylor 1961.

259. Basinger 1981: 236.

260. See also Ramberan 1978: 214.

261. Basinger 1981: 236.

262. Pugh 1977.

263. Basinger 1981: 235, 237–38.

264. Basinger 1981: 236–37.

265. Ramberan 1978: 205.

266. Ramberan 1978: 206.

267. Ramberan 1978: 208–10.

268. Ramberan 1978: 210–11.

269. Nielsen 1962a: 113–17; 1965b: 2–3; 1966a: 28–36; 1974b: 207–8. See also Trethowan's 1966 response to Nielsen 1966a on Crombie.

270. Crombie, quoted in Nielsen 1966: 21.

271. Crombie, quoted in Nielsen 1966a: 21.
272. Nielsen 1966a: 23–24.
273. Crombie, quoted in Nielsen 1966a: 25.
274. Nielsen 1966a: 27–28.
275. Nielsen 1969b: 37–38, quoting Robinson.
276. Nielsen 1969b: 40.
277. Nielsen 1969b: 38–39.
278. Nielsen 1962b.
279. Nielsen 1962b: 249–50.
280. Nielsen 1962b: 250.
281. Nielsen 1962b: 254.
282. Nielsen 1962b: 255.
283. Nielsen 1962b: 253.
284. Nielsen 1962b: 253.
285. Nielsen 1962b: 256.
286. Nielsen 1962b: 256.
287. Nielsen 1962b: 249, 253; emphasis added.
288. Nielsen 1961a: 270–71, 281; 1970c: 5.
289. Nielsen 1962b: 259.
290. Nielsen 1962b: 257–61; 1963a: 279; 1974b: 204–6; 1974d; 1975d.
291. Nielsen 1974d: 226–27; emphasis removed.
292. Nielsen 1963a: 279.
293. Nielsen 1963a: 279.
294. Nielsen 1963a: 279–280.
295. Nielsen 1974d: 225. See also his 1971b: 448–72.
296. Nielsen 1962b: 259.
297. Nielsen 1974b: 201–7. See also Thorson 1968 regarding Polanyi's ideas.
298. Quine and Ullian 1970.
299. Nielsen 1974b: 203, 206.
300. Nielsen 1962b: 260.
301. Nielsen 1974b: 207.
302. Nielsen 1962b: 260–61.
303. MacIntyre, quoted in Nielsen 1962b: 261.
304. Nielsen 1964c, esp. p. 19.
305. Nielsen 1964c: 18.
306. Nielsen 1962a: 113–14. See also his 1965b: 2–3.
307. See, e.g., Diamond and Litzenburg 1975: Chaps. 9–10, esp. p. 439; Tooley 1975.
308. Clifford 1968: 346.
309. Nielsen 1968b: 15–16.

Chapter Four

"God" Required: Why the Scientific Method for Theology

Gordon Kaufman and Kai Nielsen face the same challenge—namely, modernity's confrontation of religion—and both respond ineffectually. The reply ought not, like Kaufman, relegate the supposed reality God to something so far from people's lives and possible experience that God becomes irrelevant to living and, as the previous chapter pointed out, theology becomes a system of ideas merely functioning in particular ways. Neither ought the response, like Nielsen's, only throw cold water on theological ideas without helping to reconstruct them more adequately. The reply needs to face the challenge head-on with a factually meaningful theology that answers modernity's secular challenge and still centers on the reality God. Theologians need to do theology fully scientifically, but not lose the wisdom from human experience over the past many millennia or the moral critique necessary to guide and admonish how people live: a difficult, but not impossible challenge.

Why should theologians do this?

It makes a large jump to suggest theology adopt the method of the sciences. Several groups emphasize separating the two—from the extreme empiricists, who want to show religion has no worthwhile content, to the religiously minded, who want to defend religion against secularity or carve out an isolated niche for religious language—and do this to such an extent that for theology to side with science's method could feel like a sell-out to an antireligious enemy. Proceeding in the suggested proactive way will face resistance. It will not remove the fears to point out, as in the next chapter's presentation on scientific method, that one of the enemies, scientism, has had its claws manicured; this may only help ameliorate some worries. To establish the claim that theology should adopt the scientific method requires something more.

Theology adopting the scientific method expresses the ideal that would integrate the two fields. Many writings explore the relationship between science and theology; many extol the need for their mutual relevance and integration.[1] This chapter will touch on several reasons for these beliefs. It will hence help bolster the rationale for this book's trying to bring science and theology together at the foundation of their enterprises, namely in their methodologies.

A CONVERGENCE OF SCIENCE AND THEOLOGY

"Science and religion are both universal, and basically very similar." Charles Townes reflects on the convergence of science and theology, writing that they "become almost indistinguishable" when one peeks "at the real nature of each."[2] They differ mostly superficially. He spells out their "near identity" by commenting on their goals: science tries "to discover the order of the universe and to understand through it the things" people sense around them, including themselves. The principles and laws of science express this order and strive "to state [it] in the simplest and yet most inclusive ways." Theology, in comparison, tries to understand and accept the meaning and purpose of the universe and how humans fit into it. People often try to find this purpose by positing a "supreme purposeful force" (which some call "God") as the "unifying and inclusive origin of meaning. . . . Understanding the *order* in the universe" does not equate with "understanding the *purpose* in the universe," Townes continues. Neither are they that different. The Japanese call physics "*butsuri*, which translated means simply *the reasons for things.*" Thus inevitably arises, Townes suggests, the close linking of the purpose and nature of this universe.[3]

Townes's argument leads him to believe science and theology will join together. Both attempt to understand the universe and both deal "with the same substance."[4] New strength for each arises through their convergence.[5]

One attempt at their inevitable confluence seeks their methodological unification.

JUSTIFYING THE CONVERGENCE

William Shea talks about the "revisionist" theological approaches of Langdon Gilkey and David Tracy, considering their work to follow the lead of the American pragmatist and instrumentalist philosophers, especially John Dewey.[6] According to Shea, Dewey's analysis of what constitutes enquiry, taking natural science as the paradigm, lays the path for secular theology.

Townes's and Shea's comments support Michael Polanyi's foundational work on human knowing.[7] He emphasizes a tacit dimension and argues that the process of discovery, the linchpin to all understanding, unites two methods: the one by which scientists gain their knowledge and the other by which theologians gain theirs. This idea of the creative act builds a theory of knowledge that challenges the object-subject dichotomy of extreme positivist-empiricist understandings of science and sees all acts of knowing as facets of the same thing, on a continuum. Even theology can sense discovery and learn new things. As science is a creative human enterprise, so is theology; they work together at knowing. Theology, according to the commentator Richard Gelwick, can therefore feel "confident of knowing toward truth in its own (proper and valid) way," a way similar to science's.[8]

To justify theology's adopting science's method—that it be descriptive—goes beyond noticing the convergence of the two fields. It also needs more than exhortations and Shea's and Polanyi's observations. However, despite desires, no irrefutable deductive argument will prove theology must adopt the scientific method. Only suggestions, like those above, accumulate to make it a better way to proceed than its competitors.

The most forceful justifications may flow from the recognition that, for modern Western culture, the paradigm for creating knowledge comes from the scientific method. Three indicators especially point to this:

1. *Theology should be rational and empirical, like science, because it invests in truth.* "Out of a concern for the wrestle of theology with truth," John Godbey writes, a theology "must wrestle with the best human knowledge available in the historical epoch in which [the theologian] writes." Many of the great theologians down through the

ages (Origen of Alexandria, Thomas Aquinas, Friedrich Schleiermacher, and Paul Tillich, for instance) did this. Today, Godbey continues, the method of science offers the "best human knowledge available."[9] It provides the modern West its preeminent truth-giving way
for collecting knowledge. Science speaks the voice of contemporary
truth. Hence, current theologians—in as much as they want to invest
in truth—must wrestle with using the scientific method.

A biblical position such as the Epistle writer Paul's insists on the
relevance of the Gospel in that it contradicts ideals and forms of life,
setting its own standards of relevance, asking its own questions, and
generating meaning incomprehensible unless the believer believes.
However, Paul, in his theology and preaching, still wrestled with and
used his contemporary thought forms.[10] Current postmodern attitudes rightfully ask respect for each of the multitude of approaches
to knowledge or truth.[11] But only the scientific offers the potential in
current Western society to express truth decisively, universally, pow-
erfully, and compellingly.

2. *Theology dare not drift too far from science's method lest it not communicate with society and thus fail to change or effect secular life
and institutions, losing in meaning, proper function, worth to the
community, and relevant message.* Like it or not, the scientific
method usually constitutes modern Western culture's paradigm for
producing truthful, useful, and meaningful knowledge. People today
rely on the "tried and tested" approach. The central motivation for
theology's adopting the scientific method will therefore probably
arise from a desire to serve secular life and experience, the theologian's secular being, and to help theology face the challenges of individuals and societies in this secular world. Society needs "an
empirically-based theology," Brian Cooper writes, that formulates
"religious affirmations and creedal statements . . . in a manner analogous to scientific formulas and natural 'laws.'"[12] It needs a scientific method for theology to give the theological enterprise of knowing weight and vibrancy. The God-world relationship must make
God seem fully relevant to everyday life for religion to be religion.
If theology does not do this, its religion will probably receive little
or no compliance and will result in little or no directing and unifying
of individual lives. It may well fail as a religion.[13] (The same argument as applies with Kaufman's approach where "God" is merely a

functional word.)[14] This may help explain why proportionally fewer people today hold to traditional religious moralities; as chapter 1 mentioned, the wider the gap between religion and secular life, the less people believe in the forcefulness, even reality, of the traditional God for which these moralities stand.

3. *Theology needs to adopt this method because of psychological and social needs.*[15] Current social and individual chaos and uncertainty largely derive from the use of modern technology and scientific knowledge. Challenges include:

- overpopulation because of better health practices;
- environmental degradation from industrial and consumer demand;
- global warming, in part from the gases that technological civilization emits;
- genetic engineering of plants, animals, and humans;
- the rapid transmission of information and ideas through electronic communication; and
- terrorists' use of explosives and munitions, potentially even nuclear and biological devices.

All of these contribute to the plague of moral dilemmas. Then, how best to use the discoveries of science? What discoveries not to use? How to guide potentially dangerous research? On what basis ought society to allocate its resources in the face of global and local threats? Society lacks a convincing morality. People need wisdom to help guide them. This used to come through religion, but religion has become either irrelevant to secular modernity or it has tried to build other but doomed, backward-looking worlds in parallel to it. Religion can even make the world a worse place with terrorist and military clashes between ardently held religions (militant fundamentalist Islam versus militant fundamentalist Christianity).

To help make the world a better place for humans and humanity's kin, theology—the system of understanding that emerges from religious wisdom—ought to embrace modernity and guide secularity's latent spirituality. Theology might take a first step in this direction by developing and following a truly scientific method for itself. A theology resulting from this may stand a better chance than current candidates of creating a meaningful and powerful theology to help solve, for example, technology-produced social problems.

In one sense of myth, scientific knowledge and theology are mythologies; culture and its individuals need an adequately functioning mythology, something not at present in existence. Theology's first step entails it as a mythology articulating itself, telling some of its stories again or telling new stories, according to the format the common secular-scientific mythology makes definitive.[16]

THE CAMELLIA MODEL

Several previous expositions of this challenge and advocacy of this solution have relied on the "ladder model" for the relationship between science and theology.[17] This ladder model offers an image of an ideal toward which thinkers might work in seeking to relate these two spheres of human activity. In it, both subject themselves to the world of experience (the "ground" on which the "ladder" stands), and build up two lines of knowledge (the "poles" of the "ladder"), parallel but separate because of their different respective assumptions, explanatory objects, and social aims. A number of points of contact and shared segments of knowledge (the "rungs" of the "ladder") join them, and through these the two might take a common stance. A common scientific methodology could therefore enter as a bottom "rung" of the "ladder," a method modified according to the aims and peculiarities of the individual disciplines. Here could continue the flow between the two—this time from science to theology—working toward their integration. Moves on other rungs might also go from theology to science, as with Stanley Jaki's and Pierre Teilhard de Chardin's theology-inspired hypotheses for physics and biology.[18]

This model for the science-theology relationship, while it proves helpful, meets its limitations (especially the oversimplification implied in having only two poles) and requires revising.[19] The "camellia model" appears a better guide to join science and theology.[20] Imagine a camellia tree flourishing and forever flowering in rich soil and a moist subtropical climate. The leaves and petals of its flowers represent aspects of each of theology and science. Some connect through the center of the "flower" they belong to, while others connect through the "twigs" and "branches" between them. Each relates to, feeds, and depends on the rest. Though each "petal," "leaf," and "stalk" is separate from the others, they form an intricate whole that eclipses the parts.

Applying this model to the relationship between science and theology directs attention to the numerous points of contact and shared segments of knowledge (the "petals" of a "flower," the "stalks" and the "branches" of the "tree") over which scientific and theological theories can hold things in common. The two become a whole where all parts and aspects connect. A shared method becomes a substantial "branch" or "trunk" through which connections and flow can occur.

Theology's adopting the scientific method could grow, in the vision of the camellia model, a vibrant, colorful, and living complex.

ADVOCACY

This book advocates theology's adoption of the scientific method. It repudiates attempts to show theology has naught to do with the objective. Many theologians strongly discourage the use of the scientific method for theology, and many theologies follow nonobjective or nonscientific methods:

- Wolfhart Pannenberg suggests Karl Barth would not concede for one moment to the scientific nature of theology.[21]
- Langdon Gilkey also thinks theology should not proceed by a method analogous to science's.[22]
- Karl Rahner writes: "Every science is *per definitionem* a particular branch of human knowledge, but . . . this does not apply to divine revelation and theology, at least so long as these do not betray their own true nature."[23]
- Theologians do "not come near the essential element in theological thinking and speaking," writes Heinrich Ott, if they "attempt to describe it as objective thinking and speaking."[24]
- M. D. Chenu asks whether theology is rightfully a science. If this involves "the valid and fruitful task of rationally and systematically using the methods and resources of the intellect in accordance with the capacity thereof," he answers with a resounding "Yes." He answers "No" if science requires "testing every statement by experiment,

according objective validity only to" this sort of knowledge, "criticizing all results by tried and proved methods of demonstration and verification and . . . proclaiming the intelligibility of the real world through a rational study of its relations and laws."[25] Theology cannot treat its subject matter—namely God—in this way. Theological method, Chenu says, is superscientific; humans can only reach the mystery of God by and within faith.[26]

These all point out the fault of the theologies, something to change in the way theologians work their craft. Theology can be both rational and empirical. Theologians can do theology the way Chenu says they cannot.

This attitude to science is not scientism—an uncritical worship of science—any more than is the use of a computer or the turning of a light switch. It in fact upholds a critical approach to all knowledge, whether theological or from any of the usual sciences. Neither does it see the results of science as universal truths that triumph over competitors willy-nilly. It merely asks all attempts at knowing to subject themselves to reason and transpersonal experience.

Some theologies follow an empirical approach in an unfortunate way. The chapters above pointed out the descriptive nature of fundamentalism, its incompatibility with secularity, and hence the irrelevance of its religion to much of life, or the direct conflict and schism it places within people's lives and minds. Fundamentalism is compatible with the scientific method given biblical inerrancy (which provides objectivity, the data of theology comprising the words of certain scriptures) and theology as a restatement of supposed biblical truth. This book will not pursue that approach, however, because the reasons for accepting such authority turn out to be circular and hollow. To say, as do fundamentalists and traditionalists, that "faith only comes from God through grace" has, as Nielsen would point out, no factual meaning, though the statement presents itself as factual. It also proclaims an irrational dualism. Nor will this book follow other fundamentalisms, for instance an ecclesiastical one in which an ultimate doctrinal authority (such as the pope) can "falsify" at least portions of theological theory.[27] It will view the data of theology differently.

The proof of this pudding is in its eating. If the proposed method fails—if it produces theologies that all future believing communities feel inadequate and which therefore rot on library shelves, or if it fails to produce any theologies at all, or if it logically falls to pieces—then theologians should change from this methodological diet.[28]

CONCLUSIONS

Methodological construction for theology should start with certain assumptions like the need for its and science's mutual relevance and hence for building their relationship according to something resembling the camellia model.

This book purposefully started with the secular. Hence, it loads the dice for science since the secular espouses the scientific method. Science has become so ingrained in Western society that, when modern Westerners reach for truth, they use a scientific approach. A theology striving toward integration with science thus ought not only to take note of scientific results, but ought also to use scientific method. This does not refer to the details of the technical laboratory method of some sciences; it does not mean test tubes and formulas as with the image of science stuck in the popular imagination. Rather, it means science's general approach to questions: the belief, roughly, that an idea has truth if many people, maybe everyone, can unequivocally experience it. In theology, it means openness to ordinary normal experience.

Theology with a scientific method might act more effectively as a moral force and thus more adequately help direct and unify individual lives. A better-functioning Western society requires the factually meaningful and truthful nature of theology and religion.

Theology should not sidestep this challenge, but accept it head-on. Scientific method offers the best way for modern Westerners to understand God and the spiritual perspective on the universe. The task now is to produce an account of how to do theology scientifically in a way that, for example, answers Nielsen. This does not require automatically tossing out theological ideas as untrue. It means asking about their factual meaningfulness and truthfulness. Theologians would search with the scientific method for an image of God in which God has real interactions with the universe. At first, this approach may feel rough, approximate, messy, strange, but passionate. Later, it should feel natural and safe.

Theology constitutes science of God: to know, scientifically, what God is. This book proposes one such scientific approach to God knowledge, how to do science of God.

NOTES

1. See, e.g., Sharpe 1984.
2. Townes 1966: 301.
3. Townes 1966: 305.
4. Townes 1966: 310.
5. Sharpe 1984.
6. Shea 1976.
7. Polanyi 1964.
8. Gelwick 1975. See Polanyi 1964; 1959. See also Apczynski 1977; 1979; Gill 1969; Lonergan 1972; Reist 1979; Scott 1970; Wiebe 1974b; Woods 1958.
9. Godbey 1970: 208.
10. See Kerr 1953: 143–45. See also Comstock 1971: 625; Diamond 1975: 52–54.
11. Ferré 1976.
12. Cooper 1969: 11.
13. MacLaren 1976: 78; Ruse and Wilson 1986; Sharpe 1984.
14. See also Sharpe 1979; Trigg 1973.
15. See also, e.g., Gallus 1972–1974; Godbey 1970: 194–95; Sharpe 1978: 135–39; 1984.
16. See Sharpe 1978; 1984. See also Bambrough 1969; Godbey 1969; 1970: 208; Sachs 1976: 46; Swimme 1996.
17. Sharpe 1984.
18. Jaki 1974; 1978; Sharpe 1982a; Teilhard de Chardin 1959.
19. Sharpe 1984; 2000.
20. Sharpe and Walgate 1988.
21. Pannenberg 1972: 6–10.
22. Gilkey 1970; 1971.
23. Rahner 1975: 95.
24. Ott 1967: 133.
25. Chenu 1959: 48.
26. Chenu 1959: 11–13, 22–25. See also Austin 1967: 1, 6–10.
27. Quay 1974: 356.
28. See Gellman 1977. See also Dowey 1958; Hall 1974.

Chapter Five

"God" Constructed, yet God Real: Help from Philosophy of Science

The 1960s and 1970s saw much happen to the understanding of how science operates, mostly from the revolution in the philosophy of science that the work of Thomas Kuhn epitomizes. Kuhn highlights an attack against a strongly empiricist and sometimes positivist scholarly and popular understanding of the doing of science in which science accumulates knowledge toward a perfect mirror of reality itself. Critics off on the other extreme see scientific knowledge as humanly constructed with little rational reference to reality, if that indeed exists; Paul Feyerabend says only irrational reasons lead to changing paradigms. Between these extreme positions—and given the pioneering work of such people as Norwood Hanson, Kuhn, Michael Polanyi, and Karl Popper—the discussions converge, dating the previous extremes.[1] Subjective elements do appear to influence the development of scientific theory, yet paradigms in science do change and people can communicate between cultures and spheres of discourse.

Society's health requires the integration of scientific knowledge and theology, if only for the integrity of those whose thinking takes them into both camps. This book thus seeks how to apply the method of the sciences to theology. The next issues in this trajectory concern the form such an application of scientific method might take, and whether it can remain honest to both science and theology. It cannot, however, say how theology could follow the scientific method until it describes the scientific method. The philosophy of science—which tries to delineate science's method—therefore plays an obvious and important role in such a study. This chapter aims to outline that method, especially as it develops from the contributions of the sociologically oriented philosophers and historians of science.

The depiction of the method of science relies on this compromise between objectivism and subjectivism, learning from each of the extreme positions. The step away from a severe logical positivism on the one hand and an outright relativism on the other must occur for theology (an obviously more subjective enterprise than science) to use the scientific method. As with the previous chapters, the discussion emerges from the 1960s and 1970s, in dialogue with the literature current at the time. It especially draws on the relevant portion of the convergence as Ian Barbour details it in his *Myths, Models and Paradigms*.[2] Barbour concludes that the structural and philosophical features of the explanations of science and religion parallel each other, though they differ in some functions and emphases.

Repeating some clarifications might also help at this stage. The word "science" generally refers to the knowledge of the natural sciences. "Empirical" means a more general form of "scientific." A "descriptive" statement or theory means one with factual claims and that can become empirical if investigators want to check out the claims' truth or falsity. "Rationality" refers to the manner in which people make empirical judgments; the philosophy of science aims to spell out what constitutes rationality.

THE ELEMENTS OF SCIENCE

Following is Barbour's general framework within which fit the continuum of methods of the various sciences:[3]

- A scientific discipline comprises *research traditions*. One tradition often dominates a discipline and each embodies itself in core examples (or exemplars or *paradigms*) that, through teaching and modeling, initiate a student into the methods of attacking problems acceptable within the tradition. They also guide the tradition's research programs.
- A research tradition also assumes *metaphysical beliefs*, for instance about the kinds of entities that exist in the world. Newtonian mechanics, once a universal paradigm, relies on a collection of ontolog-

ical commitments concerning the regularity, causality, and action-at-a-distance properties of the universe.[4] A number of traditions can share one set of such beliefs.

The doing of science—at least "normal" science, which is the focus of this description—within a research tradition requires the construction and evaluation of models and theories. This involves four steps:

- Scientists picture in their minds a *model* (a theoretical model in particular), usually in the form of a mechanism or a process.[5]
- Then they take as analogous the particular phenomenon under investigation and the model. They develop a *theory* by correlating some of the observable terms of the phenomenon and some terms of the model.[6]

  The classic "billiard ball" model for the behavior of a gas provides an example. "Consider a box full of gas, such as air," Barbour asks, and imagine the gas consists of "very tiny elastic spheres bouncing around."[7] Also assume "the mechanical behavior of the hypothetical spheres" resembles the "behavior of colliding billiard balls." From these develops the scientific theory called the Kinetic Theory of Gases. This theory involves equations that interrelate the mass, velocity, "energy, and momentum of the hypothetical spheres." No one can observe these properties, but the model does suggest some of them relate to properties of the gas one might observe; a physicist might, for example, figure out the change in momentum of the particles when they collide with the walls of the container under the force of the gas's pressure.

  An act of creative imagination uses a familiar and intelligible situation as the basis by analogy for a theory that helps in understanding some other aspect or part of the world.[8]

- Scientists assess theories by a variety of *criteria*, including simplicity, coherence, and agreement with experimental evidence. "Agreement with experimental evidence" provides the leading criterion and means that the theory should accurately account for known observations and yield precise predictions of future measurements; the theory should especially lead to the discovery of novel types of phenomena. Scientists, however, may subject theories to more than observations. In particular, they may invoke "simplicity." This not only refers to simplicity in the form of the theory and the minimum number of independent assumptions, but also to an aesthetic element, the "beauty," "elegance," or "symmetry" of the theory. They may also require "coherence," which refers to a systematic interrelating of theories into a comprehensive unification of separate laws and a portrayal of the underlying similarities in otherwise diverse phenomena.

* A *comprehensive theory* usually develops from the paradigms of a research tradition as its attempt to understand all that lies within its area of study.

This division of scientific knowing may easily become—and will later become—a vision of different levels of knowing. The idea "levels" can both ease and distort the framework. It is artificial. The levels do not watertightly separate the aspects bulleted above; metaphysical beliefs, for instance, permeate all of them, and a change in a metaphysical belief comes about because all the aspects conspire together to force it.

EVALUATION AND CHANGE IN SCIENCE

Thus, the knowledge of science grows. The most controversial aspect of this concerns objectivity and the extent to which subjective factors influence knowledge change. A law stating relationships between observables may find itself more at the mercy of discrepancies than may theories, which reside further from data than do laws. This means scientists do not necessarily confirm or infirm theories by referring straightforwardly to a set of public and objective observation data; other criteria, such as simplicity and coherence, can come into play. Further, while to some extent data appear public and objective, to an extent they also depend on theories and observation processes. No clear line divides observational from theoretical terms—this applies to all facets of scientific knowledge—the objective from the subjective.

Does any rationality underlie theory change? This question especially applies to those rare moments in the history of science when theories in a discipline revolutionarily overthrow the reigning ones.

To highlight the seriousness of the question, avenues may open to a scientific community enabling it to hold on to a theory for which discordant data exist. Scientists can, for example, create auxiliary hypotheses to explain the data, or look in the data for errors or inadequacy, or hope someone will someday find reasons to undermine the data. Sometimes, good methodological reasons back resistance to such change.[9] But sometimes such instances can also show a scientific community irrationally failing to change.

The issues of how to judge between theories and how they might change therefore engender much dispute in the philosophy of science. Nevertheless, besides conformity to data, rational criteria (including aesthetic ones) exert some control over theories, despite the lack of clear rules to guide their unambiguous application.[10] Proponents of rival theories usually also share an observation language based on common data not in dispute, thus helping provide a base for rational decision making.

Comprehensive theories resist falsification even more than do theories, using much the same defensive tactics. Discordant data usually do not overthrow them. Rather, alternatives with "greater promise of explaining known data, resolving anomalies, and predicting novel phenomena" replace competitors in trouble.[11] Shared observation statements and criteria suggest some objectivity in the decision to abandon a comprehensive theory, when scientists judge the growing list of anomalies, inconsistencies, and unresolved puzzles serious, for the promise of a proposed new one. The stage at which this happens with a theory under attack is not clear, though authors propose some suggestive clues.[12] The same happens with research traditions.

Metaphysical assumptions lie even further away from observations than do comprehensive theories and research traditions, further away from direct empirical confirmation or infirmation, but still not totally immune to change. This can happen with the coming of new emphases in existing research traditions, or the introduction of different basic ideas with new traditions. Changes of interest in science or other areas of human experience can call into question the wider application of a tradition's metaphysical assumptions.[13] Their change appears somewhat rational.

The descriptive nature of a science can surface not only in rational debates but also in the long-term movement of disciplines. But these changes may involve other factors. The different facets of scientific knowledge (metaphysical assumptions, research traditions based on paradigmatic exemplars, comprehensive theories, theories built from

models, and laws relating observables) all can change. And the changes
in each case may be partly rational and public (more as moving down
the list), and partly irrational, or better, a-rational (less as moving down
the list). This compromise reflects Barbour's philosophical position, itself a compromise between naive realism and conceptual relativism (or
instrumentalism), which he calls "critical realism."[14]

CRITICAL REALISM

Conceptual relativism sees all knowledge as completely subjective: the
human imagination constructs knowledge without referring to the universe outside the knower. The tree that falls in the forest does not make
a noise if no one hears it. The opposite extreme—naive realism—sees
knowledge as (at least potentially) completely objective, perfectly mir-
roring or corresponding in detail to independent physical reality. Red
apples are really red because people see them this way on the tree. Both
positions misguidingly suggest they know something of the nature of
truth and then attempt to place it in specific and accessible places: to
know ideas are true—or no ideas are true—requires knowing something
truthful.

Barbour's critical realism—which Arthur Peacocke also espouses
and develops[15]—steers a middle path between these two extremes. It
says both objective and subjective factors play a part in knowing. Reality independent of the knower does exist and knowledge somehow reflects it, but beliefs and circumstances also influence knowledge.

The version of critical realism used here also says no one can separate the subjective and the objective from knowledge. What parts of a
term does theory provide and what parts does observation provide? No
one can ever know for sure. Science involves both, wrapped in a helix
so intertwined that people cannot prize them apart.

Critical realism challenges because many degrees separate the two
ends and it is difficult to specify and describe the peg between them on
which to drape an intermediate position. No one can catch and hang on
to truth; it forever eludes. Thus rises "the unresolved ontological question," writes Ernin McMullin, "of the *extent* to which [one can regard]
the work of science . . . as a disclosure of a real order, independent of

[humanity] in its genesis. In this age of science," there scarcely arises "a more important question."[16]

Critical realism also raises the question of why ideas work in manipulating the world (maybe this asks too obvious a question to register on intellectual screens). The correspondence theory of truth tries to answer this by saying correct science perfectly images reality and hence people can successfully manipulate the world using science as their guide. Problems loom with this answer, as the Kuhn revolution points out. This book will not pursue this topic further, but it emerges as something interesting perhaps to look at later.[17]

Critical realism applies not only in the approach to science, but also in theology and daily discourse. The word "infinite" exemplifies a class of constructs important for theological discussions; it arose with Gordon Kaufman's work and numerous times with the writings of Kai Nielsen's antagonists. Other words in its class include "absolute," "universal," and "unconditioned." Within them emerges critical realism.

A dictionary defines the adjective "infinite" as:

> 1. lacking limits or bounds; extending beyond measure or comprehension: without beginning or end; endless 2. very great; vast; immense 3. *a) Math.* Indefinitely large; greater than a finite number however large.[18]

In people's experience, something always remains unknown and unexperienced beyond all that is known and experienced; they find they cannot identify or understand everything. Their minds take them, from this realization, further. The adjective "infinite" appears to derive from imaginatively contrasting its subject with everything experienced (which people qualify as limited, bounded, ended, measurable, exhaustible, or countable), by saying it exceeds all of them. Nothing known through the senses can constitute or contain anything infinite because, if people can experience something in its totality, they can put bounds on it and make it finite. Similarly with the adverb "infinitely." People talk about the infinite this, the infinite that, something going on and on infinitely, for infinity, or ad infinitum.

The human imagination produces the qualifiers "infinite" and "infinitely" from the experience of finding more things beyond bounds, but then people also concoct a noun, the idea "infinity" or "the infinite."

They imagine something existing that nothing they might take as it actually constitutes it. They project this imagined thing onto reality and
read it off of reality, thinking infinity and the infinite objectively exist.
They identify the infinite. Some people even worship the imagined object of the word. "Infinite" as an operation or process—a conclusion
about limitations from experiences—projectively turns into a real entity
with religious or metaphysical overtones.

Rodney Needham maps the word "belief" in a similar way.[19] People
tend to think of beliefs as ideas with special status, but "a belief" really
means "an idea held to." The elevated status of the word melts away
when one asks what makes it special, like Paul Tournier's attempts to
understand "the person": "through having its successive envelopes
peeled off one by one," the "person" vanishes in the hand.[20] Needham
uses Ludwig Wittgenstein's idea of meaning as use and not some supernatural or idealist substance that floats around.[21] Words like "absolute," "ultimate," and "infinite" work in similar ways to "belief": in
language, people construct and manipulate them so they appear to have
real referents, though they may not.

The words "freedom," and "happiness" also act similarly, showing
that critical realism not only works in science and theology but also in
daily discourse. No one can say explicitly what "freedom" and "happiness" mean or what it means to live fully free or fully happy. The feelings and status pointed to in their use are things no person can ever fulfill, yet people project their incarnations onto real things (for example,
life in the United States as free; having a lot of money as feeling happy).
Some people pursue freedom and happiness all their lives and yet never
ask what it would mean to obtain them or why they should go after them.

On the other hand, a natural human process creates these words. People, in the act of living, construct the wholeness of these words and develop their meanings and referents. Humans are not usually conscious
of the building-up-of-meaning process because it slowly emerges as a
product of life day to day. The words and their purported referents may
come to have a valued, necessary, and rightful place in lived lives.

The mind-set of critical realism suggests one ought not to say "the infinite" and "freedom" exist objectively. Neither do they only exist in the
imagination. The object of each word falls between the two extremes
and no one can prize apart the constructed element of their meanings
from what objectively exists.

RIVAL ACCOUNTS OF
SCIENTIFIC RATIONALITY FOR THEOLOGY

Not only do the details of Barbour's critical realism rouse critiques, but so does his presentation of scientific method. For example, in some scholars' eyes his list of criteria does not provide a full or adequate description of scientists' process of assessing theories.[22] Neither is he the only one to present, either thoroughly or in passing, a summary of post-Kuhn developments in the philosophy of science.[23] Or the only one to look at theological method as following some particular understanding of the method of science.

A tradition of consciously seeking to create a scientific theology started around the time of Friedrich Schleiermacher and continues through to the present via the inspiration of such people as Henry Nelson Wiemann.[24] Besides those considered below (William Austin, Sanborn Brown, Kaufman, Carl Kordig, George Schlesinger, and Don Wiebe) and those in the next chapter (Wolfhart Pannenberg, Thomas Torrance, and David Tracy), others add their voices. These include Bernard Lonergan, Kenneth Klein (using David Rynin's philosophy of science), Bernard Meland, Martin, Ian Ramsey, and Michael Tooley (who attempts to demonstrate the factual meaningfulness of theology by accepting a criterion of verification but requiring a specific sort of transcendence)[25] Those considered here therefore only represent a sampling.

Schlesinger considers that an observation confirms a hypothesis (in science or in any sort of study, including theology) when it increases the credibility of the hypothesis.[26] He spells this out in the form of two principles. The first adjudicates between rival hypotheses by favoring the one that predicts a higher probability for a piece of evidence. This evidence would then confirm that hypothesis more than the other one. The second principle uses simplicity as the means to adjudicate between hypotheses similarly related to all available evidence. With these principles, Schlesinger finds theism (the belief, he says, that there exists a Perfect Being "with such properties as omnipotence and omnibenevolence") more confirmed than naturalism.[27] The evidence he uses for this includes actual observations (the existence of evil and the predictability of human choices) and possible observations (for instance, miracles) if someone actually made them.

Schlesinger's account of normal science may not reconcile with Barbour's nor may it present science adequately:

- It does not compare two theories with respect to criteria relevant to
  the facts they hold in common, but starts with the evidence and asks
  for the relative probabilities of the evidence with respect to each
  theory.
- It may ignore the question of predictions and the theory-ladenness of
  evidence.
- What decides whether something constitutes evidence for a theory,
  and whether a scientist has compared a theory against all possible
  pieces of evidence relevant to it?
- When it comes to comparing theism and naturalism, skeptics usually
  take Schlesinger's evidence as confirming naturalism against theism
  rather than—with Schlesinger—the reverse. In his account, would all
  evidence count for theism? Has something gone wrong here?

Austin examines the question "Is theology a science?" by looking at
the nature of paradoxes in science and theology—especially the paradox of the wave-particle duality of light—using the principle of complementarity and its potential for theology.[28] He notes that J. M.
Bochenski and Alfred North Whitehead similarly observe this analogy
between the methods of theology and those of physical science.[29] "Theology . . . aims to provide a theoretical interpretation of the 'religious
experience of [humanity],' as physical science aims to provide a theoretical interpretation of sense experience."[30] "Religious experience" includes not only nonsensory ("mystical") types of experience, but also
"events (historical events such as the Exodus, and occurrences in the individual religious [person's] experience as well) in the sensible
world."[31] With this, he says the same as Barbour. "Theology, like science, aims to explain" (given experiential statements) "by finding theoretical statements from which" to deduce the experiences, and from
which the researcher can also deduce "additional testable statements."[32]
Austin agrees that other theologians might object to his saying the primary purpose of theology comprises knowledge of God and not the interpretation of experience; he also suggests his may offer a secondary
aspect or function of theology. The method presented in the next chapter will say that gaining knowledge of God constitutes the primary task

of theology, but that theologians can achieve this from all types of experience and by submitting ideas back to experience.

Brown suggests ways theology might learn from the method of physics, his discipline.[33] Scientists test the credibility of a model, he writes, "in every way . . . imagination can suggest." A model must find agreement with experiment "to a sufficient accuracy to differentiate an acceptable model from an unacceptable one." The level of accuracy demanded varies with such factors as the refinement of the model and whether it offers a fresh suggestion or only a slight modification of an old-standing explanation. Because the various intellectual disciplines do not differ in the way they acquire knowledge, he advises recasting the theological search for truth "in the same mold" as he describes. Theologians could then create a model and check its validity against what people believe is true.[34]

Another attempt comes from Wiebe.[35] He adopts Michael Scriven's understanding of scientific method, listing what constitutes a proper scientific explanation as: "a set of presuppositions which, if false, make the argument incorrect; . . . the assumption of connections between phenomena, which, if irrelevant, make the argument incomplete; and . . . a context" that makes an explanation "either appropriate or inappropriate."[36] To explain something implies commitment to—and the availability of the grounds for—the truth of the propositions, to the adequacy of the connections, and to the appropriateness of the explanation. Wiebe maintains religious explanations have this same structure and form, despite the problem of delineating what its explanations try to explain.

Kordig makes a similar presentation to Barbour's, especially over paradigms and the nature of rationality.[37] He claims causality as a standard or criterion by which to evaluate scientific theories, irrespective of changes in research traditions.[38] "It demands that constructs should contain causal laws," which means that a "specifiable state or condition of a physical system" time-wise follows another "state or condition." The causal nature of a scientific theory leads to identifying its predictions, and therefore to confirming or infirming it. This fits with what Barbour calls supporting experimental observations: a theory has value "if it accurately accounts for known observations and yields precise predictions of future measurements."[39] (In comparison, some writers consider predictability unimportant for making the object of the theory intelligible.)[40]

Note how closely Barbour's criteria and those given above parallel Kaufman's guidelines (stated in chapter 2) for constructing a theology. Kaufman makes the overall criterion that the theology must lead toward fuller humanization. A difference in the methods' emphases arises from Kaufman's first criterion, namely the formal relationship between God and the world in which God limits absolutely. This reflects Kaufman's choice for a basic theistic symbol—God as the ultimate limiter—which, in Barbour's list, could come under "supporting evidence."

The accounts of scientific explanation given by Schlesinger, Austin, Brown, Wiebe, Kordig, and Kaufman allow theology to seek scientific confirmation or infirmation for its theories. Do these analyses of science match Barbour's? Wiebe's three components of a proper explanation fit respectively into Barbour's classes of conceptual assumptions, models, and theories. However, the major tool in the evaluation of a theory (and which might incorporate or reconcile the work at least of Austin, Brown, Wiebe, Kordig, and Kaufman into or with Barbour's) is the criterion Barbour labels as "agreement with experimental evidence." Most Kuhn-informed philosophies of science do match Barbour's scheme taken flexibly. (Schlesinger's account, on the other hand, may not fit with Barbour's—but it appears questionable anyhow.)

Barbour presents a broader account than do the others of the structure and nature of scientific rationality (as opposed to the *formal* specification of what it entails for a scientific theory to explain some phenomenon).[41] His analysis may therefore prove more useful in this current context than could the others.

This discussion merges into that of chapter 3 on Nielsen and the question of factual meaningfulness. The stricter and parallel question to Nielsen's, the one associated with Antony Flew, asks about the verifiability of supposed truthful statements and not just about their meaningfulness. Barbour thinks his book, *Myths, Models, and Paradigms*,[42] answers Flew's more severe challenge to theology by showing that both scientific and religious statements are partly descriptive and partly nondescriptive (though religious beliefs fall more on the latter end of the scale).[43] Scientific statements—the paradigms of empirical truth and meaning—may therefore not meet the standards required of religious statements and critics should therefore not apply such criteria to religion. One reviewer of Barbour's work, Leroy Howe, considers this to constitute Barbour's single achievement regarding the descriptive nature of theological language.[44] For Schlesinger, however, Barbour's account does not satisfactorily reply to Flew because, he argues, though an adequate account of scientific rationality has not yet appeared, it could, and when it does (Schlesinger thinks his provides this account, Wiebe thinks Scriven's does), theologians should apply it to theological claims.[45] The next chapter applies this methodological quest to theology.

CONCLUSIONS

Different types of logic exist between and within cultures (in Western culture, for example, that for everyday life and that for quantum mechanics). However, a basic rationality probably exists innate to humans, the fundamental method for gaining knowledge; perhaps the "tried and tested" approach to life encapsulates this rationality. People differ over how they apply it: over the type of reasons they consider valid (for example, biblical versus scientific statements), the data they refer to (the contents of scripture versus quantitative measurements), and the importance ranking they use for different statements ("Jesus as true God and true human" versus a lack of contradictions). Both science and theology fall into this general, natural family of logics.

The use of Barbour in this chapter attempts to present the empirical method of science, a delineation, as critical realism, that pays special attention to reconciling the objective and the subjective. His ideas offer a good place to start. The next chapter will look at theology with the eyes of a critical realist and analyze it as comprising—like science—metaphysical beliefs, research traditions (with paradigms), comprehensive theories, theories (with models and criteria), and laws relating observables.

NOTES

1. See, e.g., Reardon 1955.
2. Barbour 1974: esp. chaps 3 and 6, summarized on pp. 142–46.
3. Clayton 1989a; 1989b.
4. Barbour 1974: 113, 117. See also Michael Polanyi 1964: 160–71.
5. See, e.g., Barbour 1974: 184–85; Leatherdale 1974.
6. See the references in Barbour 1974: 42–44; MacCormac 1976: chap. 3.
7. Barbour 1974: 31.

8. Barbour 1974: 30.

9. See Barbour 1974: 102.

10. Machan 1977.

11. Barbour 1974: 114–16.

12. E.g., Kuhn 1970; Mitchell 1973.

13. Barbour 1974: 117.

14. Barbour 1974.

15. Peacocke 1984.

16. McMullin 1974: 675–76; emphasis added.

17. See Sharpe 1984; 2000.

18. *Webster's New World Dictionary.*

19. Needham 1972.

20. Tournier 1957: 71.

21. Wittgenstein 1968.

22. Barbour 1974: 92, 115.

23. See, e.g., Carnes 1982; Klein 1974; Pannenberg 1976; Schlesinger 1977; Sharpe 1984; Wiebe 1976.

24. See Martin 1972; Meland 1969; Peters 1976; Ramsey 1964.

25. Klein 1974; Martin 1972; Meland 1969; Tooley 1975 (but see Martin 1978).

26. Schlesinger 1977b: 17–28; 1977a: 3.

27. Schlesinger 1977a: 1.

28. Austin 1967.

29. Bochenski 1965; Whitehead 1925.

30. Austin 1967: 8.

31. Austin 1967: 8.

32. Austin 1967: 8. See also Schilling 1962.

33. Brown 1966.

34. Brown 1966: 16–17.

35. Wiebe 1974a; 1976.

36. Wiebe 1976: 38.

37. Kordig 1971; MacCormac 1976. See also Barbour 1974: 188–89; Doppelt 1978; McMullin 1974.

38. Kordig 1971: 111, 114–15. See Margenau 1950: chaps. 5, 6; Thagard 1978.

39. Barbour 1974: 92.

40. See Pannenberg 1976: 336; Montgomery 1966: 77; Thom 1975: 321–23.

41. Barbour 1974.

42. Barbour 1974: chap. 7. See also MacCormac 1976; Mitchell 1973.

43. Howe 1974.

44. Howe 1974.

45. Schlesinger 1977a: chap. 20.

Chapter Six

"God" the Lens:
Key-Theology as a Science

How might theologies be scientific, descriptive, or empirical? They generally do not function this way now. But could they? What does theology seek to explain? What explanatory role might the term "God" play?

Scientific knowledge does not contrast with theological knowledge, as would the purely objective with the purely subjective; these extremes do not distinguish science's expression of truth from theology's. Both of the qualifiers apply to each of the two types of understanding. An adequate descriptive explanation of scientific rationality, in other words, must take account of the nondescriptive aspects of science—one of Ian Barbour's points. Similarly, an adequate descriptive explanation of theological rationality must take account of the descriptive aspects of theology. These two points could allow theology's method to participate in the rationality of science. Herein lays the chance to develop theology as a science.

The picture of science that chapter 5 presented draws on Barbour's critical realist portrayal of science as comprising metaphysical beliefs, research traditions (with paradigms), comprehensive theories, theories (with models and criteria), and laws relating observables. Theology can also comprise these elements, as this chapter will elaborate. The chapter will also discuss the descriptive nature of theology and the assumptions concerning truth that this approach implies. Most of the sources for the chapter draw from the 1960s and 1970s, as with previous chapters, written in the face of challenges such as Antony Flew's and Kai

Nielsen's, and responses to them; a later chapter will compare the theological method developed with recent proposals. Theology has yet to answer adequately this challenge to its method. It tried to at the time, but did not succeed and the challenge and the questions remain open. This chapter will help take the discussion further in an open, honest, and constructive manner.

MARGENAU'S CHALLENGE

During the 1950s and 1960s and the end of the stranglehold of logical positivism, Frederick Ferré and Ian Ramsey helped start theology's exploration of the method of science with their talk of models in religion.[1] The physicist and philosopher of science Henry Margenau was one of the first people within this context to carry the vision further and propose theology adopt an empirical scientific method.[2] The rest of this chapter, which expands on the structure and method of theology under a scientific methodology, develops from Margenau's groundbreaking work.

Margenau's description of scientific method isolates from human experience two elements that help constitute knowledge:

1. one he labels P (for immediate perception, a sensory datum, an observation, a fact acting as a "protocol"); and
2. the other he labels C (for mental constructions, thoughts, ideas, mental images, fancies, concepts, the results of reasoning).

Something belongs to the P-domain when people recognize its truth and can accept it. Thus, writes Margenau, experience confronts the person with a P-plane, but "its complete lack of organization and coherence" defies understanding. To help alleviate this bafflement, the person sets up a "correspondence between these factual experiences and certain constructs."[3] The P-plane bounds this constructional plane, called the C-field.

A scientific construct validly represents P-facts if it satisfies two collections of criteria:

1. it must exhibit "logical fertility, extensibility, multiple connections, simplicity, elegance, and several others" (a metaphysical requirement);[4] and

2. it must successively and successfully predict what should occur on the *P*-plane.

Margenau's development of a formal structure for theology asks what comprises the *P*-plane of religious experience. No one can stand back and observe God, he says.[5] People do, however, experience "such things as the feeling of gratitude that springs up in [human hearts] . . . on a joyous day, the monitoring awareness of a conscience that regulates the lives of most of us, the feeling of awe in the face of overwhelming beauty, the guilty contrition that follows a sinful experience, the sentiments of misery and abandon at the insufficiency of human power before hate, the longing for grace and for redemption."[6] Margenau finds it difficult to specify the development of a "science of religion" beyond this because the method employed will develop as attempts to do so mature.

He insists, though, that such attempts must subject theology to the same metaphysical criteria as those he lists for science and must offer it to empirical confirmation. This requires rejecting certain "peculiar kinds of theology"—for example Calvinist predeterminism and Enlightenment deism—because theology cannot honestly test them.[7] The "fossils in the rocks at creation" response to evolution provides another example. These theologies do not seriously consider the outcomes of tests because they claim God would have foreordained the results and set them up that way at the beginning of time.

One way to answer the empiricist challenge to theology sidesteps it or denies its existence. Allan Eister suggests the study of religion may require something other than the scientific method.[8] Mary Hesse rejects the empirical method of the natural sciences for theology because she finds it inadequate for the social sciences.[9] Margenau thinks otherwise.[10] The scientific method may eventually gain knowledge of realms other than the quantifiable physical, though, he warns, the pioneers will not find it easy. The proposal in this chapter rallies behind Margenau and tries out his approach. His ideas need developing, however; for example:

- his understanding of the doing of science (hence his understanding of truth) needs supplementing with advancements in the philosophy of science;[11] and
- his restriction of the *P*-plane to religious experience needs revisiting.

The proposed approach starts by breaking down theology's method the same way as Barbour breaks down science's method into metaphysical beliefs, research traditions (with paradigms), comprehensive theories, theories (with models and criteria), and laws relating observables. This structure of Barbour divides into three: conceptual assumptions (metaphysical beliefs, research traditions, paradigms, comprehensive theories), models and theories (including laws relating observables), and criteria. The proposal would also analyze theological knowledge in terms of critical realism the same way as Barbour philosophically analyzes scientific knowledge.

What is a suitable name for this approach?

- Ralph Wendell Burhoe employs the term "scientific theology" to mean a theology that uses the findings of science, especially the theory of evolution. However, this proposal to use Barbour's analysis goes further than Burhoe's use of scientific research.
- Thomas Torrance employs the term "theological science" to mean a theology that looks to some theories from contemporary physics, but is scientific only in its efforts to unfold the truth that lies within Christian scripture. However, no scriptures restrict "truth" for the proposal that follows in this chapter.
- Bernard Meland employs the term "empirical theology" to mean scientific with respect to religious experience: it provides the data on which theology builds its theories. However, this chapter's proposal would develop a theology scientific in method but with data broader than experiences someone calls religious; it builds from any and every experience.

Burhoe's, Torrance's, and Meland's terms and approaches do not suffice here. Rather, the term used will be "key-theology," "key" in the sense of the key in the door opening into a new vista for theology to explore.

CONCEPTUAL ASSUMPTIONS

Key-theology is to some or a large extent metaphysical because it thinks about the general nature of life and the world using broad ideas such as "God." In comparison with science, much of key-theology lies at this high level, containing more of comprehensive theory, metaphysical assumptions, and paradigms than of lower-level theories and laws. Yet science, as with any system of thought, also involves metaphysical beliefs—to an extent unjustified empirically, to an extent justified empirically—similar to how the religious believer accepts a standpoint on faith.[12] "There exists," writes H. A. Hodges, "a significant comparison between the open-minded, existential stance of the natural scientist and the faith-commitment of the religious believer."[13]

This chapter's outline of a scientific method for key-theology begins with this class of ideas. In particular, this section will treat together all high-level aspects of key-theology—its metaphysical beliefs, research traditions, comprehensive theories, and paradigms (the conceptual root of believers' faiths)—because they relate so closely.

Circular Methods: Inadequate Data

When they adopt their methods, key-theologies assume metaphysically that they *can* know about God, at least imperfectly or in part. They also assume *how* they can know about God. All these adoptions and assumptions usually occur unconsciously. Christian theologies may do both of these in their discussions on Christology or revelation, for example. Even those theologians who say no one can know anything about God assume they know something about God, namely that God is such that no one can know anything about God.

The theologian, like any thinker, must make metaphysical assumptions. The core metaphysical element a theology assumes—the most fundamental theological assumption—is the word "God." Theology centers on this *theos* part of "theology." It distinguishes theology as a discipline from, say, biology or sociology. When developed into whatever the theologian takes it to mean, the God idea centrally organizes and dominates the theology, the notion on which all other ideas depend and with which they fall in line.[14]

A theology takes the word "God" and starts to fill it into an idea and a model. It thinks about things essential to the nature of God by developing the relationship between God and its second primary idea, the "world."[15] When it further specifies what it thinks—more of what it means by the words "God" and "world"—it more clearly fits into a key-theological research tradition. Many such traditions hold sway in current theology, including feminist, liberation, and those based on the writings of Thomas Aquinas, Karl Barth, Friedrich Schleiermacher, and Alfred North Whitehead.[16] Each tradition often discusses theological method and proposes ways to proceed, on its way to developing its comprehensive theories and paradigms.

Four major theological methodologies follow. Do any of them function universally, applicable to all theologies? To stand as a candidate for this, a method must allow the consideration of, among other things, any understanding of God.[17]

Gordon Kaufman

Kaufman's *An Essay on Theological Method* says the theological use of the central idea "God" must build on its ordinary use as the ultimate limit or point of reference for everything, in other words that "to which all action, consciousness, and reflection can lead."[18] To summarize what chapter 2 details, Kaufman thinks theology proceeds in three stages:

1. To construct an idea of world with metaphors and models that depict it as people feel it really is and that the idea "God" can transcend.
2. To fill out the formal understanding of God (God as the ultimate limit) with other models, especially those that picture God concerned with humanity. This stage of theology describes the relationships between God and the world, showing how God transcends the world as the first stage pictures it. And,
3. To revise the idea of world to make it fit with the freshly developed idea of God. This produces a theological world.

The ideas of world (as a whole) and of God are, for Kaufman, wholly theoretical, pure constructions. No one can describe God or the world. Theologians create the two ideas to produce a theological world that supplies unity and meaningfulness to life, and using a transcending (or limiting) idea "God" to help bring about this unity and meaningfulness in their fullness.

Kaufman's method builds on the belief that the core of the word "God" lies in its function to transcend everything totally. Barth brought this assumption forcefully into the twentieth century and founded the neo-orthodox research tradition, which many theologians either struggle with or, in the case of Kaufman, elaborate. It receives criticism for many reasons, including the logical inconsistencies that Kaufman's presentation brings out.[19] More important in this context, Kaufman's proposed theological method relies on his idea of God. The theologian cannot, within his method, differ with this God idea and start theology from scratch by examining initial assumptions. Kaufman does not offer a universal method for theology.

Paul Van Buren in his book, *The Edges of Language*, tries to answer the critics of the use-theory of language (which Kaufman's approach follows), saying where "God" resides in this functionalist enterprise.[20] However, his defense as with Kaufman's maintains the nondescriptive, purely functional nature of theology. This does not suffice for today's society. God as really existing—God as an object or being; theology as descriptive—keeps recurring as a human need, including for contemporary Westerners. To take "God" as a functional word still requires taking seriously the descriptive nature of God language.

Wolfhart Pannenberg

Wolfhart Pannenberg proposes another scientific theological method. He applies a modified version of Heinrich Scholz's minimum requirements for a descriptive science, which resemble the criteria Barbour elaborates for scientific (and, as will come up later, religious) knowledge.[21] Pannenberg starts with the idea that God is the reality that determines everything,[22] and continues by describing theology as the science of God so understood. However, because of the dispute about God's reality and because of God's all-determining nature, theologians cannot take God as the subject of theology. Theology must rather, Pannenberg thinks, focus its investigations within the world itself and seek the implications of the implicit presence of God in everything. Theology ought particularly to investigate the nature of God as shown in the historical development of religions and in the philosophical analysis of existence. Such historical and philosophical-hermeneutical techniques enable attempts to verify theological statements as statements about life. Theologians should also make a theological theory continuous with other current theologies and apply it within present experience.

Pannenberg's method for theology rests on his belief that God has primarily to do with religion and the human sense of being. His analysis does not conclude with an openness of theological hypotheses to confirmation or infirmation in what they say about the physical world, including the biological and social, as opposed to that personal and historical. He disregards this when he advocates the testing of statements about God against what they say about "meaning as implied in present existence."[23] Theologians need not progress, as Pannenberg does, from God statements, to those about the world, to those about the totality of experience, to those about meaning in present experience.[24] Rather, if key-theologians were to assume Pannenberg's basic God idea, they could progress from statements about God, to those about the world and its constituent parts, to those about meaning in present existence. Key-theology should not restrict itself to the subjective world and automatically gloss over the physical. After all, according to Pannenberg, God determines everything and everything includes the physical world.

Pannenberg starts his method for theology with the idea of God as the reality that determines everything. Is this a universally acceptable (Christian) idea of God? Perhaps his two attributes of God—namely, God as the *reality* that *determines* all things—do not adequately reflect the nature of God. Why should theologians choose these as basic to God, and not some other idea, for instance God as "that reality that everything affects"? Pannenberg's idea of God, therefore, ought not to determine key-theological method. Be that as it may, his idea probably does form a foundational plank for key-theological construction after delineating the method; it offers a high-level metaphysical idea upon which the model of God might build.

Thomas Torrance

Theologians may associate the phrase "scientific theology" with Torrance.[25] Theology must start with the "gloriously ultimate transcendent God revealed in Jesus Christ," Torrance writes.[26] Theologians then can describe the reality God based on the scriptures in a manner that parallels how science describes its subject. With this assertion, Torrance thinks he adopts a realist method (his understanding of the term "realist" differs from Barbour's).[27]

Torrance unfortunately makes his finite principle of "divine ultimate transcendence" an ultimate principle. Chapter 2's critiques of Kaufman accordingly swing into action: Torrance's criticism of liberal theology (with it, he says, theologians obtrude themselves into the place of God) applies also to his own system (with it, his assumption and his theology obtrude). A consideration of Torrance's position also ought to take into account problems in delineating the theology of the Gospels and the propriety of their cosmology for today.

Torrance's method appears scientific. However, he finds theology's data in what he initially assumes, namely that the Gospel records of Jesus Christ provide what theology needs to know about the nature of God. He ignores humility before all the data of experience. His method also deviates from science because it does not allow the questioning of all theories and conclusions. (Perhaps if he availed himself of the revised understandings of scientific method, which acknowledge the subjectivities involved in science, his overly strong revelation stance might weaken.) Yes, theology could constitute a science, it could work empirically, but it need not, as with Torrance's approach, describe the revelation once-and-for-all given. Theologians need to step back and ask about the criteria relevant to their discipline: should they ascribe to the "incarnation" such a dominant, assertive, and unquestioned role?

Torrance believes each object of study has its own particular though related mode of rationality. For evangelical Christian theology, his method may offer an appropriate scientific approach. But not for theology in general. His method might work with his God, but not with all understandings of God or as a general approach to God.

One of the fundamental differences between Torrance and this book lies in their starting points. This book at first seeks an empirically based way to talk about divine reality or at least about the fundamental words of theology. Torrance, on the other hand, starts by trying to talk about and understand what he sees in the New Testament. In general, theology's initial task comes logically prior to Torrance's.

David Tracy

David Tracy provides one of the more widely discussed liberal proposals for theological method.[28] His revisionist approach to theology proceeds in four steps:

1. identifying theology's criteria and arguments with those of various concerned disciplines, particularly with secular faith;
2. investigating phenomenologically the religious dimension in common experience (the first source for theology);

3. delegating Christian symbols and records (the Christian fact: the second source for theology) to supply data through historical and hermeneutical investigation; and
4. feeding these data into the theology-making process.

Tracy works from human experience and from received data such as the exegesis of biblical records.[29] He correlates the results of these two investigations, thereby supplying the ground in common experience for the notion of God. (He thinks this also answers the empiricist challenge to theology.) The meaning of the basic human faith thus equals the meaning of the symbols of the Christian witness; the common ground of human experience might thereby even justify a particular idea of God.[30]

Tracy's method, like Pannenberg's, bypasses the physical world. It also assumes something about God, namely that basic human faiths entail God, especially in the disclosures of limiting experiences (the religious dimension in common experience). Despite this, the historical, hermeneutical, and phenomenological analyses in Tracy's method could provide—for theology's consideration—data and criteria, and potential models for God and other theological subjects.

The above four proposals—those from Kaufman, Pannenberg, Torrance, and Tracy—lie within traditions and none offers a universal theological method that allows the development, exploration of, and choice between the multitude of God ideas. In general, to find out whether or not a method depends on an idea of God requires asking how it responds to scientific methodology; does it fully face the challenge and accept scientific method and results? Does it not restrict the data it could consider? A theological method cannot depend on any particular idea of God or the God-world relationship if it wishes to avoid circularity. The objective is a comprehensive or universal theological method that allows the exploration and evaluation of a multitude of theologies and God ideas.

The challenge is to provide another methodological proposal for theology, one based on scientific method, one that builds on the suggestions of Kaufman, Pannenberg, Torrance, and Tracy, and one that answers the skepticism of Nielsen. The scheme offered will take the deliberately constructive nature of theology from Kaufman and, from Tracy, the subjection of it to the various concerned secular disciplines.

From Nielsen, it will acknowledge the relevance and importance of the empiricist challenge, incorporating it into its key-theological method. The proposed method goes even further and promotes ways to confirm or infirm theistic models, and ways in which to critique the theological construction process.

Using the Word "God"

The challenge is to start methodology again, trying to develop one that does not depend on a particular notion of God. To begin with, key-theologians might say the core word their theologies assume is "God." But why should they use this word?

The process called secularization causes something to happen with knowledge and experience of God. People used to experience God as real, as having real existence, and God used to show this reality in interactions with people. They could take this as primary. They also attempted to understand something of the nature of God and so created theologies and special theological symbols. The current problem lies in these older theological ideas (especially those concerned with the being or nature of God) proving inadequate. Such ideas perforce relate closely to people's overall understanding of the nature of things, their cosmology or mythology. This has changed, leaving understandings of God stranded and unrelated to it.[31] Further, ideas of something define it to an extent (more in some cases than in others) and the reality the idea purportedly refers to defines ideas of it to an extent; this admits to critical realism. It means ideas of God partly define God, and the reality God to which the ideas supposedly refer also partly defines them. Thus, current experience of God, insofar as ideas determine the experience and the ideas differ from those of the past, will diverge or grow from experience of God in the past. In a sense, people come to know more about God, or knowledge of God grows, as does experience of God. What is the God people now experience? God is real, people's experience of God is real to them, and they need to understand the nature of God in such a way that they know God as real; their understandings need adequately to portray the reality of God.

God's reality needs no apology. God does not exist only as a word that functions in a certain way (an instrumentalist approach to theological language).[32] Key-theologians therefore could accept God's existence—without saying anything else about God—and work from there; key-theologies could say God exists without implying what they mean by the word "God." In fact, they could assume God exists and later ask what sort of God exists. "It seems clearly possible to have good reasons for holding some things more tentatively . . . some things as more firmly established than others," comments H. D. Lewis. This does not apply to "the existence of God," however; "everything else [known] . . . about God depends upon some kind of evidence."[33] Perhaps some pictures of God prove grossly inadequate.

This minimally means, at the initial stage of elucidating key-theological method, that the word "God" offers a worthwhile term to use. To do key-theology requires a commitment—for whatever reasons—to use the word "God." All key-theologies center on the word "God." Then key-theologians need to see how the word functions fundamentally. Third, they need to develop further knowledge of God. And, fourth, they need to ask whether any of the pictures of God are accurate and thereby do discern the reality God. The questions for theological method, given an empirical mind, thus become:

- Beyond that key-theologians need to use the word "God," what ought they to assume? Obviously, not all dogmas. But how much do they require to make a coherent basis from which to ask questions toward developing the remainder of the idea "God"? What else do they need to assume about the nature of God and the God-world relationship so their key-theologies can adequately know or put into words God's forms of existence, character, and behavior?
- How do key-theologians fill out the basic ideas of God into an adequately functioning theology?
- Then, how do key-theologians find out what sorts of God ideas accurately portray God, and which ones do not?

This section addresses the first of these questions, and the following two sections the second and third questions.

"God" as a Lens

Key-theology starts with the word "God." How does this word fundamentally function?

The discussion on Nielsen mentioned that theologians sometimes compare the highly metaphysical term "God" with theoretical terms in physics such as "electron" or "field," ideas with referents within the physical world. Consider a different comparison: to parallel the term "God" with science's highly metaphysical term "(quantifiable) physical reality." Both science and key-theology attempt to explain the world with their core notions, "quantifiable physical reality" on the one hand and "spiritual or divine reality" ("God") on the other. Call these two core ideas "lenses."

The two lenses act to isolate aspects of the world for focused explanation. Science centers its explanations on "physical reality" and may, in the case of physics, see the world as comprising such things as matter, physical forces, and fields, with properties such as mass, velocity, and valence. Key-theology centers its explanations on "God" and may, in the case of Christian theology, see the world as comprising such things as spirit, creator, and divine action, with properties such as values, love, and hope. Physics usually uses mathematical models, versus key-theology's usual use of anthropomorphic ones. Physics may see the world in mechanistic terms, whereas key-theology may see it more in personal ones.[34]

Back in 1919, Douglas Clyde MacIntosh perceived the idea "God" to function in theology similarly to how the idea "physical reality" functions in science: empirical theology contains a presupposition peculiar to it, just as every empirical science contains a presupposition special to it.

> The empirical sciences assume the existence, and the possibility of empirical knowledge, of the objects they undertake to investigate. Thus chemistry assumes the existence of matter; psychology, the existence of states of consciousness; psychology of religion, the existence of religious experience, and so on. [Each discipline assumes] . . . , commonly on the basis of pre-scientific experience, the accessibility of the object to further knowledge through further experience. And what [holds for the sciences holds for] . . . empirical theology. . . . Ordinarily, [empirical theologians will, as expected,] . . . posit the existence of God—defined, to be sure, in a preliminary fashion—because [they already feel] . . . practically sure, on the basis of religious experience, that God already exists. . . . [They investigate,] through scientific theological observation and experiment under the guidance of definite working hypotheses, . . . what God is.[35]

Need Key-Theology Start by Identifying God?

Key-theologians first accept the potential explanatory importance of the word "God" (at this stage this word is empty). Second, they look at the world through a "God" lens. What then constitutes the subject matter of key-theology? It would appear to comprise the world. But does it?

Does key-theology describe God? Does God constitute the subject matter of key-theology? The notion that key-theology describes God may suggest it can identify the referent to the word "God." To identify God ties closely with describing God. Perhaps key-theology needs to identify God so it can compare proposed descriptions of God with experience of God to decide their suitability. No one can point to God in a simple way, however. No one can say, "Yes, there he is. He is the bald one with brown eyes, a gray beard, is about as high as a house." Between them, cultures and individuals believe hundreds of ideas of God—some of them mutually incompatible—all related in a similar way to how Ludwig Wittgenstein relates games or members of a family; a pair may share something, but not all games—or all members of a family—need share some one thing.[36] To which God does a key-theology refer? Maybe key-theology cannot identify God. How can it describe God, then, if it cannot point to God? If it cannot describe or identify God, how can it distinguish between "God" ideas to find the better ones?

Three attempts to answer this identification-description matter follow, two of which unnecessarily assume the importance of identifying God. They become circular, basing their initial identifications—and hence their methods—on their ideas of God.

Paul Gastwirth

Paul Gastwirth writes that theology needs to state properties of God before it can identify the referent of the word "God." Description logically comes "prior to questions about existence. The referent may or may not exist," but theologians can only make that decision after they have stipulated "a specific set of conditions" from which they can define the idea "God" they wish to discuss.[37] Otherwise, says Gastwirth, they become theological relativists where their decision between competing ideas for God does not depend on the reality God; each God idea becomes as good and as true as any other.[38] Certainly, theologians can decide if a particular God exists only once they stipulate what they mean by that term "God." But Gastwirth says more than this, namely that theologians can only identify God through the specifiable contents of the idea, and that variations in "God" ideas mean each refers to a different (existent or nonexistent) God.

Use of language does not work this way, however. The phrase "John Smith" summons to the minds of one group of people a warm and benevolent man because they experience him this way. For another group, "John Smith" summons a hurting, pushing beast because he appears like that to them. Both refer to the same John Smith. As with a human like John Smith, so key-theologians need initially to specify God without elaborating further the idea "God"; then they can compare the proposed ideas for God with experience of God to judge their suitability. Logically, knowledge of God's character does not rise before the question of God's existence.

Robert Oakes

Robert Oakes considers God an observation term. He writes that, while theologians may have "a good deal of empirical evidence for the existence of God (as many theists undoubtedly want to maintain—for example, the 'orderly processes of nature')," tradition views God as "a being who is not (and cannot be) a 'perceptual object.'" However, Oakes adds, God logically can "be an object of sense-experience"; theologians can construe "God" "as an observation term."[39] To justify this, he assumes:

- the intelligibility of the position called epistemological dualism;
- the intelligibility of the idea "God"; and
- the logical possibility that God can supervene a "God experience" onto the experience of some object (Oakes suggests that the omnipotence of the theistic God renders this possibility probable).

With these suppositions, Oakes thinks it possible to experience God through the senses in ways whose truth theologians can investigate. In that one can observe and describe anything from a truth-examinable experience of it, people who think they experience God may experience God and may observe and describe God. "God" is therefore an observation term.[40]

The argument behind Oakes's conclusion, however, depends on the theology he assumes, a theism that accepts the omnipotence of God. He therefore does not prove the descriptive nature of theological theories in general. Neither does he propose a watertight case for the descriptive nature of the theistic idea of God because he assumes the experiences of God that make God an observational term happen at the whim of God; they could occur in private and uniquely and therefore perhaps not be examinable for their truthfulness.

This chapter suggests the descriptive nature of theology in ways that do not depend on theism, as in Oakes's case, or on any other theological theory. He thinks theologians need an approach like his because they usually consider the term "God" wholly theoretical. They need not retreat, though, into the "wholly theoretical."

Berent Enç

Berent Enç proposes a third way to determine or identify the reality God. He wants theologians to select a set of sentences they would consider essential to the nature of God and part of their eventual theological theory:

- such sentences must state what kind of thing God is;
- they must therefore provide God with properties or dispositions with which to explain the phenomena they associate with God; however,
- the theory cannot explain the properties;
- it cannot use the properties to recognize (the presence of) God; and
- the properties cannot state observable consequences of God.[41]

The five bulleted points above may not all appeal, but at least Enç's approach does not depend on what he thinks God is. It is not necessary to identify God to talk about how to do key-theology.

Key-Theology's Subject

A way to pursue the question of whether or how key-theology can describe God requires asking what key-theology describes. What comprises the subject matter for key-theology?

Because God does not sit there for anyone to describe like a physical thing, theologians would have to know, suggests Pannenberg, how to "distinguish God from the affirmations of theologians and already-committed believers."[42] Something else than God must therefore form the subject matter for key-theology and, through studying this, key-theologians discern the nature of God.

The answer appeared a few pages above: "God" functions as a high-level metaphysical lens for looking at the world, just as "physical reality" does. The subjects of both lenses therefore are real, are the same, are the world. This deserves some elaboration. Augmenting what Donald Wiebe writes about this, theology's data include:

1. "the daily round of experiences" that makes up people's lives;
2. the empirical world;
3. the world in the sense of the world's "totality and the sum total of . . . personal experience";
4. records of people's (individual and collective) religious journeys and thoughts received via scriptures and dogmas or less important theologies, mystical narrations, poetry, art, and so forth; and
5. the type of experience that differs from "mere sensation" and that some people call religious experience[43] (as Margenau, Tracy, and Henry Nelson Wiemann suggest; in fact, for liberal thought from Schleiermacher onward, this offers the final arbiter for theology).[44]

Difficulties arise when theologians believe the subject of theology comprises exclusively either the third, fourth, or fifth of these, the whole that constitutes the world, religious records, or religious experience:

• As chapter 2 noted, Kaufman thinks theology becomes purely constructive and nondescriptive when it takes the world-as-a-whole as its subject. Chapter 4 argued, however, for the descriptive nature of key-theology. Society badly needs this. Further, Kaufman suggests, no one can readily know about the whole, not only because humans lie within it, but also because nothing can stand in distinction to it. Key-theology ought not, therefore, to focus only on wholes.

• Kaufman also argues that too many problems arise when constraining the data of theology to religious experience, dogma, scriptures, or a combination of the three. The difficulties occur even when including under religious experience nonsensory (mystical) types of experience, or (as William Austin phrases it) "historical events such as the Exodus, and occurrences in the individual religious [person's sensory] experience."[45] One circularity admits that a theological or religious understanding can induce or isolate experiences or aspects of them as religious; theory can infuse data. Cultural relativism could also arise when choosing a limited referent. Theologians cannot consider religious experience sufficiently free of doubt to say someone definitively experiences God.

- A religious experience is, rather, a natural—if maybe unusual— experience, just an experience until someone interprets it as religious.[46] Instead of starting with such events, key-theology could try to find a perspective on, understanding of, or explanation for experience considered religious. It could apply consistency with the experience as a criterion for assessing theological theories. A key-theology finds strength if it can point to actual experiences it claims as religious, show how and why they are religious, and indicate their significance. Charismatic theologies find such strength with glossolalia.

Thus, the subject matter of key-theology—an arbitrator between key-theologies—includes the world, as a whole and as people experience it, potentially all phenomena and all experience. Key-theology's subject encompasses everything and anything. The word "God" forms the fundamental core explanatory tool for key-theology, with which it tries to explain all of reality. Key-theology reclaims what theology traditionally claimed.

The subject of natural science, like the subject of key-theology, potentially encompasses everything, ideally even one-off and subjective events (for instance, the evolution of *Homo sapiens*, and the experience of pain). Key-theology cannot claim its corpus let alone its central idea "God" as unique (though it could consider them peculiar). The two do differ, however. Science and key-theology employ the same subject, use similar procedures (as this chapter explains), but aim at different objects with their explanations. Key-theology aims to know about God, its object; science aims to know about physical reality, its object.

Science and key-theology may also differ in the types of ideas and models they use in their explanations. For instance, the word "God" has a history of use from which key-theology might isolate a cluster of attributes essential to God and areas in which people claim to experience God and God's activity. These differ from the ideas of the sciences.

Key-Theology Describes God

The subject matter of a discipline equals what it describes. Science describes the world (if science does not describe it, what does?) and so its subject is the world. Science assumes a basic metaphysical symbol (its object, "physical reality") through and with which it then proceeds to describe the world and its facets. This indicates the theoretical nature of science's idea "physical reality" and yet maintains science's foot in the descriptive. Key-theology similarly starts with a fundamental metaphysical idea (its object, "God") and similarly describes and explains both the whole and the content of the world by filling out its basic symbol "God." The subject of key-theology is the world. As with science, the theoretical nature of key-theology's idea "God" still maintains key-theology's foot in the descriptive. Key-theology describes as science describes.

Key-theology describes its subject, the world; does it also describe its object, God? Does science describe its object, physical reality, as it also describes its subject, the world?

Western culture commonly assumes the object that science seeks to know and little debate rages over the existence of the referent for this symbol. Today's mind produces a particularly science-oriented, physical-world biased age, with minimal considerations of anything ethereal. (The idea "physical reality" does change. Ongoing investigations into paranormal and other phenomena on the edge of what consensus now accepts as real, for instance, may force a broadening of the present image of what constitutes the reality science can investigate.) In this light, talk about science as descriptive of physical reality usually makes sense.

Science has it easy compared with key-theology. Unlike science's physical reality, not everyone experiences the object of key-theology, God, or assumes that God (whatever the conception of God) exists. Neither do those who think God exists necessarily regard God as a readily describable object. Because of these factors, key-theologians may hesitate to consider their models and theories descriptive of God. So, how might key-theology describe God, especially if it does not identify God?

A key-theology fills out the basic symbol chosen as God. In this, key-theology describes God but only secondarily in the sense that the key-theological corpus arising from its idea "God" sees the world through this lens. Whatever constitutes God, key-theologians describe God not by pointing to or identifying God as an object, but by describing the world theologically.[47] Science too describes its object, the physical world, in a secondary sense by looking at the world through its particular lens of the physical.

A more pointed version of the question in the above paragraph comes to the surface. The world provides the data, the subject for key-theology. "God" therefore refers to the world. Could "God" also refer to God? The answer: Maybe, but maybe not. A dualist may see theology's object, God, as completely separate from the world and therefore from any experiencible reality. What people do experience (the subject of theology) may then result from the God-world relationship and, from this dualist perspective, this does not constitute God. "God" at most refers to the God-world relationship. A monist theology, on the other hand, may see the world as the referent for "God" and, in this case, "God" can refer to God.

Another approach to describing God is possible. As in the dualist position, key-theology elucidates the "God" idea by building an understanding of God's relationship with the world. Key-theologians know God via what happens in the world; they know the object of key-theology via the God-world relationship. The paramount or core working idea is therefore "God-world." Key-theology may thus describe God inasmuch as key-theological descriptions of the world (the results of the God-world relationship) refer back to God. To spell this out more, assume God grounds the world;[48] for example, with Pannenberg, assume God constitutes the reality that determines everything.[49] It makes sense with this stance to consider the world as a reflection of God, its determiner. It also makes sense to think of key-theologians' ideas of God (God's character, behavior, and forms of existence)—because they attempt to describe the world—as trying at the same time to describe, put into words, or refer to the world's ground, namely God. Key-theology can describe God.

Changes in High-Level Ideas

Key-theology describes the world in any or all of its aspects using a God idea as its lens. In this, the notion "God" resembles a very high-level scientific assumption. Do such assumptions and terms depend only on observation and involve no theory, or do they all depend only on theory? Are decisions between competitors subjective or objective? Barbour considers the debate on this within the philosophy of science and concludes that all assumptions and terms of them rely to some extent on theory and all of them depend to some extent also on observation. Competing research traditions, for instance, share terms that rely on commonly held theories and these common terms offer bases for discussion and decision making. Science's comprehensive theories, paradigms, research traditions, and metaphysical beliefs resist but can change and change rationally. Discussion and decision between competitors can thus occur, as evidenced in the move from a Newtonian type of physics and metaphysics to one based on quantum physics and relativity.[50] The same holds true for key-theology and the idea "God": "God" is both a theoretical and an observational term. Rational discussion and decision between competitors can occur in key-theology, the criteria for which this chapter will discuss in more depth. They allow the comparison between various God ideas and a decision between them, and this upholds the descriptive nature of theology.

MODELS AND THEORIES

Chapter 1 introduced the role theology plays. The theologian, it said, attempts rationally, coherently, faithfully, and systematically to express and spell out a set of beliefs including, primarily, beliefs considered religious. The discussion now turns to what many might normally associate with this central role of theology: its models and theories, Barbour's next level of knowledge down from conceptual assumptions.

Models to Theories to Key-Theologies

As suggested in the discussion above on Gordon Kaufman's proposed theological method, a thread common to all uses of the word "God" may not exist. Key-theologians, therefore, need to choose the essential contents of their God lens. That deist, process, and theist approaches to Christian theology offer many choices for this lens says the foundations of theological systems can vary and take many shades within the same school.[51] Theologians may not consciously choose their basic model, however, for it may come to them as part of the language use of a community to which they belong for reasons other than belief choice. Despite this, and as consciously and deliberately as possible, the key-theologian critically chooses a basic idea for God.

Having chosen this initial God key—for instance, thinking of God as "the ground of being"—the key-theologian more fully develops God and world models from it and then, based on criteria discussed below, forges them into theories. This development also involves working out the implications of and relationships between the models, deciding on positive and negative analogies, comparing them with other theologies, and applying them to points of interest (including creation, Christology, politics, and anthropology). (Models use analogies. Such use of analogy in theology has a long history, including the approach of Aquinas in the thirteenth century. In modern times, Ramsey helped reinvigorate the deliberate model-making spirit in his defense of theology against strong empiricism and positivism.[52])

Sources for theological models would vary considerably, rightfully so since key-theology must try to encompass a wide swath of the world. Key-theologians might look for models in, for example, biology, hermeneutics, history, phenomenology, philosophy, politics, physics, and social studies. Some of the differences between key-theologies may boil down to their pulling their models and ideas from quite different places.

Religious dogma, scripture, and experiences also offer models and elements for key-theology. Hypotheses from any received Christian, other religious, or indigenous wisdom can perform this role in key-theology. All these only offer potential models, however, because they—like any other proposals—need evaluating before acceptance or rejection. Doing key-theology comes logically before the biblically, experientially, or traditionally given;[53] traditional, experiential, or biblical categories and ideas become suggestions for starting points, but may not determine or represent the outcomes. On the other hand—this will come up under the discussion on criteria—key-theologians could include faithfulness to that which Christians consider inherently Christian or biblical as a possible principle for evaluating a Christian theological hypothesis; tradition may help decide the appropriateness of models and theories. Key-theologians could also build up to, or show to be rational, a model they consider particularly biblical, without assuming biblical fidelity as the primary source or the overriding criterion.

This proposal for key-theological method allows for the development of any type of key-theology. Whatever their interests (biblical exegesis, liberation from social oppression, the natural world, profound experiences, social concerns), key-theologians base their work on a set of beliefs developed into models. They also build their ideas under criteria, which also reflect the beliefs.

Descriptive or Existential?

Does key-theology focus on description or on fulfilling the existential functions usually associated with religion (such as focusing values, influencing lifestyles, inspiring worship, promoting service to others, and providing purposes)? This question has arisen several times above in different settings, but now it needs a longer discussion. The answer may influence the content of the theological models developed and their relationships with religion.

Theology used to espouse theories descriptive about the world—the structure of the universe centered on the earth, the creation of the cosmos in 4004 B.C., where lightning strikes—but science proved it wrong. Positivism and scientism also dismissed theology as factually groundless. To prevent further raps on their empirical knuckles, some theologians follow a subjectivist view that says no one can test either theology or science; any knowledge is factually as good as any other.

Some other theologians protect their knuckles with an alternative approach that orients their ideas away from the physical world and plays down, dismisses, or disregards in them the physically descriptive. An opposition exists, these theologians surmise, between subjective theological statements and testable scientific ones. Theologians cannot confirm or infirm theologies, they think, and so they turn to existentialism, demythologization, functionalism, and language-game fideism. Their works frequently follow Ludwig Wittgenstein's later writings or those of J. L. Austin, among others, and avoid subjecting their theories to the world science examines. Sometimes they consider an analogical model incapable of doing justice to the world of persons and so they require theology to use something more like disclosure or paradox.[54] Ferré and Tracy, in a parallel move, take theology's metaphysical nature to an extreme and talk of theology as purely metaphysical. Empirical claims in theology do not function at the same level as those in science, says

Tracy, because the religious dimension forms the base for all others and accounts for all experience. This means for him that theologians cannot confirm or infirm theological claims in an ordinary way.[55]

Approaches such as these allow theology to promote its existential functions. These tactics, however, may also narrow its vision to the contextual or functional approach to the truth and meaning of theological language. Theology then either refuses or finds it difficult to make its way back to where it can suggest physically descriptive statements without—as in fundamentalism—throwing the results of empirical science to the wind. As said before, this weakens theology's ability to speak meaningfully and helpfully to the modern person.

Theologians reduce the empirical in their subject because of its greater subjectivity than science's, and because of the philosophy of extreme separation. They sometimes think that symbols offer the only way to talk about things beyond cold hard objects here and now. They need not react this way, for several reasons touched on before:

- Scientific models also involve the nonempirical, for instance, because of the analogical or more broadly metaphorical nature of scientific language. The language of models need not imply reductionism and physicalism. To talk fully about the "cold hard things here and now" requires metaphor, and to talk fully about things beyond them also requires objective language. All knowledge involves both analogical model making and empirical grounding. Science and theology therefore each include both objective and subjective factors, though theology leans more toward the subjective than does science. An extreme separation of the two promotes fiction; theologians should rid their minds of the now-melted positivist picture.[56]
- Empirical evidence to an extent controls metaphysical ideas because they can alter under changes in theories and research traditions; they can adjust under the pressure of experience. In addition, theology seeks not only to explain the whole of the world (as Tracy assumes), but also its parts, and knowledge of the parts changes. Theology is more metaphysical than science but, ideally, theologians can still test it.
- Models use metaphors that, when read literally, can generate contradictions and appear odd in their expression.[57] Descriptive theology and its twin, science, employ such models. Inasmuch as the models'

metaphors do justice to the subjective world, so too can the models that include them. Roger Hazelton would probably oppose this reasoning on the same basis that he criticizes Tracy, namely for wanting to restate symbols (metaphorical theology) as testable ideas.[58] Theologians can speak the truth in metaphor, he suggests, and it offers a more appropriate language for theology. Both Hazelton and, to a lesser extent, Tracy probably suggest an unreal dichotomy between descriptive-empirical (model making) and metaphorical knowledge. Theology can open itself to models—which function theoretically and descriptively, and metaphorically and symbolically—as adequate person-explaining notions.

The descriptive nature of key-theology may exceed the existential (or nondescriptive); the factual truth of key-theological statements concerns the key-theologian more than their providing meaning for living. Key-theology develops models in a rational way and need not concentrate on the existential functions of religious language. It may happen to help in this—and perhaps should help by, say, giving the existential aspects a larger or theoretical perspective—but it primarily acts as explanation to aid in understanding the world and people's relationships with it. In fact, if it comes to meaning, the testable, descriptive, or empirical meaning of theological statements (as Nielsen's challenge requires) interests key-theology more, despite protestations to the contrary.[59] Other forms of meaning associate with other types of religious statements. Key-theology can excuse itself for this interest; that constitutes its task. The theological "God" need not aim at functioning as the religious "God."

Key-theology does not divorce itself from living, though. The relationship between the descriptive and existential elements of key-theology is more complex than simply ignoring the latter. The existential does enter descriptive key-theology. John Miles grants that Barbour establishes the descriptive functions of religious language yet, he says, it must also function—and even primarily function—evocatively. "For if it is *merely* [descriptive,] . . . how many will trouble with it?"[60] He takes his case too far with "even primarily function." The "merely descriptive" can involve the evocative. Compare Miles's statement with a comment by Ferré that Barbour quotes: "Seldom, if ever, do people hold metaphysical models and therefore even more so theological models, their 'visions of ultimate reality,' . . . entirely dispassionately." Metaphysicians' views of their world and themselves, plus their "sense of order and intelligibility," become wrapped into their conceptual models.[61] Key-theology not only concerns the world, but also relationships with it.

Key-theology's descriptive and existential aspects do reconcile. One of its evaluative criteria (which the next section will detail) concerns whether the theory works for worshippers; meaning for living is an existential criterion. Further, suppose a key-theology describes and explains the physical world as well as the person world, and empirically succeeds at this—what a powerful and evocative theory. Perhaps the more successfully a key-theology descriptively explains the physical and the person worlds, the more evocative it becomes. The better a key-theology performs its descriptive functions, perhaps the better it performs its existential functions.[62]

Key-theology should focus its model making and theory building more on description than on the existential functions usually associated with religion, but it should not forget them.

Religious Beliefs or Key-Theological Theories?

Theories play a clear role in science, but the status of theories in key-theology is less clear. Which equates with scientific theory: key-theological theories or religious beliefs? The answer to this may influence which functions dominate: the descriptive ones of key-theological theory or the existential ones of religious practice.

"The data of religion are experiences and events" that "imaginative models" interpret, Barbour writes. "As scientific models lead to theories by which [scientists order] observations . . . , so religious models lead to beliefs by which [believers order] experiences." Barbour chooses religious beliefs rather than theological theories as the counterpart to science's theories.[63]

Which dominates the other: the models of religion or the theories of theology? Barbour would probably say the models of religion as intertwined with religious beliefs. The word "beliefs" implies more of a permanence than does "theological theories" because, for the believer, beliefs ought to be true. The life commitment of believers is a more serious enterprise than the speculations of theologians. Theology functions as a theoretical and rational enterprise, trying to tease out beliefs and thus engaging in the hypothetical and tentative. Religious models, closely related to beliefs, must therefore dominate theology's theories. One side of the issue—Barbour's side—may think this way.

Ferré suggests—and Barbour reiterates—that, in science, the theories that develop models govern the models because science aims at theory building. Key-theological theories could similarly dominate *key-theological* models. On the other hand, *religious* models (because of their existential functions) dominate the formal religious beliefs or doctrines derived from them.[64] Do religious models also dominate the theories of key-theology?

Key-theology, as an intellectual vehicle seeking truth, needs to inform beliefs (religious models) because the beliefs may not (or may no longer) appropriately depict the truth as modern Westerners have come to know it. Truth grows on people and so models for it need to change. This leads to a tension between key-theology's theories and religion's models. Because key-theology serves less of the existential and more of the theoretical functions, key-theological theories could inform religion's models; key-theologians can suggest alterations to or disposal of them "according to the dictates of theory."[65] Key-theology does not subject itself to the models of religious belief.

The theoretical aspect of religious language concerns the discussion on key-theological method; thus, key-theologies, rather than religious beliefs, serve as the counterpart to science's theories. To rephrase Barbour, then: "As scientific models lead to theories by which scientists order observations, so key-theological models lead to key-theological theories by which key-theologians order experiences."

CRITERIA

A key-theologian chooses her or his basic understanding of God as a starting point and then builds models and theories by describing and explicating this symbol, especially as it relates to other symbols. The key-theologian thus constructs a key-theology by introducing appropriate ideas and integrating them with the foundational idea of God.

Once in possession of a key-theological theory, the key-theologian needs to evaluate it. Against what ought key-theologians to do this?

How might they test a proposed system, rudimentary though it be, to see how good it is? What do the words "test," and "good" mean?

Start with the word "test." Present and past understandings of scientific method differ over how they visualize the evaluation. A scientist usually compares rival theories using certain criteria and usually not, as philosophers used to think, an isolated theory against set criteria and objective facts. A key-theological theory similarly needs evaluating against rival theories. Suppose you meet a theology that demands you repent because it says you continually and horribly sin in ways of which you are unaware. You would probably dismiss it if you knew of alternative theologies that to you make more sense of your life. People usually hold to a theory—especially a comprehensive one—if they know of no better alternatives, while searching for another.[66]

Next, turn to the word "good." Barbour considers the list of criteria for scientific theories and then applies them to religious beliefs:

> Any system of thought [should desire] *simplicity* . . . (e.g., minimum number of independent assumptions and conceptual categories); but it . . . seldom [becomes] a major consideration in either science or religion. *Coherence* involves both internal consistency (the absence of contradictions) and systematic interrelatedness (the presence of connections and implications between statements). But *supporting evidence* . . . [offers] the most important criterion. Religious beliefs must give a faithful rendition of the areas of experience taken . . . [as] especially significant: religious and moral experience and key historical events. But they must also adequately interpret other events in [people's] lives as active selves. Hence [the list includes] *extensibility* of application (fruitfulness) . . . as an additional criterion. Finally, *comprehensiveness* in the coherent ordering of diverse types of experience within a systematic metaphysics is desirable, though . . . secondary to other criteria.[67]

Note that supporting evidence becomes paramount for evaluating religious beliefs and theological theories.

Theologians disagree over the criteria suggested for their discipline, similarly to how scholars disagree over a list of scientific criteria such as the one Barbour enumerates for science. For instance, compare Barbour's above list for religious beliefs with those outlined previously from Kaufman's *An Essay on Theological Method*, or with those by Sanborn Brown, John Carnes, Alan Duthie, Alfred Glenn, Leroy Howe,

John Montgomery, Shunji Nishi, or Maurice Wiles. Collectively the others suggest theology can seek to confirm a theology by looking at:

- coherence;
- its fit with scripture;
- how well it presents church dogma with an eye on economy; or
- its relevance for today's situation, adequacy in speaking to all of life's essential concerns, or meaningfulness to modern life.[68]

These criteria fit into Barbour's list for religion under coherence, supporting evidence, and extensibility. It thus seems appropriate to say Barbour's list probably offers a comprehensive enumeration of the criteria for theology.

Barbour's list also applies in the evaluation of rival key-theologies. In fact, Barbour's list of criteria—the same set—can help evaluate key-theology's metaphysical beliefs, research traditions (including their paradigms), comprehensive theories, theories (including models and criteria), and any laws relating observables—and are extrinsic to all of them.[69]

Several of the criteria merit further discussion.

Evidence and Extensibility: Subjective Experience

The criteria fall into two types, paralleling the previous distinction between the existential and the descriptive functions of theology:

- social criteria, which refer to the ability of the key-theology to undergird a properly functioning religion;[70] and
- theoretical criteria, which rely on the meanings of the key-theology and its potential to explain.

Below focuses on the social criteria, and the next subsection looks at the theoretical criteria.

The criteria of supporting evidence and extensibility parallel science's criterion of experimental support. They refer, Barbour says, to several types of occurrences, including "religious and moral experience and key historical events," plus "other events in [people's] lives as active selves."[71] A key-theology finds strength if it feels true in relating to personal and communal life orientations and interests. In particular,

- A key-theology finds strength if it points to communal and individual experiences it claims as religious, shows their unique religious nature, and indicates how they relate to other aspects of life.
- A key-theology finds strength if it makes sense of people's modern secular lives, of events not usually considered religious (though a key-theology may induce or isolate some experiences—or some aspects of them—as religious).
  - ○ Thomas Brownhill answers Thomas Langford's question, "How can one adjudicate between rival visions?" with Paul Tillich's suggestion that the life process experimentally tests ontological knowledge. (Brownhill also considers this unrealistic.)[72]
  - ○ Earl MacCormac writes similarly: a theology finds "confirmation or disconfirmation in human experience. [People] do lose their faith when adversity strikes while others persist through the same events."[73]
  - ○ Ferré evaluates theologies this way:

    [People find them] reliable, and thus candidates for reasonable adoption, to the extent that [they organize their] experience of life as a whole (not, remember, just specific bits and pieces of experience) . . . in this manner without distortion, forcing, or ill fit; and to the extent that the total account of things that they suggest is consistent, unified, and free from uninterpreted disconnections.[74]

    (Ferré may imply that conclusive testing of a theology can only take place once human life has finished and all the possibilities encountered; confirmation of a theology comes at the eschaton.)

  Key-theology is empirical in that it can organize experience—the human world and perceptions, people's lives personal and communal—pointing out patterns and parallels, explaining or putting into perspective events felt important, and predicting future ones. If a key-theology does not make sense of occurrences, if it says untrue or meaningless things about people's lives, then, to that extent, it proves itself an unsatisfactory explanation for those people. This demand proves decisive in the lives of many moderns: theologies fall because they require specific religious experience not in fact experienced.[75]

- A key-theology finds strength if it leads to a more fertile life.[76] Extensibility for key-theology ought to do more than illuminate, integrate, and organize present and past experience, more than explore it hermeneutically.[77] It also ought to provide a basis for ethics, serving and molding the community. Key-theologians ought to ask if the core idea of a key-theology leads to, in Kaufman's terms, a "fruitful life, in the broadest and most comprehensive sense possible."[78] Key-theologians ought centrally to ask what sort of social order and interpersonal behavior an aspiring key-theology upholds and promotes. The Bible records the Hebrews suffering "travail and anguish" of the worst sort through which anyone could survive. "But it is more than survival," Brown comments, "it is survival with a development of thought and quality of being, a chronicle of an ethical development, and an enlarging sensitivity to the essential interrelatedness of life."[79] Such survival and qualitative growth represent the ethical extensibility criteria for judging and testing the credibility of a key-theology. "From very early times the Church has inclined to the view that a person's faith affects his [or her] performance," continues Brown. "The effectiveness" of a key-theology lies in "the fact that it makes people act differently."

The above criteria boil down to experience. A key-theology ought to make sense of, embed in, and lead the lives of each person plus the cultural context in which people live. The fall of communism in Eastern Europe over the years 1990–1991 caused major changes throughout the world, some hopeful. A key-theology needs to speak personally and communally for this world of change and this world of hope. It needs to speak personally and communally for this world of tragedy and this world of despair (in the death camps of the 1940s, in Vietnam of the 1960s, in New York of 2001, in Sudan of 2004, in the Middle East since forever). The world is also evolving and developing. A world connected through communications, trade, images, and impressions. A world that defines yet objectifies morality. A world that humanity creates for God, good or bad.

For a key-theology to account adequately for significant areas of experience, people must perceive and know its truth. The basic God model needs to feel true; people need to sense this God exists; their common discourse needs to use "God" as real and essential. "God" needs to provoke, feel full of deep mystery, and become the symbol for living. Then people may consider the "God" they discuss indeed refers to God. They may incline to follow the ethical code to which the key-theology points. "God" may generate a sense of authority and compassion.

Who are the people who might think this way? Perhaps the ability to proselytize with a theology can partly gauge its strength or weakness. For a key-theology to head off competitors and to make compelling sense to potential proselytes, the populace must feel the God as real. A key-theology probably cannot create this sense unless most people already experience it, unless almost everyone knows that the referent of the key-theology's central God idea exists and is essential.[80]

For most people to feel the truth of the basic God notion of a key-theology may require supporting evidence and extensibility that convince. Not that such a "conversion" would necessarily happen overnight. A difference still separates a key-theologian's forging a well-supported symbol as basic for the idea "God" and the person in the pew or the street seeing that symbol as representing the reality God. This vision may not catch (though pew sitters and pedestrians might recognize the existence of the symbol's referent) because they fail to associate the referent immediately with the word "God." The catching of the vision may require time. If the key-theology succeeds in terms of the criteria laid out and it receives wide acceptance, gradually the idea suggested as God might become for most people an adequate description of God, and thus the basic idea become identified with the reality God.

Evidence and Extensibility: Objective Experience

All theologies say something about the subjective world and so theologians could to some degree or other test their work against it. Barbour's category of supporting evidence should also include that a key-theology should make sense of experience and knowledge of the *physical* world. Where does this objective side to a key-theology lie, however?

The three relevant sentences in Barbour's list of criteria help to answer this question. He writes:

> Supporting evidence is the most important criterion. [Theologies] must give a faithful rendition of the areas of experience taken to be especially significant: religious and moral experience and key historical events. But

they must also adequately interpret other events in [people's] lives as active selves.[81]

Following from Barbour,

- The phrase "key historical events" refers to the objectively historical, as opposed to the subjective and purely personal. Key-theologies can thus rest on historical events; for instance, to disprove the historical facts of the life of Jesus may falsify many forms of Christian belief.[82]
- Key-theologians can test their theories by comparing what they say about the meaning of life and history with philosophical, historical, hermeneutical, or phenomenological studies.[83]
- As the ideological, political, socioeconomic, or philosophical aspects of culture change, the theological ideas closely connected with them also alter. The Bible records the Hebrews evaluating and changing their theological models as these aspects of their culture changed.[84]

Key-theology's potentially objective nature exceeds these points, however. A key-theology makes factual assertions beyond personal or communal, private or public subjective experience. Ferré, in his enthusiastic review of the book by Barbour that forms the backbone of this chapter, makes a point on Barbour's critical realist compromise between naive realism and reductive instrumentalism: Does it or does it not assume

> some structural correspondence . . . between the model and the reality modeled? If so, then a type of literal picturing relation, however "tentative," is present; if not, then . . . [theologians work] with a conceptual instrument whose justification [lies] . . . in its usefulness in the widest possible sense—explanatory, unifying, heuristic—and whose "truth" [theologians can assess] . . . by its continued reliability in these respects in the long run.[85]

By not adhering to instrumentalism, key-theologians need more than usefulness as a criterion. Some type of "literal picturing relation" exists: wherein lies this picturing? Theology must account, says James Miller, "to the universe for its confirmation."[86] "Theologians offer statements expressive of human experience as confirming doctrinal claims," echoes MacCormac, "and . . . [these] include some factual and historical statements."[87] What comprises these factual statements?

Key-theology contains several types of objective statements besides those mentioned pertaining to history, social, and personal experience. For instance, it can make statements about:

- the nature and creation of the physical universe;
- the structure of society;
- human personality, or psychology;
- experiences claimed as common to all people, for example, the findings of social psychology;
- the age of the universe;
- the end of the universe at some date;
- people becoming wealthy and successful because of their good lives;
- the evolutionary process causing a convergence toward an Omega Point;
- the omnipotent and omniscient God also loving everyone absolutely; or
- the sociopolitical sphere as in Two-Thirds World, Black, and women's theologies.[88]

Some aspect of the human experience of the universe anchors any key-theological statement; all key-theologies involve factual (human and physical world) assertions about their subject matter, which covers subjective experience and history, and the biological, physical, and social worlds in all their aspects. All of these claims also lie within, or impinge on, the subject areas of other disciplines. Key-theologians should thus test their key-theologies against the collection of contemporary knowledge, including modern science. They could do this by striving to base their claims on those that other disciplines have already established. Or they could open their ideas to assessment in each relevant discipline. (Confirmation in cosmology of the theological suggestion that the universe moves only once from a beginning to an end [as opposed to oscillating from big bang to a collapse that initiates another big bang, ad infinitum] would confirm it in theology.[89] Discrediting it in cosmology means theologians should put it aside.) This constitutes the "revisionist method" for theology, though with a wider subject area than usually envisioned for this approach.[90]

A key-theology can find further strength if it successfully predicts the future. Jerry Gill likens theological models to high-level models of science, which he thinks of as analogies and whose confirmation or infirmation partly lies, he says, in their "ability to . . . predict and suggest new possibilities concerning future experience."[91] Such a process is practical and experimental, but also flexible and complex. It includes uncertainty and mystery.

Brown provides an application of the extensibility criterion similar to Gill's. Theologians ought to apply their theories in boundary conditions: a valid theory, he writes, "must predict sensible results elsewhere."[92] He asks, in particular, that theologians consider the validity of their theories at the point of the emergence of the human species, and whether and how they define human goals and purposes when the solar system obliterates human life on earth. Only "worrying more about the extremes in time than about the present" solved "some of the most difficult problems" of science. If theologians were to "look at the boundary-value solutions," he adds, they "may well make more progress toward an ultimate theology for the present."[93]

Another of Brown's methodological suggestions that might help key-theology subject itself to the objective world derives from changes in physics' subject matter. Nineteenth-century physics focused on individual particles and on increasing the precision for measuring every physical parameter and quantity. Physics in this and the last century, on the other hand, studies nature as "statistically random phenomena where not only would the older method of attention to every element no longer be profitable, but where to deal with the details of each particle would actually prevent arrival at a solution." To explain the behavior of individual units with greater precision than before, physicists close their eyes to the behavior of the single entity and treat "the vast collection of particles as a statistically fluctuating continuum." Theology could follow the same path: "by dealing with the problem as a whole . . . [theologians might] understand better the nature of the individual, better even than [they] did by concentrating on the individual alone."[94]

This opening itself to the knowledge and testing of science means that, to some extent, key-theology's ideas and proofs depend on scientists' presuppositions—an appropriate and exciting thing.[95] It also means key-theology may change as scientific knowledge changes— also an appropriate and exciting thing. All gaining of knowledge offers adventure with a concurrent uncertainty and never a final resting place.

Coherence

The above subsections discussed the primary criterion, evidence, looking at subjective and objective types. Other criteria also need elaboration.

Coherence falls next in the line, though in this case it requires only one further point.

Coherence, according to Barbour, "involves both internal consistency (the absence of contradictions) and systematic interrelatedness (the presence of connections and implications between statements)."[96] To help adjudicate between rival key-theological visions, key-theologians can look for contradictions within them and opt for the one with the least number—though it may be impossible to eradicate all internal contradictions from a theology (including key-theologies) or build it from fully adequate assumptions. Differences in a vision of the world may occur within a community bound together by a faith because different areas of research reveal different aspects of the world. These partial insights may not fit together coherently. No contradictions would exist with complete knowledge of the whole of the world, assuming the consistency of the world. Yet no theology can achieve this.[97]

Community Criteria

Similarly, because an individual can only perceive a partial version of a key-theology (a mind and brain reaching the edge of its capacity), one person probably cannot judge a key-theology decisively. Immersion into a vision usually precludes emotional room for other visions, and so a person can probably only immerse him- or herself in one vision at one time. An individual caught by a vision thus may not evaluate it adequately.[98] A contradiction within a vision may only appear to a bystander. A key-theology may involve a person less emotionally than does a vision, but still an individual adhering to it may see fewer internal contradictions, or find them of less significance than does someone outside it.

Communities must therefore conduct the testing of a key-theology. Theology is, after all, a collective endeavor. Brownhill writes that those with a significant stake in the theories decide on the adequacy of rival theories or visions but, before they do, the broader societies of believers must judge theological visions.[99] The replacement of one theology by another indicates the community of faith jointly judges the former inadequate in relation to the latter. This guards against charlatan proposals. "By what criteria," asks Joseph Runzo, "can theologians or believers distinguish these 'proper' conceptions of God . . . from other conceptions masquerading as the concept 'God'?"[100] They will do this, continues Brownhill, based on "the visions the community has already received and accepted."[101] Faithfulness to what Christians consider inherently Christian constitutes a criterion for evaluating a Christian key-theological hypothesis. This remains too vague for practice, however; all members of a community (especially a religious one) seldom agree, so who decides for the community whether a proposal fits with the already accepted visions?

Communities tend to conserve. Thus this community process for adjudicating theologies sets theology up for traditionalism and stonewalling, shunning the crisis and challenge that face faith communities in the modern secular West. It also remains to find out two things:

1. whether anyone can adequately isolate what specifically constitutes a Christian theology and, if someone can do this, what constitutes this identification; and
2. in what ways key-theologies should echo traditional knowledge, and specifically who decides if they echo them adequately.

Chapter 1 described theology as attempting rationally, coherently, faithfully, and systematically to express and spell out the religion's beliefs (or the beliefs of what the theologian considers an important group of people) in order to understand the religious life. Chapter 1 then added two twists to this picture:

1. theologians can also play leader roles for religious beliefs, language, and life by suggesting matters beyond the accepted beliefs; and
2. theologians may also consider it important to spell out or remain faithful to a set of beliefs other than those they associate with a religious tradition.

A tension thus exists that the conservative option overlooks. Yes, key-theology cannot act only as an end unto itself and has to behave communally as well as theoretically; the theoretical aspects of religious language usually cannot stand without the existential or socially embodied. This may mean the pioneering conflicts with the conservative. Nevertheless, key-theology aims more at the theoretical than the existential and so matters related to the former may take precedence

over those related to the latter. Two other approaches to this issue
come to mind:

1. To find acceptance in a community, key-theologies must fit into its
   knowledge; tradition sees certain questions and categories as important, and a key-theology may fit by responding respectfully and relating to these important elements. For instance, to offer a truly
   Christian idea of God—in other words, an idea that adequately
   echoes what Christians have known and experienced as their God—
   the key-theologian needs to show a continuity between the proposed
   core symbol "God" plus its explication, and the formulations, understandings, and experiences of God from the Christian past.
2. Alternatively, the key-theologian may make the identification of the
   decision-making community a key issue. This community need not
   comprise a group of Christians or the whole collection of communities that consider themselves—or that others consider—Christian.
   The community that decides could even be an interreligious one or a
   secular one, but it needs to be a specific society that can reflect on
   its experience.

Such personal yet social decisions that lead to change in community
beliefs require time to effect. The process reveals the truth of the world
slowly, especially if the new vision questions those the community already knows. Coincidence or the enthusiasm or social connections of an
individual researcher may spark or spearhead a change, but history
eventually decides on theological visions.

Criteria Changes

Science "has developed a remarkably successful attitude of mind,"
writes Brown, in which consensus between scientists of the same spe-
cialty sifts acceptable and usable explanations for phenomena from the
unacceptable.[102] This attitude has developed, however; the agreed-
upon criteria have changed as science has grown, and the method of
science inherently recognizes the need for such change. The ancients
thought self-consistency alone leads to scientific truth because they
used predictability and order as their criteria. Greek logic, founded on
self-consistency in premise and conclusion, rose and fell; this formal-

ism did not suffice as a general method for science. Theologies have similarly changed their criteria, and key-theologies should continue to develop theirs.[103]

Criteria Weights

Authors vary in how they define the criteria of science and what they assume each means in practice. More significant, perhaps, is the relative order of importance different scholars assign to them.

This also happens in key-theology.[104] Barbour may be correct in thinking that supporting evidence constitutes the most important criterion, but "supporting evidence" can contain many different things and the question remains as to the relative importance of these. In fact, the various ways theologians ply their trade may differ primarily because of the different priorities they place on the various criteria. For instance, as asked above, is it more important for a key-theology to reflect secular experience than for it faithfully to represent a religious tradition (both of these fall under the criterion of supporting evidence)? Alternatively, should tradition rage over secular relevance? Avery Dulles goes further: "Does the community of faith have any legitimate autonomy vis-à-vis the community of secular inquiry?"[105]

A key-theologian makes decisions such as these when approaching and performing the craft of theology.

In science, each research tradition consistently places the weights and interpretations on each of the criteria. Traditions that share interpretations and knowledge can, because of this, discuss and decide on theories. Less inter-research tradition objectivity probably exists in theology than in science. Different communities of faith or different theological traditions within a religion place varying relative weights on the theological criteria. Within their research traditions, though, theologians ought to share criteria, criteria meanings, and relative weights of criteria. Key-theologians thus perhaps ought to decide on the relative weights and meanings of criteria before theologizing commences, including on the relative weights of the secular versus tradition criteria. They may, having done this, partly overcome what Malcolm Diamond sees as a difference between science and theology, namely that scientists know what they mean by the terms they use and how to resolve their differences, whereas theologians do not.[106]

Many general questions apply to a set of criteria. From where do they come? What gives them a standing over thought systems, and should key-theologians accept the allocated status? Is the choice between criteria only a relative one? Should a key-theologian test a set of ideas in all their parts, as a whole unit, or in small segments? When does a test decisively prove against a system? How much secondary elaboration should key-theology tolerate? Considering the criterion of humanization in particular (one of Kaufman's criteria), is a theory really testable against it given that the process of proving it may take a lifetime and the theory might then find itself outmoded? Moreover, ought key-theology by default to leave a handful of people with the task of deciding what should constitute humanizing, determining the best possible way of life for all people?[107] Key-theologians cannot answer such questions as these in any final sense; they can only look for criteria their communities share, propose and promote solutions, and allow history to arbitrate.

THE GOD IDEA AS INFIRMABLE

A key-theology first assumes the central importance of an idea of God. Then it uses the word "God" as a central focus for a coherent system of explanation that helps in understanding the existence and nature of the world, life, and human experience. Each God idea focuses on specific aspects or approaches to these, but all attempt to know about God. Once developed, a key-theology undergoes testing based on the criteria the previous section described.

Key-theologians ought to create key-theologies based on different notions and that try to explain different ranges of things. They should develop their ideas to bring out the factual implications of each key-theology—its testable implications fully exposed—and then test them.[108] From what one key-theology means by God, key-theologians can create another key-theology with an alternative, more adequate, and more promising God idea—a better knowledge of God. By becoming involved in this discovering process, key-theologians develop key-theologies that are more fitting and thereby explain the world more ably. "God," in a way, resembles fire; while humans accepted the reality of fire countless generations ago, succeeding people changed their understanding of it, for instance from fire as the release of phlogiston to fire as combustion.[109] Key-theologians examine how adequately the God idea understands God when they evaluate a key-theological theory;

"God has property X" offers, in principle, a confirmable or infirmable claim. Ideas of God are descriptive.

Scholars such as Flew and Nielsen question the testable nature of theology because they notice theologians resist or flatly refuse opening their core ideas—especially that of God—to confirmation or infirmation. When challenged, most supporters of a theology will extensively qualify it and the descriptive statements derived from it. This protects the whole theory and especially its central ideas, but at a price. Too much qualifying and the integrity of the theory withers or dies. Competing theories then may make more sense.

A large-scale theory such as a key-theology acts like a web or network of ideas.[110] Experience impacts the whole or parts of the web, making its adherents reshuffle and embellish it, but not necessarily abandon it or major parts of it. This protects the core beliefs.

On the other hand, circumstances can eventually count against high-level beliefs and comprehensive theories. It is impossible to specify at what point the status of embattled beliefs and theories changes to false and alternatives need entertaining, though it is possible to recognize the descriptive nature of theological statements and high-level ideas such as "God," and it is also possible to evaluate rival theories. To change often means transferring allegiance to another web based on other high-level beliefs.[111] Sometimes it requires the death of the adherents and the ascension of new blood.

Suppose people cease to assume the validity or importance of all God ideas as ways to look at and try to understand the world. Suppose all potential theologies succumb to systems of understanding rooted in non-God ideas, such as a Marxist or a physicalist system, ideas that do not flow from previously acceptable ones of God. If this happens—and it has not—it would mark the failure of all God ideas against non-God alternatives and evince, as much as empirically possible, that God does not exist. As the root of a web of ideas, "God exists" offers, in principle, an infirmable claim.

DIFFERENCES BETWEEN KEY-THEOLOGICAL AND SCIENTIFIC METHODS

Barbour's book, *Myths, Models, and Paradigms*, grants religion and science roughly the same philosophical status, that of a critical realism, which he characterizes as "broadly empirical."[112] In a paper published earlier than *Myths, Models, and Paradigms*, Barbour compares science and religion and proposes these similarities (his later works differ in their finer details, not in thrust):

- both involve the interaction of experience and interpretation;
- both depend on the experience of communities;
- both use symbolic or analogical language to interpret experience;
- both take processes and relationships, as opposed to objects, as constituting the world (though some scientists may disagree with this);
- both require the full use of reason and apply the criteria of consistency and comprehensiveness; and
- neither allows a complete and final certainty.[113]

They also differ. Barbour writes that science and religion ask different questions, even about the same event:

- science selectively looks for mechanisms, the means, while remaining ethically neutral, and religion attends to purposes and ends;
- science aims for reproducible knowledge, for understanding derived from repeatable phenomena and relationships expressed in general laws, whereas religion seeks "configurational" understanding, how the parts of a unique whole interrelate; and
- science seeks to minimize observer involvement by enforcing an impersonal and detached approach, quite the opposite to religion that requires personal involvement.

This book primarily concerns theology, though, and not religion. Inasmuch as theology serves the purposes of religion and inasmuch as religion includes theology, theology entails existential functions science need not show.

Barbour thus assists those who wish to analyze the similarities and differences between theology and science,[114] to find a tool for understanding the practice of theology, and to look at the present (and a potential) scientific methodology that key-theology might employ. Barbour's ideas provide a useful and intelligent springboard from which to launch the details of the construction, which similarly emphasizes the commonalities in the methods of science and theology. In the light of critical realism, science and key-theology resemble one another, falling on the same continuum of knowing.

They are not identical, however. Barbour's three points highlighting the dissimilarities between religion and science state this, the discussion above on the existential functions of theology reinforce it, and the five differences outlined below bring it out even more. The issue becomes whether the differences require knocking one or both of them off the proposed continuum of knowing.

Orientations

Key-theological and scientific explanations differ because they employ two sorts or levels of adequacy. They look at the world through two different lenses. The idea "physical reality" orients attention toward things whereas the idea "God" orients attention toward and involves persons, dealing with its subject matter in qualitative terms.[115] Barbour suggests that religious beliefs correlate models with human experience, including religious and moral experience, key historical occurrences, and "other events in [people's] lives as active selves."[116] Science, on the other hand, concerns itself with objective, quantifiable phenomena. Science and key-theology offer alternative and complementary explanations of the same things from different points of view.

This does not require having to choose between their complementary explanations of the same thing—two mutually exclusive realms, as the writings of D. M. MacKay and Karl Heim, for instance, promote.[117] Key-theology provides a broader context that clarifies experiences—including subjective experience—beyond what the idea "physical reality" can explain;[118] it includes the objective as well as the subjective. This overlap means they are not completely different.

Tentativeness

A second potential distinction between science and key-theology focuses on tentativeness. The method scientists employ requires skepticism about the hypotheses and, though less so, the theories of their disciplines. Ideally, scientists are open to find hypotheses wanting in the light of (new) experiences and to replace them with better attempts at explanation. While key-theology seeks a similar skepticism about its hypotheses and theories, most theologians would probably not think of their work in this way.

Barbour asks if a holder of religious ideas finds tentativeness important when testing them.[119] This again highlights the existential functions of theology. Perhaps tentativeness cannot accompany a religious life because religion decides, not only on the theory, but also on the significance and direction of a person's life. Too tentative an attitude may undermine religion's most crucial experiences. Barbour concludes that an openness to new insights, together with holding onto beliefs "for which you would be willing to die," offer the difficult combination that "constitutes religious maturity."[120]

Turning from Barbour's topic of religion to key-theology means the dichotomy between life-risking belief and tentativeness loses some of the forcefulness. The word "beliefs" implies more of a permanence than does "theological theories"; "theology" feels more potentially hypothetical and provisional. Religious faith and religious life focus on metaphysical assumptions and models (the realms of beliefs), whereas key-theology and its testing focus on theories based on such assumptions. A failure of testing to support the assumptions of religion can and does call them into question. This occurs more rarely, however, than the changing and development of key-theology's theoretical level; here it holds ideas tentatively in the hope of finding more adequate explications of its basic assumptions. This includes the fact that key-theology bases some of its theories on scientific knowledge (for instance, theories of creation) and therefore could change. How much tentativeness versus certainty a key-theology can tolerate for its theories or its basic assumptions offers another topic for investigation.

Differences in tentativeness between science and key-theology may relate to differences in the extent to which people feel the immediacy or tangibility of the physical world versus how much they feel this with respect to God. Modern secular Westerners cannot point to God and God's actions. Many people used to feel they could indicate the God that tradition depicts, and some still do, but nowadays most Westerners do not think this way. Instead of concluding that an insurmountable barrier separates science and theology, the issue offers a challenge. Can key-theology generate an understanding of God that enables modern culture to see incontrovertibly that God exists and that God acts? Some contemporary theologians think they can do this. It happens, for instance, with the God of Burhoe's theology (God as nature, the world as in science) and with that of Schubert Ogden's (and following him Langdon Gilkey's and Tracy's: God in human limit experiences).[121] Observational aspects of God may exist. Key-theologies derived from them may lead to greater belief in their truthfulness and hence to a more successful religion and a more adequate ethics.[122]

The testing of key-theology may exhibit less tentativeness and openness to fresh insight than does the testing of many sciences. This does not support the extreme, though, that pits the tentativeness of science against the stance of the key-theologian. Scientists can resist others proving them wrong and key-theology can open itself to new ideas and infirmation under testing. The distinction offers a relative and not an absolute difference.

Mathematics

The third apparent and often real difference between the scientific and key-theological methods shows in the use of and desire for mathematical models and theories in science and the lack thereof in theology. "The world as mathematical" constitutes the root metaphor for science, MacCormac suggests.[123] As with tentativeness, however, this may not offer a watertight division between key-theology and science. The lack of mathematics in theology may say more about the humanities background of most theologians than about key-theology's possible use of mathematics. Perhaps key-theologians ought to mathematize key-theologies to help them offer a greater range of explanatory ideas and perhaps an easier dialogue with the sciences than with words alone. Perhaps mathematicians could develop a mathematical language in which to express humanities' notions and models—including those of key-theology—and to state the breadth of such ideas. With this, the world, both scientific and spiritual, becomes potentially mathematical. Neither do mathematical ideas always entail a quantitative approach (which theologians might fight as reductionism) rather than the qualitative one that matters human often require; general topology, for instance, is qualitative.[124] Further, mathematics proves useful in the study of humans and people, as with sociology's and psychology's common use of probability theory and statistics rather than deterministic models.[125] Despite Hesse's view, the successes of these two sciences overpower their shortcomings when looking back over their short histories. Their mathematical models are still developing. Even more in its infancy, the mathematical possibilities of key-theology still lie dormant.

Unanimity

The unanimity of science—the agreement between scientists on results—offers the fourth possible difference between science and key-theology. Properly performed scientific experiments achieve more or less the same results no matter where, when, or who carries them out; the physical universe behaves consistently. With this comes the possibility of general laws of nature. This aspect of science means its method has difficulty with purely private or unique events.[126] In comparison, Barth, Dulles, Søren Kierkegaard, and others think theology treats purely private and unique events. Several theologians consider their discipline quite different from science, a special class of knowledge, because God does what God wishes to do.

The most potentially non-unanimous aspect of theology's criterion of supporting evidence may concern religious experience.[127] Religious experience apparently is subjective, purely private, and each instance unique. On the other hand, Tracy emphasizes the religious face of ordinary limit experiences and MacCormac talks about theology's testing the common experiences that religious terms and symbols interpret. Theology still differs from science, MacCormac continues, because these experiences frequently involve an individual's desires and feelings, which other people may not observe.[128] MacCormac goes too far: such religious experiences do not require the private and unique nature of common religious experiences because, though personal and subjective, many people can have them.[129] Dulles also disputes the approach of Tracy and MacCormac because he thinks extraordinary experiences, not common ones, play the primary role in evaluating theologies. Again, a response can say a religious experience is not purely private and unique in that more than one person can undergo it and an investigator can subject it to shared criteria. The existence of common natural roots of religious experience, referred to earlier in this chapter, also suggests this.[130] Key-theology might therefore reach some agreement or consensus—not necessarily unanimity—based on this public subject matter.

Disagreement over theology's criteria, the content of each criterion, and the relative weights given to each, speak to a second reason why theology may less frequently exhibit unanimity than does science. While theologians may agree with the criterion of supporting evidence, for instance, they differ as to what counts as supporting evidence; ought they to look to Bible verses for support and exclude religious experience or historical facts? Theologians also differ over what they consider more important among the evidence; they may accept the above three sources of evidence, but should they consider biblical support paramount over the others? They can use public and shared criteria, and still the results may depend on the tradition and the theologian.

The lower level of consensus in theology reflects its greater level of subjectivity than science's. Theology should not expect unanimity. John Godbey writes that theologians who use the method and findings of the sciences should disagree with each other because theology contains "such extra-scientific things as elements of the philosophy of science and the cultural religious heritage." On religious grounds, he continues, theologians should not desire unanimity "because of the absolutely indispensable nature of honesty in one's religious witness."[131] They relatively comprehend the non-ostensible God of theology. Theologians should expect in their subject what they see in it: a proliferation of theologies and theological research traditions, each claiming truth and each building on different criteria, relative weights of criteria, and initial God-ideas. More unanimity might appear, though, within each theological research tradition and confessional family because each should mutually build its theology and reach plateaus of agreement.[132] For similar reasons, more unanimity might also appear among key-theologies.

The proposed distinction between science and key-theology based on unanimity further softens with the realization that scientists sometimes disagree with each other. Thomas Kuhn's assessment of rival research traditions in science and their lack of unanimity teaches this. In the past, two equally respectable theories in genetics—each satisfying the relevant criteria—offered alternative and rival accounts of the same phenomena.[133] Similarly, generations of physicists found the energy and caloric theories of heat and the theory of the dual nature of light useful and acceptable.[134] Different models can sometimes simultaneously explain the known data with similar adequacy.

Predictability

The fifth potential difference between the scientific and key-theological criteria concerns predictability. Barbour's criterion of "supporting experimental observations" for science includes the valuing of a theory that provides "precise predictions for future measurements."[135] Barbour includes no equivalent criterion in his list for religious beliefs, even under the categories of supporting evidence and extensibility. Scholars tend to think of theology as more to do with living and providing values, taking account of religious experience and applying it to living, than as predictive. Modern Western Christians tend to gloss over such topics as heaven and hell as reward or punishment for how people live. Barbour's extensibility criterion therefore concerns more the interpretation of known experiences or happenings rather than forecasting new ones. Is this a major difference between science and key-theology, that key-theologians do not seek out far-ranging causal laws from which they can predict future events?[136]

Is predictability in fact a hallmark of science?[137] Scholars dismiss the common picture of the inerrant, indisputable predictive method of science; scientists cannot, for instance:

- completely divorce observers from what they examine or the machines through which they observe;
- completely trust human senses;
- repeat all experiments;
- guarantee philosophically that a repeated experiment provides the same results;
- remove experimental errors; and
- avoid the occasional odd experiment or a process that goes inexplicably wrong.[138]

Still, predictability does play a role in science, though a more ambiguous role than commonly thought.

Further, several scientific disciplines—such as cosmology and biological evolution—do not present a repeating world. They may test mechanisms (gravitational attraction, genetic replication) with predictions but, for the canvas on which they paint, their reality—like that of history—does not repeat; confirmation and infirmation involve a time-scale beyond people's lives, and the events of their subject areas make prediction difficult if not impossible. Postdiction (the confirmation and infirmation of a hypothesis by accumulating evidence of past events) offers a more helpful route.[139]

Key-theology similarly often deals more with the unique unfolding of human history and of a person's life than with repeating natural phenomena. Thus, predictability may not play an important role in key-theology. It also works more with the value and subjective orders—therefore relating more closely to the methods of the human sciences—than with the material order and the method of the physical sciences. This makes predicting more difficult; but even the human sciences make predictions.

A key-theology resembles a metaphysical system. A metaphysic works with general categories and tries to account for all major types of experience; it assumes no new types of experience will occur in the future and hence it cannot predict novel events.[140] Its center of gravity acts at a higher level of knowing than does that of a science and it lacks the preponderance of the science's lower-level laws necessary for predictions. Inasmuch as a key-theology is more metaphysical than is a science, it will probably make fewer predictions of novel events. However, key-theologies are not fully metaphysical and all-encompassing, and therefore potentially can make some forecasts. The more a key-theology deals with repeating events and causal laws and the less all-inclusive the terms it employs, the more it can predict the future.

One way to test a key-theology may lie in its fruitfulness to anticipate and plan.[141] The biblical prophets prophesy, saying that, if you continue to behave in such and such a way, so and so will happen to you. In such ways, predicting the future plays a role in some theological traditions—probably including some key-theologies—but ambiguously and secondarily.[142]

Paul Quay attempts to show the inadequacy of Kuhn's depiction of normal science because theology also satisfies the characterization; he thinks any proposed method for science should decisively distinguish it from theology.[143] The case presented above has not reached Quay's conclusion, only agreeing with him that theology follows Kuhn's characterization of normal science. Science and key-theology share the same method and do not differ decisively, but only in degree over such things as orientations, tentativeness, mathematization, unanimity, and predictability. On the other hand, key-theology does not stand out with this demarcation. The different sciences do not all apply identical methods, varying as they do by the degree to which, in each of them, one aspect of the method presides over another.[144]

TRUTH IN KEY-THEOLOGY

Does the contention that key-theologians select a basic symbol for God mean they do not deal with the real God but with some symbol they construct and make God—though they select the symbol for a God they feel exists?

Objectivity in Key-Theology

Having rejected subjectivism for key-theology, the need for understanding the role of objectivity in it becomes even more important. Science has a rationality and an independent physical world to which it refers, and these produce its objectivity. Objectivity in key-theology can exist if it too has an accepted rationality and referent. It has these: something exists independent of key-theologies that allows for communication between them and appraisal of them because they refer to it. That something is the world.

Objectivity does not exist across current theologies. They could, however, glimpse objectivity:

- If they saw objective truth as coming from one quarter or from some bulwark the various quarters have in common. Instead, current theologies see truth as coming from many, sometimes conflicting sources: biblical revelation, religious experience, church dogma, and common language.
- If all theologians sought to conceptualize the same existent God and they agreed on channels for and the relative importance of aspects of knowledge of that God. They do not do these.
- If, as Kaufman suggests, all theologies derive from the common use of the word, namely the idea that "God" acts as "an ultimate point of reference." Chapter 2 argued, however, that no such use exists. Or
- If all theologies sought, as a criterion, to "humanize" the world out of

their various religious traditions, or if all acknowledge the ultimate authority and literal meaning and truth of the same scriptures. However, they do not all invoke the same criterion as primary; each uses criteria based on its own presuppositions.

Certain approaches to theology, for example biblical fundamentalism, could behave objectively, but objective only against a narrow set of data (in fundamentalism's case, a literal reading of scriptures). However, nothing could act as an objective criterion for all the various present theologies. Nor do they seem to have a common referent or source for truth. A common objectivity, therefore, does not appear to exist across current theologies.

Key-theology, on the other hand, is objective because it has a referent and rationality. It subjects all its theories primarily to the world (the requirement of supporting evidence). Though the remainder of its list of criteria (their relative weights and what each means) may remain a little open, further mutually acceptable criteria could appear in it out of ongoing and developing discussion.

Key-Theology as Description

Societal systems of belief define for members of the society what constitutes the real and what exists, and hence what society members can describe. In the past, theological description built from culture's belief in the objective existence of God, however it perceived that. The majority of modern people no longer believe in these objective existences. The supernatural and the spiritual world (usually associated with God and existing independent of the physical) have ceased to comprise part of the real because culture has ceased to believe in them. Modern Westerners cannot describe them with credibility. Not surprisingly, the phrase "theology as description" sounds inadequate and contradictory for nonfundamentalist approaches, and their criteria for assessment have become more socially pragmatic and humanistic.

The relevant beliefs of present society essentially center on the ultimacy of the material; the physical and bodily world (including the mind as emerging from the brain and nervous system) constitute the real. Modern Westerners can describe them. Key-theology can consider itself descriptive if it can access God's nature through—and can subject understandings of God's nature to—data society feels have objective validity. It does this by looking through a God lens at the same world the various sciences do, elaborating on its ideas via model and theory building, and adjudicating confirmation and infirmation via empirical criteria against the world. Society will judge God ideas against their potential and the sense they make of the world and the experience of modern westerners. Key-theology, therefore, is descriptive. To describe the world this way is the closest humans can come to describing God.

Disagreements

Science and key-theology share truth.[145] They share the same method and describe the same world according to their respective assumption or lens. If the two descriptions refer to the same thing, they should either say the same or complementary things about it. What if they disagree about something? Scholars should even draw out of their theories potential disagreements with other theories in their own or other disciplines. Such conflicts should not lead to the retreat of key-theology from the empirical realm, however. Rather, key-theology and its combatant discipline should apply their shared rationality (with shared criteria and observations) to adjudicate between their competing hypotheses, even if it means calling some assumptions of one or both into question.

This suggests a single truth exists. Hence, while differing, nonconflicting perspectives (physics and chemistry, analytic and social psychology, science and key theology) can all be right, no one perspective can taste truth in its fullness. The obsession of the West that a unique truth exists means, in principle (let alone practice), no one can ever have it. Not even arrogant, self-righteous perspectives achieve truth, and all approaches need always to continue in their search for it. Perspectives can therefore conflict and, with time, objective and rational resolutions of conflicts can lead to more wholesome knowledge for the combatants. Different, mutually compatible perspectives all contribute together to knowledge of a whole.

This philosophical position needs elaboration.

Reality Lies beyond Knowledge

The ideas "God" and "world" have changed and can differ for each significant cultural shift. What people know as the world and what they know as God alter with culture and experience. The "world" used to comprise the heavenly spiritual spheres as well as the physical realm—just as real as each other—but now people generally only consider the latter as real and they think "world" refers to it alone. In tandem with this, what constitutes a "person" has changed (most people no longer consider the soul as real as opposed to personality or personhood) as well as what constitutes "God."

Does this mean the world, the person, and God have changed or that people's perceptions of them have changed? Do they remain fixed while human knowledge flutters around them?

On the other hand, for modern Westerners, reality has real, independent, universally accessible, and consistent existence. The word "reality" has a meaning and a referent ("what underlies appearances")[146] that helps mold the word: people's experience of reality can inform and correct what "reality" means. The word unavoidably connotes these things. Thus, reality is not purely a human creation. What constitutes reality may even change independently of humans knowing it. Similarly, God is not purely the human creation "God," because:

- as the understanding of what is real changes, the symbol "God" can lose its objective weight and become inadequate;
- key-theologians subject the idea "God" to experience;
- the understanding of "God" builds on experiences of God; and
- the symbol chosen as "God" may have sufficient mystery and sense of beyondness that people feel they do not have control over it.

Humans cannot know what comprises independent reality beyond the idea, however, because all descriptions of it use language (language traps its users). Similarly with God, the person, and anything else. None are a fixed (or even changing) set of things existing out there, and people experience and define them differently over time and cultures. Rather, what people experience and define differs, and what really exists out there lies beyond human knowledge.

Critical Realism

Hazelton writes: "Truth must always remain . . . a thought in the back of the head." The point at which it moves to the front, becomes explicit, or forms into criteria one can apply, it ceases to govern and effectively displaces itself. "Then it becomes its own worst enemy, a caricature of itself."[147] No one can catch and hang on to truth; it eludes the grasp.

The unreachable ideal of truth comprises an exact or perfectly accurate replication of the world, but the world comprises a lot more than anyone can imagine or know. This assertion advocates a weak version of the correspondence or picture theory of language and meaning. From it develops critical realism.

Some theologians and philosophers criticize critical realism, though usually only the details of certain versions of it, while accepting it broadly. Its philosophical holism offers an epistemological insight with ontological possibilities.

Critical realism says that both objective and subjective factors play a part in knowing. As chapter 5 argued, reality independent of the knower does exist and knowledge somehow reflects it, but beliefs and circumstances also influence what the knower knows. The version of critical realism used here also plies the inseparability of the subjective and the objective aspects of knowledge. What parts of a term does theory provide and what parts does observation provide? No one can ever know. Knowledge involves both of them so intertwined that not even the greatest philosophy engineer could prize them cleanly apart.

People construct all knowledge including the idea "God." God transcends models of God as a thing transcends all pictures of it; key-theologians model God (or, better, God-world relationships), but the reality of God marks an inferential jump beyond the model. Having said this, two qualifications become necessary. First, this does not mean God does not exist. That people construct their knowledge of their closest friends does not mean the buddies do not exist. Second, a key-theologian who believes God exists will then ask, using the guidelines of this chapter, what this God is like. It may not mean God has the properties other people may think God has.

Because of the unreachable nature of truth, the reality God (as with the reality world or any part of the world) will always hide; no one does, will, or can know God utterly.[148] In particular, key-theology will fail to provide a complete or definitive description of the world viewed theologically; neither can it provide a complete account of God. God (as with everything else) transcends human knowing. On the other hand, key-theology may offer the most adequate vehicle for contemporary society to attempt expressing truth theologically.

How does a reality relate to constructs about it: the physical world to scientific knowledge, and God to key-theology? Does the available constructed "God" equal in some way the real God? Does scientific knowledge—the available, constructed theories of physical reality—equal in some corresponding manner real, physical reality? If so, to what extent? No one can answer this type of questioning. Whatever the theories and whatever the number of failures or successes they may have with any number of tests, no person can know whether theories correspond accurately to what they refer (their percept). No one can escape knowledge to test or check its accuracy with the percept in question; its reality lies beyond ideas of it. This means admitting to an "epistemological agnosticism."[149]

Neither can anyone ascertain the relationship between the knowledge of something and the thing itself. This does not deny a relationship could exist between ideas and objective reality, but it affirms humans can never know that relationship. Scientists and key-theologians aim to picture, to attain truth, and never can know whether their theories accurately picture, or whether they reach or even approach truth.[150]

Scientists can and do, however, assume an accuracy. Westerners tend to think an objective reality independent of humans exists to which ideas (and the basis for their critique) ultimately refer. This idea remains an idea;[151] it constitutes a basic belief or myth of Western society.[152] Nothing objective (as opposed to pragmatic, historical, or hypothetical) could prove it. Science involves faith as well as testing and reason.[153]

Because no one can know if a theology really pictures reality—even if some or even all people assume it does—key-theology can only apply the tests it has, the tools it has for choosing the most adequate description. It may provide a true description of reality but, because of epistemological agnosticism, one can never know. Key-theology, in adopting the scientific method, thus also acknowledges this place for faith.

Criteria and Truth

The elusive nature of truth also surfaces through the criteria for making empirical decisions. A delineation of an exhaustive and accurate set of criteria, an authoritative and definitive set, has not emerged to describe the process of empirical rationality by which scientists judge a theory or between theories and with which, therefore, key-theologians might adjudicate their theories. Four reasons suggest this:

1. Scientists' decisions about and between theories involve relativity and subjectivity. Criteria carry different weights and varying applications between different groups of researchers, for instance, and the criteria change over time.[154] Moreover, as also discussed above, criterial procedures cannot always decide between competing theories.
2. Kurt Gödel's theorem for an arithmetic system logically demonstrates the incompatibility of consistency with completeness.[155] Satisfying consistency may not allow scholars to think they have completed their depiction of some thing or process.
3. Describing the rational process of scientists is an act of knowing and subject to at least the same limitations as scientists' attempts to know the physical world. The observer cannot fully delineate rationality.
4. To provide a complete set of criteria (and their relative priorities) for gaining objective knowledge lays hold of truth, and truth can only act as the carrot in front and never consumed.

No one can fully specify the criteria or how to follow them. In fact, the decision on scientific truthfulness resides more in living, in this case living as a scientist. Truth breathes more in action rather than in statements of belief.[156]

This has implications for the proposed method for key-theology. Philosophy of science attempts to describe how science gathers its objective knowledge and key-theology adopts this method. The key-theologian does not fully know what to do to follow the method, however, because it (including its criteria) does not open itself to complete specification. Rather, key-theologians need to become scientists, learning method from their fellow scientists. Key-theologians can in turn help determine scientific method as it changes and develops.

Growth in Key-Theology

Key-theological truthfulness equals scientific truthfulness and lies in depicting the world as accurately as possible with empirical techniques, along the channels of each discipline. This assumes or hopes that:

- Criteria allow rational and empirical arbitration between theories. The world judges and arbitrates between theories by directing the constructs and descriptions, calling them into question or applauding if they follow the right path. This leads, in the long run, to:
- The rise and fall of theories. In turn, this implies that:
- Knowledge (scientific and key-theological) progresses and accumulates. (Hesse suggests only applications of science [pragmatic knowledge] accumulate, not theoretical knowledge.[157] She retreats to this in the light of the subjectivist critique of objective knowledge, but does so unnecessarily. Neither need her claim apply to key-theology.) This means that:
- Knowledge approaches truth and greater accuracy. Science comes more and more to know the nature of the physical world. Key-theology will come more and more to know the nature of God and God's world.[158]

To prove this series of claims (or Hesse's for that matter) begs the point and chooses something as the perfectly accurate arbitrator of truth.[159] These declarations constitute assumptions related to the belief that an objective reality independent of humans exists and to which ideas ultimately refer.

Society not only ought to assume something like these claims, but it needs to assume them. Though no one can ever know whether what key-theology or any theology knows of God and the world is really true of God, society not only ought but needs to assert some things as true (or more true than others) to create authority, feelings of certainty and security, and moral conviction. Similarly in science: science ought and needs to assert some things as true so society can control part of the environment and thus develop technologies and improve people's lives. Experience shows nothing as certain, yet provisional certainties allow people to live fully day to day. Human beings need to think they can choose the most correct idea.

This need not require hanging on to an idea until the death. A person can hold something as the most adequate description of the world—and therefore like the embodiment of truth—yet realize a more adequate description may appear later to supersede current knowledge. Under critical realism, to claim something as true means remaining open to the possibility of error. This approach espouses the need for variety or chaos so that theorizing via its method keeps trying out ideas. An unstable, dynamic, physical situation keeps experimenting with different states until it finds an equilibrium, albeit a temporary one. People ought to affirm "a working commitment to truth as authority for . . . choices," writes Walter Thorson.[160] A working relationship with the truth is more important than feeling in possession of it; such a commitment accompanied by risk acknowledges truth's authority and ultimacy.

CONCLUSIONS

Two books, *Discerning the Mystery* by Andrew Louth and *Axiomatics and Dogmatics* by Carnes, represent the majority of nonfundamentalist approaches to theology's method in the light of science.[161] For Louth, science does not fulfill what society claims for it and therefore theology ought not to follow an empirical method. For Carnes, theology should work empirically with spiritual experience as its data and conform to the sciences over other domains. Both approaches fail because they cordon off theology from the scientific method—the organ of truth in contemporary Western society—or create a domain of experience for theology exclusive of science's. Their Gods do not or need not interact with the world science describes, and hence neither approach allows theology to speak helpfully to the majority of modern people and to the future that needs building.

God has to make a difference to the world. Where? Is this an empirical question—finding where God as already conceived acts—or is it better to ask this question the other way around: Can empirical methods help determine what God is like and hence where God does or can make a difference? This choice between questions equates with another one: To what is theology responsible? Tradition or new insight? Institutional church or humanity at large? Spiritual or everyday experience? Revelation or scientific findings?

This chapter has suggested how to do theology responsible to all these things yet without separating it from science. *Science of God* argues theology (as key-theology) ought to work empirically, in terms of both what it finds out about the world and what it says about God and God's relationship with the world. Science and key-theology share the same empirical method. Therein lies science of God.

The construction of key-theology's method, in summary form, grows like this. It first draws on Barbour's portrayal of science as comprising metaphysical assumptions and research traditions, theories and models, and criteria for the evaluation of theories. It then contends that key-theology also comprises these same three general types of elements. While this emphasizes the commonalities in the methods of science and theology, it does not claim they are identical, but considers their differences to represent variations in degree rather than absolute distinctions.

The method continues. The *theos* part of the word "theology" constitutes the most fundamental theological assumption and the one that, to a large extent, defines theology as a discipline. A key-theology thus centers on a metaphysical idea of God (whatever it takes that word to mean); a God idea centrally organizes and dominates any key-theology, the notion on which all other ideas depend and with which they fall in line.

Key-theology aims to know about God; God thus constitutes the object of theology. How might key-theologians decide what the word "God" means? How can they know about God? Better: What comprises the subject matter of theology? What does theology study and from this discern the nature of God? The subject of key-theology comprises the phenomena of the world, reality as a whole and as people experience it, potentially all things, processes, and experience. Key-theology includes the subject matter of all other disciplines. By studying these, key-theology knows about God.

Both science and key-theology thus similarly describe reality in that each attempts rationally and empirically to explain it both as a whole and also its content. Science describes in the sense that it looks at all through its particular lens of its fundamental model, the physical. Key-theology too describes in the sense that the larger theological corpus arising from its fundamental metaphysical model of God sees all through the lens of this model. Key-theology knows about God as science knows about the physical world.

Key-theologians first choose an initial God lens. Then they develop models from it for God and for the world, constructing these into a theory. This involves working out the models and their implications and relations, deciding on positive and negative analogies, comparing them with other theologies, and applying them to points of interest. Sources for key-theological models vary considerably. Religious dogma, scripture, and experiences can offer some of these models and elements, but only potential ones for they—like all other proposals—need evaluation before acceptance or rejection.

Once key-theologians create theological models and theories, or even during the construction phase, they need to evaluate them. Barbour considers the list of evaluative criteria for scientific theories and then applies them to religious beliefs, thus making a useful starting point for those of key-theology. As quoted above, he writes:

> Any system of thought [should desire] *simplicity* . . . (e.g., minimum number of independent assumptions and conceptual categories); but it . . . seldom [becomes] a major consideration in either science or religion. *Coherence* involves both internal consistency (the absence of contradictions) and systematic interrelatedness (the presence of connections and implications between statements). But *supporting evidence* . . . [offers] the most important criterion. Religious beliefs must give a faithful rendition of the areas of experience taken . . . [as] especially significant: religious and moral experience and key historical events. But they must also adequately interpret other events in [people's] lives as active selves. Hence [the list includes] *extensibility* of application (fruitfulness) . . . as an additional criterion. Finally, *comprehensiveness* in the coherent ordering of diverse types of experience within a systematic metaphysics is desirable, though . . . secondary to other criteria.[162]

A key-theology, however, makes factual assertions beyond personal or communal, private or subjective lived experience. Key-theology contains several types of descriptive statements besides the obvious ones pertaining to history, social, and personal experience. In fact, a key-theology can make descriptive claims for any part of its subject matter, which, as said above, covers human experience and history, and the physical, biological, and social worlds in all their aspects. Some facet of the universe and human experience of it anchors any key-theological statement. Each of these aspects falls within the domain of some discipline of knowledge, and so key-theology's statements impinge on the subject areas of other disciplines. Key-theologians should see that these disciplines evaluate each such statement.

Key-theology can be a science. This requires more than simply saying key-theology does follow a scientific method, end of matter,[163] or theology is scientific in the broad sense of being rational, but not confirmable or infirmable (as in the first of M. D. Chenu's approaches above).[164] Neither does it take the commonality between the methods of science and key-theology to mean the inadequacy of this characterization of scientific method.[165] Rather, it forges key-theology into a science in practice. An empirical system of key-theology starts by assuming the vital importance of God ideas; it takes "God" as a high-level and central assumption. Then it seeks the nature of God using confirmation-infirmation techniques on proposals whose content refers to the world. A key-theology develops a theological epistemology and philosophy, its constructive nature centered on a God idea, judged by certain criteria, drawing upon all experience (not only religious experience), and in principle attempting to explain all.

This means key-theologians need to examine their fundamental models for God by empirically criticizing systems built from them. It means engineering the descriptive aspects of key-theologies, developing and bringing to the surface their testable parts, and then opening them to confirmation or infirmation. Though theology already follows this scientific method to some extent (think of the work on model making in theology by Ferré, Kaufman, and Ramsey, for instance, and how many theologians have consciously assimilated this approach into their methodological tool kits), theologians need to become more aware of this and more consistent in what they do about it.

Science and key-theology share the same method and each attempts a description of the world according to its respective essential assumption or lens. Science and theology share truth.

Key-theology's adoption of the scientific method may result in new theologies based on ideas of God different from current ones. Innovation in theology may result from such changes in method.[166] A coherent set of basic assumptions—one lens—might arise that, when worked out fully with the empirical method, leads to both key-theology and science. Starting with a common root, the assumptions could develop in two interrelated and coherent branches, one person-oriented (key-theology) and the other thing-oriented (science), differing from present theology and present science but continuous with them. Key-theology and scientific knowledge become incorporated into one another, developing key-theology into a science that does not become fanatical, fringe to regular theology, or that received theology need reject.

The last chapter will attempt the start of such a key-theology. It will employ the scientific method, seek an explanation of the world, and peer through a God lens that assumes a person rather than a thing orientation. It will ask key-theology initially to address human happiness. Starting with the sciences that examine happiness—particularly biology and genetics, psychology, and social psychology—it will seek to understand something of the spiritual nature of human beings and thereby of God.

NOTES

1. See Barbour 1974: 60–64; Peacocke 1984: 40; Scharlemann 1973.
2. Margenau 1947; 1950; 1955; 1960a; 1960b; 1964.
3. Margenau 1960b: 106.
4. Margenau 1960b: 107; emphasis removed. See also Margenau 1950.
5. Margenau 1950: 10.
6. Margenau 1960b: 115.
7. Margenau 1960b: 116.
8. Eister 1978 (e.g., p. 356).
9. Hesse 1975b: 385–400. See also Cauthern 1967; Clayton 1989a; 1989b; Jaki 1975b: 60.
10. See Margenau 1964: chap. 2. See also Negrotti 1971.
11. Margenau 1950: 15, 23–26.
12. Borhek and Curtis 1976; Sharpe 1984.
13. Hodges 1978. See also Sharpe 1984.
14. See Kaufman 1975: 9–11.
15. See Kaufman 1975: chap. 3.
16. See Capps 1972; Hanson 1972.
17. For others, see Buri 1968; Gilkey 1969 (plus Thompson 1972); Hartt 1977; Hennelly 1977; Lonergan 1972 (plus Gilkey 1971; Peter 1973); Polanyi 1964 (plus Apczynski 1979); existentialism (e.g., Macquarrie 1979); hermeneutical (e.g., Dulles 1979; Schillebeeckx 1974); historical critical (e.g., Schindler 1979; Tracy 1975a); linguistic (e.g., Burrell 1979; Nygren 1972 [plus Muser 1977]); praxis or liberation (e.g., Kress 1979); process (but see Wright 1979); transcendental (e.g., Peter 1979).
18. Kaufman 1975: 11. See also Sharpe 1979.
19. Sharpe 1979.
20. Van Buren 1972.
21. Pannenberg 1972: 6–19; 1976: chap. 5.
22. Pannenberg 1976.

23. Pannenberg 1972: 16.

24. Pannenberg 1976: 343, 305. See also Ogden 1975.

25. See, e.g., Torrance 1969a; 1969b; 1972; 1981.

26. Torrance 1972. See also Torrance 1969a; 1971.

27. Klinefelter 1973.

28. Tracy 1974: 13–34; 1975a; 1975b; 1977; 1991. See also Shea 1976.

29. Schroeder 1979.

30. Tracy 1974: 34.

31. Davies 1983; Gill 1969: 533–37; Sharpe 1984.

32. See Kaufman 1975; Tracy 1975a; van Buren 1972.

33. King Farlow and Christensen 1972: 20, n. 21; emphases removed.

34. Guthrie 1980; 1993.

35. MacIntosh 1919: 28–29.

36. Wittgenstein 1968.

37. Gastwirth 1972: 151. See also Sharpe 1979.

38. Gastwirth 1972: 152.

39. Oakes 1976; emphasis removed.

40. Oakes 1976.

41. Enç 1976.

42. Pannenberg 1972: 11; 1976: 328–30.

43. Wiebe 1976: 40, 42.

44. Peters 1976.

45. Austin 1967: 8; Kaufman 1975: 1–8. See also Schilling 1962.

46. See d'Aquili and Newberg 1999; Hamer 2004; Hardy 1966; Newberg and d'Aquili 2001; Rottschaefer 1985.

47. Coulson 1958: 9.

48. Sharpe 2000.

49. Pannenberg 1976.

50. Barbour 1974: chap. 6.

51. See Barbour 1974: chap. 8; King 1973a; 1973b.

52. E.g., Gill 1974.

53. See Kaufman 1975: 3–4.

54. Dillistone 1962.

55. Tracy 1974: 32–34.

56. Barbour 1974: 132–33. See also Fawcett 1970: 89–93; Feyerabend 1975; King-Farlow and Christensen 1972: 1–2.

57. Barbour 1974: 42–44; MacCormac 1976: chaps. 1–3. Both rely on Black 1962.

58. Hazelton 1977. See also Pannenberg 1976: 331.

59. E.g., Robbins 1972; Schlesinger 1977a: chap. 25; Wiebe 1976: 46.

60. Miles 1977: 50.

61. Barbour 1974: 65–66. See also pp. 45–46.

62. See Barbour 1974: 145–46; Diamond and Litzenburg 1975; Jones 1978: 96; Martin 1966.

63. Barbour 1974: 119. See also MacCormac 1976: 136–37, 151.

64. Barbour 1974: 49, 65–66, 68–70. See also Crow 1976; Mitchell 1973: chap. 6; Smith with Todes 1969.

65. Barbour 1974: 65.

66. Barbour 1974: 130–31.

67. Barbour 1974: 143. See also Jones 1978: 96–97; MacCormac 1976: 151. On the coherence criterion, see Pannenberg 1972: 10.

68. Brown 1966; Carnes 1976; Duthie 1965; Glenn 1972; Howe 1971; Kaufman 1975: 55 (plus Sharpe 1979: 189); Montgomery 1966; Nishi 1974; Wiles 1974.

69. Shea 1976: 279. See also Gill 1969: 555.

70. See Sharpe 1984.

71. Barbour 1974: 143.

72. Brownhill 1968: 122; Tillich 1967: vol. 1.

73. MacCormac 1976: 48.

74. Barbour 1974: 67.

75. See Austin 1967: 9; Barbour 1974: 119; Howe 1974; Kaufman 1975: 71–72; MacCormac 1976: 136–37, 151; Martland 1963; Thomas 1973: 4–9.

76. Kaufman 1975: epilogue.

77. Gill 1969: 556.

78. Kaufman 1975: 72.

79. Brown 1978: 44. See also R. Brown 1977.

80. See Wiebe 1974b.

81. Barbour 1974: 143; emphasis removed.

82. Brown 1978: 42–43. See also Barnhart 1976.

83. Pannenberg 1976; Tracy 1975a.

84. Brown 1978: 42–43. See Miller 1972: 25.

85. Ferré 1974: 730.

86. Miller 1972: 27. See also H. I. Brown 1977.

87. MacCormac 1976: xvii.

88. See Carey 1975.

89. See Jaki 1974; Sharpe 1982a.

90. Shea 1976; Tracy 1975a.

91. Gill 1969: 556. See Black 1962; Brown 1978.

92. Brown 1966: 18–19.

93. But see Brownhill 1968.

94. Brown 1996: 20–21.

95. See Lovell 1979.

96. Barbour 1974: 143.

97. Brownhill 1968. See also Langford 1966; Polanyi 1964.

98. Brownhill 1968: 121.

99. Brownhill 1968.

100. Runzo 1975: 686.

101. Brownhill 1968: 122.

102. Brown 1966: 16.

103. Brown 1966: 16.

104. Barbour 1974: 143–44.

105. Dulles 1976.

106. Diamond 1975.

107. See Campbell 1974: 4–5; Kaufman 1976.

108. See Pannenberg 1972: 12–13.

109. See Enç 1976; Sharpe 1979: 185–86; Toulmin and Goodfield 1961.

110. Quine and Ullian 1970.

111. Barbour 1974: 132–33; King-Farlow and Christensen 1972: 3–14; Mitchell 1973; Pannenberg 1972: 332.

112. Barbour 1960: 211.

113. Barbour 1960.

114. See also, e.g., Townes 1966.

115. Fawcett 1970: 89–90.

116. Barbour 1974: 143.

117. See Austin 1976; Heim 1953; MacKay 1974; Sharpe 1991.

118. Wiebe 1976: 39–40.

119. Barbour 1960: 212.

120. Barbour 1960: 212.

121. Burhoe 1975; Gilkey 1970; Ogden 1966; Tracy 1975a. See also Coburn 1969; Oakes 1972.

122. Sharpe 1984.

123. MacCormac 1976.

124. See Sharpe 1982b; Thom 1975.

125. Margenau 1950: chap. 8, pp. 55, 96–97.

126. See Carnes 1976: 513; Miller 1972: 25–26.

127. See King-Farlow and Christensen 1972: 3–15.

128. MacCormac 1976: 60.

129. Dulles 1976; MacCormac 1976: 151.

130. See, e.g., d'Aquili and Newberg 1999; Hamer 2004; Newberg and d'Aquili 2001; Rottschaefer 1985.

131. Godbey 1970: 200–201.

132. See Gill 1969: 557–58.

133. MacCormac 1976: 151.

134. Brown 1966: 17.

135. Barbour 1974: 92.

136. Evans 1968: 121, 129–30. See also Howe 1974.

137. See Barbour 1974: 92.

138. Brown 1978: 33–38.

139. Lovell 1979: chap. 1.

140. Barbour 1974: 60–67, 140. See also Daly 1969: 123–24.

141. Jones 1978: 97.

142. Austin 1967: 8–9. See also McFague 1982: 137–44.

143. Quay 1974.

144. Clayton 1989a; 1989b.

145. E.g., see Horton and Finnegan 1973; Wilson 1974.

146. *Concise Oxford Dictionary*.

147. Hazelton 1977: 21.

148. See Novak 1968; Trigg 1973: 168.

149. Sharpe 1984: afterword.

150. Hazelton 1977: 21.

151. Trigg 1980.

152. Sharpe 1984.

153. Polanyi 1964.

154. Brown 1966: 16. See also Kordig 1968: 459–61.

155. See Carnes 1976: 513–15; Miller 1972: 23.

156. Baum 1971: 354–59.

157. Hesse 1975a: 121.

158. Schillebeeckx 1968: 7.

159. See Sharpe 1979: 183–86.

160. Thorson 1968: 35.

161. Carnes 1982; Louth 1983.

162. Barbour 1974: 143.

163. Wiles 1974. Also see Pannenberg 1972: 6–10.

164. See, e.g., Brown 1966: 14–21; Carnes 1976: 501–16; Howe 1971: 385–406; Nishi 1974; Putnam 1979; Wiles 1974 (but note Winslow 1977).

165. Quay 1974: 355–59.

166. Capps 1972.

Chapter Seven

God Ignored:
Contemporary Scholars Fail

Like the prior chapters, this one draws historically from the development of ideas toward key-theology, this time set in a more contemporary debate on theological method from the point of view of science. Only those voices that draw on the modern understanding of the doing of science—that is, those incorporating the insights associated with Thomas Kuhn—come in for consideration, and of them only some—for issues of space have meant the omission of many others.[1] In particular, this chapter interacts the key-theology proposal with the ideas of Arthur Peacocke, Philip Clayton, Wentzel van Huyssteen, Nancey Murphy, and Alister McGrath. How does key-theology compare with theirs? How do they handle the concerns that led to key-theology?

ARTHUR PEACOCKE

Peacocke has positively influenced many scholars' thinking about the relationship between science and theology and has significantly helped theologians in their attempts to create systematic theology in the light of science. His book, *Intimations of Reality: Critical Realism in Science and Religion*, details the critical realism he follows and advocates.[2] Theological models and ideas are "partial and inadequate," he writes, "but necessary and, indeed, the only ways of referring to the reality that is God and God's relation to humanity."[3] Theologians must aim toward an objective understanding such as the scientific method provides. At the same time, though, they need to recognize the subjectivities that inescapably enter into any form of knowing, including into both science and theology. This attitude means theology and science interact and approach the same reality.

His description of the model-building nature of theology (its similarity to the scientific use of models) parallels Ian Barbour's:

- both theology and science speak analogically and metaphorically;
- the models in both do not produce literal pictures, but the scholar can mold them to make them as accurate as possible;
- models in both function less to picture than they do to depict processes, relationships, and structures as the patterns of the relationships (this differs a little from Barbour's understanding of the use of models, which emphasizes the picturing rather than the depicting of processes); and
- both involve community in their formulation and propounding.[4]

Peacocke's list of the differences between models in science and in theology also reads like Barbour's:

- the personal nature of religious models and metaphors means they influence more and subserve less the doctrines or theories of theology than do the models of science in relation to their theories; and
- theological models largely function affectively and hence have an evaluative and evocative role that scientific models generally lack.[5]

The subject of theology comprises, Peacocke thinks, what people take to be their experiences of God. Theology reflects and analyzes humanity's religious experience, satisfying the need to ask questions about the meaning of human existence. (Peacocke, almost as an afterthought, extends the subject matter of theology beyond this by saying that, for people to believe a theology, it will also have to appear the best explanation of the broad features of the natural world.) The metaphorical language of theological models acts referentially without coming across as naively realist and unrevisably descriptive in a parallel way to science's models referencing the natural world. What tradition terms "God" becomes in theology the referent of the experiences (God as "that which, the one who, is encountered" in religious experience) as an inference to the best explanation. "The best" here involves the "application of the criteria of reasonableness that . . . generally [serve] to assess ideas and, in particular, in appraising scientific models and theories—namely, fit with the data, internal coherence, comprehensiveness, fruitfulness, and general cogency." These criteria of reasonableness can also lead to consensus among investigators.[6]

Not only does Peacocke's understanding of theological method try to follow a scientific approach to the treatment of its data, but it also hints at the web image for theology used in developing the idea of key-theology. Theology, he says, must allow for various degrees of belief in the truth of its propositions and it must accept a hierarchy of truths, some more central than others.[7]

Major dissimilarities surface, however, between Peacocke's ideas and key-theology. Gordon Kaufman's *An Essay on Theological Method* and the above case for key-theology pointed out the circularity of using, as Peacocke does, religious experience as the data for theology; natural and reasonable explanations exist for it.[8] Religious experience therefore is too fraught with difficulties to offer theology its data.

Peacocke's construction of a theology—as exemplified in his *Theology for a Scientific Age: Being and Becoming—Natural, Divine, and Human*—tries to follow a scientific method as outlined above to critique received theology and to understand the modern world and humanity's place in it.[9] His thinking follows and develops the notion of hierarchies, an idea such people as Charles Birch previously expounded.[10] God acts in and on the world, Peacocke proposes, in a top-down way; God operates on the whole of the world, which then acts on its parts as wholes can act on their parts. The way the mind acts on the brain, for example, offers Peacocke a model for this downward action.[11] This holism leads to the recognition of emergent properties of the wholes that the behaviors of the parts alone cannot explain.

Peacocke's own system of theology takes him only so far, however. He reaches a point with his downward-acting emergent holism where he posits a God quite distinct from the world. This allows him to introduce as many traditional ideas as he needs to feel comfortable, but it renders God "an outcast," as chapter 2 above describes. He thereby terminates his scientific approach to doing theology.

Isolating a safe place for an idea of God occurs in all the methodological proposals this chapter considers. Key-theology's approach to knowing about God, by contrast, continually opens to change the understandings of God it derives.

PHILIP CLAYTON

Chapter 6 of Clayton's book, *Explanation from Physics to Theology*, provides his understanding of theological method, especially for theology seen as a science.[12] Theology, he says, has two "publics" to which it is responsible, and these lead it to have two levels. The first comprises the activity and idea world of the religious believer, the church. Theology considers its responsibilities to and place within the religious community, and so constitutes a science about the Christian tradition's beliefs concerning the world (including humans and God). For the second public, what Clayton calls the "academy," theology considers its academic status, its goals and characteristics as a science, and issues like the nature of its explanations and the criteria involved in its rationality. Theology thus distances itself a little from beliefs as stated in their religious context; it describes and clarifies how these first level statements function, what they say, and how they fit together to form a system. Theology's explanations try continually to insure the tradition's relevance to contemporary issues.[13]

Clayton can then list what theology must consider when spelling out its rationality:

1. the relationship between its statements and those of the first level;
2. its criteria as they stem from its two publics; and
3. issues arising from comparing it with other fields of study.[14]

He expands his third aspect of theological rationality—plus the second aspect as it applies to the academic public—with his understanding of theology as a science. Theology must:

- formulate its explanations to make them open to criticism;
- accept relevant research from other disciplines;
- provide warrant for the truth of its basic beliefs in the milieu of explanations that those scholars who dispute them might accept; and
- take its claims on the academic level as hypothetical with no assurance of finality.[15]

What do the data of theology comprise? Theological inquiry takes as its initial and primary data, Clayton writes, the church's beliefs.[16]

What do theology's criteria from levels one and two comprise (Clayton's second numbered point above)? Basic criteria for theology as rational and explanatory (the second level) include: "the free and public exchange of ideas, use and acknowledgement of sources, reasoned and criticizable discussions of others' ideas, and the ideals of clarity, objectivity, and criticizability." Satisfying the church (the first level) defines the primary criterion, however. Clayton wants the theologian to assess theological proposals already deemed adequate in a formal way (consistency, coherence, sufficiently comprehensive) against religious beliefs: they must cohere with the practices and beliefs of religion, and correspond with tradition. Here appears, Clayton says, the crux of calling theology "a faith science," "the science of God," or "the science of Christianity": theology serves and remains bound to the church.[17]

Assessment of Clayton's Proposal

Clayton has gone some way toward making theology a science, but not far enough. His understanding of theological method diverges from the one developed for key-theology when, for example, he thinks the data of theology comprise church doctrine; key-theology takes all of reality, all experience, as its potential data. The most pointed difference between Clayton's and the key-theology proposal has to do with the way he handles the first of his levels, the power he gives to the beliefs the church holds; he gives them a far greater role than any others by requiring adherence to them, period. "Systematic theology is the essence of the very same truths of religion" that the Bible contains, he quotes from G. J. Planck.[18] As asked above, what room remains for theology to challenge or steer the beliefs of the church? What happens when knowledge of life and the universe as the academy discerns it (for example, evolution, the biological basis of subjective and mental phenomena, or the relationship of the earth to the sun) conflicts with church-promulgated beliefs? Despite his assertions that in principle anyone can participate in theology, that no privileged premises can ground any solution, that theology cannot bracket questions of truth, that theology has to open itself to insights from discussion and research, and that theistic beliefs involve "truth claims about the way things are," Clayton has the Christian church's religion—not all or any other part of experience—doing the real arbitration.[19] This stymies the search for truth. The Theological method must allow theology an openness to pursue the truth (even perspectives on new truths) in equal partnership with the other disciplines of the academy, and not merely to give this lip service.

In the key-theological proposal, level-one beliefs can offer potential models for exploration and the theologian might include adherence to them as a criterion to satisfy along with others. These might conflict with it, however, and hence the need for discussion among the scholars and a decision about the relative weights of the criteria. Key-theology thereby follows Clayton's dictate—to which he fails to adhere—that probably the explanation most likely true is the one best approximating an ideal scientific one.[20] To make a science out of theology requires not only its accessibility in principle to all people, but also its testability by all people, including those out of the church.

Clayton's more recent book, *God and Contemporary Science*, uses a supposedly scientific idea to understand God's working within the world.[21] This approach develops Peacocke's lead by promoting the philosophy of emergence and downward causation (whole-part emergent action and properties). Unfortunately, like his understanding of theological method as following science's, this proposal of Clayton may not lie open to the actual process and findings of science. Science does not yet understand how wholes act on their parts over and above what the behavior of the parts can explain. Clayton's holism argument— a modern form of the God-of-the-gaps—will therefore find itself more and more isolated as science fills in spaces it has yet to explain. Clayton thinks his idea scientific but, being far more speculative, it does not achieve his aim. He glues himself to a questionable form of holism and, through it, can import many metaphysical notions without empirical testing.[22]

Clayton's writings also hint at a potential criticism of key-theology. He agrees with other writers that no foreign authority (such as logical positivism) should randomly sift through a theological tradition's beliefs, rejecting those for which it finds insufficient evidence; it is inappropriate to demand point-by-point verification of the assertions a theology might make. This does not excuse theology from standards as evidenced in science, he adds, but it does "soften and contextualize the standards that remain."[23] Does key-theology behave toward theology as

Clayton thinks logical positivists do? It does not (though it takes to heart the seriousness of Kai Nielsen's challenge for factual meaningfulness) because it follows the softer and contextualized set of standards Clayton refers to, which sociological and historical critiques such as Kuhn's produced when they took aim at the older philosophy of science.

The critical question, however, concerns the amount of softness and contextualization: how far can the theologian step away from the usual image of science, let alone the usual doing of science, before theology ceases to operate as a science? Theologians cannot so soften and contextualize the requirement for factual meaningfulness that they can make any factual assertion they or their church traditions like, and so create a dual standard for inquiry and verification.

WENTZEL VAN HUYSSTEEN

Van Huyssteen asks how people might hang on to religious faith amid the confusion of the modern age. In a postmodern context that celebrates cultural and religious pluralism, how can believers speak with deep conviction or passionate commitment? Van Huyssteen answers this by exploring how theological reflection relates to other modes of intellectual inquiry, especially to scientific knowledge.

The Scientific Method

His understanding of scientific method and the nature of rationality—a broad and "flexible notion"—in general diverges little from that developed in chapter 5 for key-theology, apart from the terminology used. Both derive from the same foundation ("no sharp line" can demarcate scientific rationality from other types of rationality) and claim to relate to the form of rationality that underlies most goal-directed actions of humans. Both aim, as did Barbour's, to capture the features of science that make it the rational enterprise par excellence, and both focus on the individual knower in the context of community.[24] Where they take these beginning points, however, differs.

Van Huyssteen's position develops using insights from Nicholas Rescher. All types of knowledge depend on three broad aspects of rationality: "the cognitive, the evaluative, and the pragmatic." With these, the knower deploys good reasons for, or tries to find the strongest and best reasons for, respectively, "hanging on to certain beliefs, . . . making certain moral choices, and . . . acting in certain ways." "The pull of purpose," as van Huyssteen words it, constrains the inquirer. These three dimensions merge seamlessly as a whole when engaged together to understand the best a knower can.[25] Then rational behavior occurs.

The writings of Harold Brown emphasize similar aspects of rationality, highlighting the role of critical and responsible judgment in human cognition: the rational individual has the ability, without following prescribed rules, to evaluate a situation, to assess the available evidence, and then to reach a reasonable decision. This requires acute self-awareness and the command of a body of appropriate information. Note that the rational agent can form judgments in situations that lack rules for determining a definitive outcome. This requires social mediation in the making of rational decisions, the scholar's embeddedness in and conscious commitment to living and concrete traditions and their various cultures, worldviews, strategies for reasoning, and values (like coherence, intelligibility [the most important one], predictive accuracy, and simplicity, plus more philosophical ones like empiricism, feminism, naturalism, and pragmatism). The holder usually adheres to such extra-empirical influences tacitly as standards implicit in her or his self-awareness and self-conception.[26]

Unlike the position of Kuhn, in which a rational decision occurs when most scientists in a community agree, Brown only requires that agents submit their decisions to their peers (those sharing relevant expertise) for evaluation, and that they seriously consider the evaluation. (However, does not the community eventually "agree," not in the sense of consciously forming a consensus, but in that some theories do not survive while others, the successful ones, continue, even if altered from how originally proposed? Kuhn may have meant this.) Brown's argument acknowledges the influence of the community on the individual scholar. It also highlights the other direction of feedback, from self-aware individuals to their social contexts, especially their contribution to changing the community.[27] Rationality or the continuing process of shared assessment does not require a common voice that silences a particular rational agent. Neither need a community fully represent an agent's vision of it in the present or the future.[28] Communal rationality thus has its limits.[29]

In summary, rationality involves an agent's:

1. making the best judgments possible in a particular context and community;
2. remaining open to error and change that context-dependent decision making requires;
3. awareness of the interpretive and experiential dimensions of decisions; and
4. recognizing the lack of impervious foundations.[30]

Science and theology share this common rationality.[31]

The greater subjectivity often found in theology than in science does not imply its lesser degree of rationality, van Huyssteen argues, but rather its particular focus epistemologically and its broader scope experientially. The doing of theology depends on an overlapping but different set of values to science's. This occurs because theology's actual and reflective practice focuses in a religious community and grows from the way Christians live their existence of faith. It acknowledges that ritual and story focus the religious lives of these people, and it takes to heart that noncognitive aspects of religious language often evoke adherents' attitudes and encourage their personal transformation.[32]

Answering Standard Questions

Van Huyssteen can now answer several challenges to any account of rationality and, in particular, to the above account of theology's rationality.

Truth

How does rationality relate to truth? Rescher argues, and van Huyssteen agrees, that physical reality exists independent of minds and that humans can gain information about it.[33] Scientific inquiries presuppose this realism. However, knowledge—including that of science—can never be perfect or complete; more to reality exists than humans can know. Thus, like the position advocated in the case for key-theology, van Huyssteen sees rational inquiry not approximating truth, but estimating it. Scientific theories have to settle for a better approximation to truth rather than a closer one, because no way exists to monitor a measure for "closer." On the other hand, what defines "better" as in "a better approximation

to truth"? Van Huyssteen answers: the theory built on fuller information
and exhibiting fewer deficits.[34] An inference to the best explanation, this
long-term process of theory building requires scholars to estimate or
judge as best or as rationally as they currently can.[35] This then gauges
the explanatory progress of a theory.

Conceptual Relativism

Does van Huyssteen dodge conceptual relativism, the giving of equal
weight to various supposed truths? To answer, he refers to Brown. First,
to claim a belief is rational does not mean claiming it is true. Conceptual systems of equal rationality may not hold equal truth status. Second,
while rationally to accept a claim requires assessing evidence for it,
some types of evidence more strongly warrant belief than do others.[36]
One conceptual scheme may lie closer to the truth than does another.
These two points, van Huyssteen implies, rule out conceptual relativism.

These two points, however, lead to other questions. What defines reasons as stronger?[37] What warrants the superiority of one person's versus
another person's decision as to the forms of evidence that give stronger
warrant? No clear, noncircular answers stand out. Van Huyssteen does
not provide adequate grounds for negating conceptual relativism.

As an alternative, does the solution to conceptual relativism require
rooting theories in the given that most people would acknowledge? If
so, then maybe science does have a stronger warrant for belief than does
the theology van Huyssteen envisions.

Referent for "God"

Does a referent exist for the word "God"? Does "God" only offer a hope
or an assumption, a solution to experiential issues or to conceptual
problems based on religious experience? Alternatively, can objective
reference, reality depiction, and cognitive claims occur in the theories
of theology with their open-ended and flexible networks of metaphors,
without an exhaustive or definite prior understanding or description of
the referent? Van Huyssteen, as an advocate of critical realism, answers
in the positive. Theology can depict reality, he thinks, because the theological speaker belongs to a linguistic community that has handed on
the factual meaning of the person or event, generation to generation,
right back to the original.[38]

He spells out this chain of contextual and historical communication:

> First, the Bible . . . has survived as a religious text and as a book of faith in a long and remarkable interpretative tradition of an ongoing faith context. Second, it is supported by the reality of ongoing faith experiences that this text has evoked through centuries of belief in God. . . . Of these experiences, . . . [which the faithful believe God causes,] theological theorizing provides interpretation and reinterpretation on the basis of the central metaphors of this text. . . . A third factor . . . [derives from] the metaphorical structure of biblical language, and the continuity of reference this has creatively given to religious and theological language through the ages . . . going back to the initiating events when [believers first introduced] . . . these metaphorical terms . . . [and fixed their referents]. . . . Those metaphoric and interpreted expressions around which the language of the Christian religion clusters . . . justified themselves as meaningful and referential to vast numbers of people throughout the centuries and across cultures. It is this kind of experiential adequacy, and not a justified certainty, that makes a belief a responsible belief.[39]

The tradition of Nielsen asks questions of van Huyssteen's deriving the statements of theology from a chain communicating interpreted religious experience.[40] What establishes the factual reliability of this chain? The same questions of factual meaningfulness as arise now for claims about God also arise for the meaning or significance initially given to the person or event, and for every step in the chain. Van Huyssteen's argument also ignores dramatic changes in the meaning of words and cultures over thousands of years. The same argument would conclude, moreover, the reality depiction of the religious language of Muslims and Hindus, Jains and voodoo cultists, Christian fundamentalists and Mormons; many of these conflict. Van Huyssteen's case for the reality depiction of theological language therefore does not stand.

Van Huyssteen appears to react to the extremism of logical positivism (which, he says, fixes reference with unrevisable description),[41] a straw opponent both when he wrote and now. He would serve theology better by pouring his energy into an adequate answer to the secular challenge that led to the logical positivist critique (for example, by showing the factual meaningfulness of religious language). This would achieve more for society than trying to justify liberal theology's realism by downplaying the observable in theology with the tools of

Rescher and Brown. A coherent and direct response to the challenge requires stepping back from the dogma of both logical positivism and traditional theology.

The Observable and Objective in Theology

Van Huyssteen asks his central question: "Does theology exhibit a rationality comparable to the rationality of science, and how plausible can an explanatory justification of the cognitive claims of theology be?"[42] A general form of the rationality of science applies, he suggests, not only to science but also to other investigations, including theology. How might the observable and the objective, obviously important in science, work in theology? This involves issues of data and criteria.

Van Huyssteen says that, with his model of rationality, different claims rely on different sources for their evidence. What sort of evidence or data, then, is appropriate for theology? Theology, van Huyssteen writes, "makes claims ultimately related to and based on the interpreted religious experience of a broad, complex, and pluralist Christian tradition."[43] As seen with Peacocke's similar reliance on religious experience as the data for theology, this statement moves in circles and ignores natural and other reasonable explanations for the encounters.

Turning to criteria for explanations, van Huyssteen notes that each paradigm has its own set. The uniqueness of those for theology and religion (though this also applies to metaphysical and some types of philosophical explanation) lies, he continues, in their making sense of all of experience and in their speaking to the profoundly personal. Theology's explanations make those who commit themselves to God feel secure. Theology thus judges proposed explanations better the more they solve issues from life and the religious experience that founds the community. It fulfills these functions and thereby its criteria, he says, by answering "vague and elusive questions" about ultimate meaning.[44]

The roots and rationality of theological knowledge—involving a greater degree of interpretation and experience than do those of science with its mostly empirical foundations—involve more breadth and complexity than do those of science. Science cannot answer matters of personal commitment and experience because it lacks the qualifications to answer people's deepest religious issues.[45] He spells this out:

Science can [say] . . . little or nothing about [the human] . . . experience of subjectivity, about the astonishing emergence of human consciousness and personhood, and about why [humans] have an intelligible universe. . . . Christian believers give [the name "God"] to the best available explanation of all that is.[46]

The criteria for theology, as van Huyssteen perceives them, differ from those of science.

On the other hand, science does say something about subjectivity (for example, psychology, neuroscience, evolutionary psychology), about the emergence of consciousness and personhood (for example, archaeology, evolutionary psychology, evolutionary biology), and about the existence of an intelligible universe (for example, evolutionary psychology). The science of the future may say a lot more about these subjects as well.

Further, the "best available explanation," as van Huyssteen would call God, appears a biased judgment that already committed believers previously make.[47] It is not a hypothesis offered as a potential explanation.

The difference van Huyssteen portrays between the criteria of theology and science do not hold up.

He also writes that theology should pursue a knowledge as secure as possible, a knowledge that produces maximal understanding of what Christian believers commit themselves to in faith. He says that, more than anything else, this goal determines the rationality of theology. Yet, should not this "secure knowledge" fundamentally involve the observable? Van Huyssteen thinks not: intelligibility above all other values determines rationality in both science and theology. "What is real for theology and for science is not the observable but the intelligible."[48] This cannot be correct. Systems of meaning of exceedingly warped but brilliant minds can seem quite intelligible, but not fully rational; deprecating the observable in theology promotes the specter of irrationality. In science, despite van Huyssteen's wishes, the observable plays the paramount role in intelligibility—and so it should in theology.

Van Huyssteen's understanding of rational thinking in the sciences and theology involves three things: it is never purely objective; its context influences its theory building and interpretation; and, at any point in time, it allows only a partial evaluation of research programs and their explanations. These do not mean the theologian can throw out the objective or the observable and thus allow almost anything in religion and theology to stand. Neither do they justify van Huyssteen's claim that theology cannot resemble the natural sciences and study its subjects objectively because it does not ontologically have the requisite status.[49] He appears to validate theology's cognitive claims by inappropriately and dangerously underplaying the observable and overplaying the subjective and the communal in the parallel knowing structures of science and theology. This further weakens theology in this secular age. Theology's doctrines or theories still must claim factual meaningfulness and truth, and therefore must subject themselves to accepted general procedures for the same.

Van Huyssteen's Starting Point

Van Huyssteen wants close similarities between theology and science, plus he wants significant differences in their "epistemological [foci], experiential scope, and heuristic structures."[50] The similarities in method, however, place requirements on theology that, as seen above, conflict with the significant differences he sees. He does not resolve this confusion. Why does he want to push the difference to the extreme he does? Why does he blow his philosophical smoke to try to hide the real challenge of modernity to theology?

His reasons appear when he writes:

> Religion and religious faith (and theological reflection, in spite of important epistemological overlaps with scientific reflection) . . . in many ways [do not resemble] . . . science at all: for the adherents of many religious traditions, faith involves not just a way of looking at the world, but also a personal trust in God. An ultimate faith commitment to God [resembles] . . . , in this respect, . . . trust in a friend or a spouse [more] than . . . belief in a scientific theory. . . . On this very personal level, theology and science indeed seem . . . very different kinds of activities, each with their own rules in their own domains. . . . [This thus frees] the theologian . . . to speak and reflect from within a personal faith commitment, and in cross-disciplinary conversation with the scientist, to discover patterns [potentially] . . . consonant with the Christian worldview.[51]

Van Huyssteen thinks theology and its method derive, not so much from the search for truth (reality viewed theologically), but from "the realist assumptions and faith commitments of experienced Christian faith."[52] He seeks to serve orthodox liberal beliefs and church structures, seeing theology from the tradition of emphasizing religious experience as the basic data. In this, he seems to assume a rather Western, even Protestant, individualized and doctrine-commitment view of religion. (Note the "personal faith commitment" in the above indented quote. Note also the denial of the experience of a major portion of humanity's religious traditions with his statement that "an undeniable religious dimension to human experience" exists, the understanding of which requires "reference to God or a transcendent being."[53]) In other words, van Huyssteen attempts to justify his branch of theology as it stands, with all the assumptions it makes, as a valid way of knowing truth.

He adheres to a dualism, which becomes especially apparent when he approvingly quotes from Ernan McMullin: "Science has no access to God in its explanations: theology has nothing to say about the specifics of the world." The two may overlap, however, at the level of epistemology.[54] He presumably intends with this reference to McMullin for science and theology not to overlap on the knowledge itself. But, if relevance (factual meaningfulness with respect to claims for what actually occurs) makes an important requirement—and it does—van Huyssteen's dualistic scheme does not suffice. The overlap in method must generate overlap in the content of the two systems of thought.

Does theology wish to move closer to truth or does it wish rationally more and more to refine church doctrines once given, always to support them and never to remove or replace them with more truthful insights? Is its main intent apologetics, trying to justify its doctrines with ideas from modern science? Van Huyssteen's feels like a last-ditch attempt to save Christian theology in the face of science and secularity. He needs to emerge further from the security of his fideist cave.

As a matter of the relevance of theology for contemporary Western society, it does not suffice just to voice theological liberalism. Nielsen's distinction between anthropomorphic and nonanthropomorphic or Tillichian versions of religion matches the conservative-liberal split. Nielsen's fight with the latter proved appropriate, but his dismissal of the former turned out unfortunate, with conservatism appearing at this stage in the United States to have almost won the religion wars in the popular mind (thank goodness more decisive battles still loom). The success of fundamentalist and other conservative forms of religion suggests they have something that more adequately meets people's needs than does the liberal option. As chapter 1 pointed out, that something probably has to do with certainty, which involves an empirical expectation ("prove it") and experiential support ("it works; I feel it"). Liberal theology cannot call upon this strength. Neither can it support, with van Huyssteen's ploy, believers' speaking in a postmodern context with passionate commitment and the certainty of faith.

The suggested key-theology approach responds to these issues. Despite key-theology's recognizing with van Huyssteen the limits of scientific knowing, it does not degenerate into justifying the current status and content of theology. Key-theology finds religious experience too fickle as data (since this probably comprises "secular" experience interpreted as religious) and instead takes all experience as potential data for theology. Key-theology's criteria, moreover, aim at truth over and above service or subservience to the or a church and its doctrine. Objective data exist for key-theology that make it more than just rational in the sense of coherent. The data may also help provide it with a certainty.

Van Huyssteen's attempt differs from key-theology by subtly moving the same collection of sources to go in what end up as quite different directions. He ignores the strengths of the scientific method and hence pretends that current liberal theology can mirror science methodologically. Nevertheless, van Huyssteen especially engages the key-theology approach for, more than the other proposals considered in this chapter, he comprehensively employs their common sources.

From Peacocke, Clayton, and van Huyssteen, all of whom appear liberal, the discussion turns to the conservative evangelicals, Murphy and McGrath.

NANCEY MURPHY

Murphy's most important book on theological method is *Theology in the Age of Scientific Reasoning*.[55] Basing her analysis on Imre Lakatos's theories in the philosophy of science (similar to Barbour's, but emphasizing the idea of webs of beliefs), she portrays theologies as research traditions that history judges, parallel to particular research traditions in science.[56] Her work here, however, does not speak in depth about how one ought to do theology. Rather, she orients her study historically, showing that theologies employ methods that Lakatos would portray as scientific.

Another of her books, *Beyond Liberalism and Fundamentalism: How Modern and Postmodern Philosophy Set the Theological Agenda*, more directly discusses the scientific nature of theology.[57] Asked if theology is a science, she says yes, it is. Theology comprises "referential" theories as opposed to purely "expressivist" or "experiential" ones, an opposition she uses to differentiate, respectively, "conservative" from "liberal" religious positions. The conservative refer to objectively existing things, and the liberal refer to experiences or express attitudes and values (hence the difference between her and van Huyssteen's approach). In particular, she says, theology (the referential, conservative type) follows the hypothetico-deductive form of reasoning where the theologian forms hypotheses to explain facts or observations. (Chapter 5 above builds to this same form of knowledge acquisition, but there the similarities cease.) She continues by construing church doctrines as theories that explain the facts of Christians' lives, facts whose status closely resembles those in science. The theologian rationally proposes and tries to justify reformulations of these doctrines. Various sorts of evidence or data can support such conclusions, including historical events (such as those in the Bible, including Jesus' resurrection and sayings) and church practice (such as its worship and moral life)—both of which theory and society condition, as they also do with science's facts. Such data do differ in type from those the sciences use, but then, she adds, each science chooses its own type of data.[58]

Why might biblical texts count as data, given the circularity involved? Murphy calls on the theological theory of revelation or inspiration to explain this: the Bible comes from God and, as such, theologians can depend on its truth. (She classifies this theory as one "of instrumentation," parallel, she says, to how theories in a science justify the use of its data.)[59] Christian discernment also sifts potential data coming from church practice and interpretation of history to make sure they really concern God:

> The Christian community, in virtue of the presence of the Holy Spirit, has the ability to judge whether or not practices, teachings, and prophecies [come from] . . . the Spirit of Jesus. Christians possess an *inner witness* regarding what is or is not of God, as well as *public criteria* to test these

judgments. . . . [This explains] why the judgments church members make together in prayer should . . . tell . . . something about the will of God and not merely about the church.[60]

God, through such discernment, can substantiate data from the Bible, church practice, and history.

Murphy's initial question closely resembles the one that informs the initiation of key-theology: how might theology make valid empirical claims? The parallels she draws between theology's and science's methods start by making sense (calling on the hypothetico-deductive form of reasoning) but, when spelled out, depend on the prior acceptance of theological theories and religious beliefs, and therefore make sense only for the insider. The idea of discernment, for instance, requires many ideas about God and how God acts in the world; these tell Murphy that she should trust church doctrines and biblical texts as data. She then takes them as providing the theologian with the knowledge of God from which she builds her idea of discernment.

Murphy would counter by saying the data of the sciences also depend on their theories. They do to some extent, but not so much as in Murphy's account. Her type of move would probably justify most forms of discourse as truth, even such irrationalities as flat-earth theories, and such morally irresponsible ones as Nazism. As with Clayton's account, theologians cannot so soften and contextualize the requirement for factual meaningfulness that they can claim as truth any factual assertion they or their church traditions like. Murphy's fideist proposal does not justify her calling theology a science in the sense of modern empirical science.[61] It does not shield its putative factual talk of God from outside questions of truth and meaning.

ALISTER MCGRATH

The discussion above moved from Peacocke to Clayton to van Huyssteen to Murphy, and now reaches McGrath, the five in roughly increasing order of conservatism; it traveled from Peacocke, a thinker a little distance from the key-theology proposal, to van Huyssteen, a long way from key-theology, and now to McGrath on the other side of the universe. As van Huyssteen represents orthodox Christian liberalism, so McGrath represents orthodox Christian evangelicalism.

McGrath's *The Science of God*, and his trilogy, *A Scientific Theology*, spell out his theological method by following a logical course of argument.[62] More than Murphy, he clearly proclaims his beginning point: "The roots of scientific theology are thoroughly evangelical, resting on a deep and passionate conviction" that the scriptures have to "nourish and govern" theology at every point. Theology tries to provide a coherent and faithful account of what it reads in the Bible. His version of scientific theology, he claims, neither fundamentally disagrees nor finds difficulty with the core doctrines of Christianity, for example as the Nicene Creed sets them out. In fact, he says, his scientific theology confirms traditional Christian orthodoxy.[63]

McGrath calls the Christian foundation he assumes a "tradition-mediated rationality," and considers it an appropriate universal assumption, a rationality that applies across disciplines. It therefore can justifiably ground every aspect of his approach to theology and all other knowledge. As Jonathan Wilson writes, "McGrath seeks an account of theological method that privileges the 'great tradition' of Christianity and brings it to bear on the sciences and the place of the sciences in contemporary culture."[64] McGrath thinks this because his Christian story offers, he says, a logic that fundamentally grounds and organizes it, accounting not only for its own existence, but also for those of its competitors.[65]

In addition to this fundamentalism in his approach to scientific theology, only a few other important aspects need mentioning here:

- The ontology of something (the way it is) determines its epistemology (the way humans know it). The nature of the reality of a particular thing requires that people can know it only in certain ways and to a certain extent. Humans do not have the option to decide whether and how they may know things; the things decide that themselves. This echoes Thomas Torrance's point mentioned in chapter 6 above, in which theology and other sciences each have "their own distinctive subject matters and means of investigation appropriate to that subject."[66]

  This idea shows up as an assumption in the version of critical realism that McGrath promotes, namely the one of Roy Bhaskar.[67] Barbour's and the version used to develop the idea of key-theology do not specifically include this idea, nor does it necessarily follow from them.

- The second aspect of Bhaskar's critical realism that McGrath applauds (and that differs from the critical realism espoused in the development of key-theology) promotes the idea of different levels, what McGrath calls "the stratification of reality."[68] Peacocke and Clayton also use this idea.

The two bulleted points above, along with the fundamental assumption of traditional Christian orthodoxy, allow McGrath to extrapolate the ontology of traditional Christian orthodoxy to mean:

- (the Christian) God exists independent of human knowing;
- God has a particular overarching level ontologically (the spiritual); and
- epistemologically, the spiritual requires a specific way of knowing (namely, Christian theology).

Assessment of McGrath's Proposal

McGrath's proposed method shows several weaknesses.

The levels idea—while claiming that the method of theology parallels science's in particular ways (for example, in their use of analogies)—promotes a dualism, that holds as disparate the findings of science and those of theology. It can thus justify theology going about its way of knowing the way it does, accountable only to its Christian community.[69] The same point arose with van Huyssteen's account of theological method.

A second weakness in McGrath's proposal relates to the assumption that ontology determines epistemology. Besides its anthropomorphism (attributing agency to the thing humans attempt to know), how does McGrath know first the ontology and then the appropriate epistemology? Knowing the ontology requires either an assumption or an epistemology. This applies to all fields of knowledge. To recognize this weakness in McGrath's approach need not mean falling into what Bhaskar calls the "epistemic fallacy" in which the existence of something depends on humans actually or potentially observing it.[70] Neither need it mean rejecting, as a rejoinder might claim, the existence of things humans have not observed or cannot observe, nor the necessity of making assumptions before knowing. The issue at stake is really what assumptions the scholar needs to make, and why.

McGrath's idea of method deriving from context (epistemology from ontology) is also inappropriate if he lays claim to truth in the same way as he thinks science rightly may. He cannot have it both ways. Theology cannot see itself validly or honestly on a continuum with science methodologically, or with respect to its results, if it will not subject itself as science does to factual meaningfulness.

The major weakness in McGrath's proposal, however, lies in his initial assumption from Christian evangelicalism.

Like Torrance's and others', McGrath's assumption of a starting point determines his method and much of his outcome. It assumes something as the truth and therefore, as mentioned in chapter 6 above, finds it again at the end as its truth. This does not produce *a* let alone *the* "science of God," in the usual understanding of science as an open investigation, but rather "a Christian evangelical science of a Christian evangelical view of God."

To start with a particular understanding of God and God's relationship with humanity assumes there exists only one way to know or understand God, one way to truth, and method must begin there. Many understandings of God and approaches to understanding God, however, lie in the same religious tradition, or even in the evangelical Christian approach within which McGrath's neo-orthodoxy lies. Some assume the factual inerrancy of the Bible, for instance, while others accept a metaphorical not a scientific meaning of the biblical accounts of creation. The same starting point can therefore lead to conflicting putative truths.

The theologian should not accept McGrath's base as universal. This conclusion fits well with his statement that no universally accepted criteria exist to adjudicate cleanly between fundamental assumptions. He sees the statement as implying the need to accept beliefs (namely, he says, orthodox Christian doctrines) as the base but, of course, this need not follow.[71] How can one judge between fundamental assumptions? Coherence and other logical criteria do find their place in any proposed set of criteria for making this adjudication, even conformity with what they consider their data does as well, but the relative order of importance of the criteria in each system of thought defies universalizing. Hence, criteria cannot act as the final arbiters. Perhaps the happy and just lives of an assumption's adherents may help decide its merit, but this too lies open to relative judgments. These and similar ways do help adjudicate between fundamental assumptions, but not firmly or cleanly.

This leads to the question: To what is Christian theology responsible? What adjudicates its merit? Here a split will arise. If responsible to the Christian tradition currently represented by evangelicalism, the answer is God or the Christian Bible and orthodoxy as that tradition interprets them. If responsible to (Western) society, then different issues arise involving personal and societal factors, which may end up as relative. If responsible to society, religious tradition, and to reality independent of human knowing, then—as with key-theology—another set of questions arise, related to the first two. It seeks to move beyond the confines of the others into something responsible also to the objective beyond the human.

McGrath and Openness

McGrath feels strongly about the evils of logical positivism, but he preaches his own form of triumphal Christian positivism. His approach represents a dangerous trend in religions. The beginning of his book, *The Science of God,* comments on his prior publications: "The publication of the three volumes of *A Scientific Theology* (2001–2003) has generated a high degree of interest in its themes and distinctive approach. It is already being described as 'one of the best systematic theologies in recent years.'"[72] Fred Sanders and Kirk Wegter-McNelly comment on this type of statement in another of McGrath's books: this "self-congratulatory tone . . . make[s] him appear desperate for credibility"; since he need not go to these lengths to establish his authority, why does he behave this way?[73] His self-aggrandizement—both personal (the beginning of *The Science of God* just quoted) and intellectually (for example, the title of his book professing to have set down *the* science of God)—especially when claiming the authority of God, can allow fanatics to take his words and promote universalism and imperialism. This may produce surety but, in certain hands, it also creates destructive confidence.

Too huge and too many differences separate the religious traditions, all claiming truth, for one to hold it and the others not to. Modern Western life must accept such pluralisms and try to live successfully in them; it needs to maintain them and to grow within them. This cannot involve dictatorship. McGrath and the rest of contemporary society must similarly live within secularism, learning from it and the pluralisms, and appreciating their plenitude.

On the other hand, Western society needs general moral universals whose applications require working out in each situation. Society must have these with a strength behind them. That strength entails certainty—factual and experiential (the needs that fundamentalism highlights, as expressed in chapter 1)—but a certainty that coheres with modernity. The solution to the current religious challenge must play thoroughly and completely in tune with modern knowledge and life.

Science of God offers this with a general program for research. At the beginning of the twenty-first century and its conservatism, McGrath represents a considerable challenge to the way key-theology approaches things. Nevertheless, potency lies not in the brute force of the dinosaurs, but in the markedly human trait of adaptability. It comes from caring and humility, not from violence; it rests on the time-honored search for truth (not on claims to have it) and the need for happiness and justice for all people. The approach of key-theology will more adequately meet these aims than can sword-swinging, God-claiming looking backward.

CONCLUSIONS

The major current voices in theological method draw to some extent on versions of contemporary philosophy of science, which they weight and from which they make significant leaps. They end with the theology with which they started. Their work thus forms apologetics. They do not take science seriously enough or answer social or secular critiques adequately, only sincerely taking into account how they already conceive their religious traditions.

The work of some of them—both evangelicals and liberals—parallels in important respects fundamentalism and its sibling ideology, creationism. They believe in certain immutable truths whose expression and amplification in different cultural and historical circumstances can vary only a little. Science ought merely to substantiate or elaborate the beliefs and, when it opposes the beliefs, it needs opposing, ignoring, or so qualifying to emasculate it. Edward Wilson speaks both correctly and incorrectly when he writes:

> The inexorable growth of [biology] . . . continues to widen, not to close, the tectonic gap between science and faith-based religion. Rapprochement

may be neither possible nor desirable. There is something deep in religious belief that divides people and amplifies societal conflict. The toxic mix of religion and tribalism has become so dangerous as to justify taking seriously the alternative view, that humanism based on science is the effective antidote, the light and the way at last placed before us.[74]

Wilson is right in saying the gap continues to widen and rapprochement may not be possible between science and faith-based religion. The emphasis here lies on *faith*-based religion because the humanism he offers as an alternative itself represents a form of religion. He is wrong because another alternative exists, one that allows humanity to grow in its theological knowledge.

To lay open genuinely to what humans can learn about God requires opening all beliefs to empirical examination, and learning from what science and other experience offer.

NOTES

 1. E.g., Lonergan (1972); MacFague (1982); Soskice (1985).
 2. Peacocke 1984.
 3. Peacocke 1984: 40; emphasis removed.
 4. Peacocke 1984: 42–43.
 5. Peacocke 1993: 14.
 6. Peacocke 1984: 38–39, 46; 1993: 15, 17.
 7. Peacocke 1993: 16, 18.
 8. Chapters 2 and 6 above; Kaufman 1975.
 9. Peacocke 1993.
10. E.g., Birch and Cobb 1981.
11. See also Sharpe 2000.
12. Clayton 1989a.
13. Clayton 1989a: 149, 154, 156; emphases removed.
14. Clayton 1989a: 157.
15. Clayton 1989a: 162.
16. Clayton 1989a: 155.
17. Clayton 1989a: 153, 157, 158, 166.
18. Clayton 1989a: 158.
19. Clayton 1989a: 148, 161, 166, 173.
20. Clayton 1989a: 178.
21. Clayton 1997.
22. Sharpe and Walgate 2003.

23. Clayton 1989a: 151.

24. Van Huyssteen 1997: 164; 1998: 22–23.

25. Van Huyssteen 1998: 39; 1999: 24, 128–29; emphases removed.

26. Van Huyssteen 1998: 24, 25, 30, 146; 1999: 131, 154.

27. Van Huyssteen 1998: 27, 28, 32.

28. Van Huyssteen 1998: 29–31; emphasis removed and the last statement attributed to Clayton and Knapp.

29. Van Huyssteen 1999: 151.

30. Van Huyssteen 1998: 44.

31. Van Huyssteen 1997: 262.

32. Van Huyssteen 1997: 261, 262; 1998: 26.

33. Van Huyssteen 1997: 258.

34. Van Huyssteen 1998: 34, 36, 39.

35. Van Huyssteen 1997: 177; 1998: 21; with reference to Brown.

36. Van Huyssteen 1998: 28.

37. Van Huyssteen 1997: 230.

38. Van Huyssteen 1997: 171–72; emphasis removed.

39. Van Huyssteen 1997: 173–74.

40. Van Huyssteen 1997: 171–72; emphasis removed.

41. Van Huyssteen 1997: 173.

42. Van Huyssteen 1997: 163.

43. Van Huyssteen 1998: 34; 1999: 129.

44. Van Huyssteen 1997: 177, 231–33.

45. Van Huyssteen 1998: 37, 41–42.

46. Van Huyssteen 1998: 42.

47. Van Huyssteen 1998: 42.

48. Van Huyssteen 1997: 163; 1998: 22–23.

49. Van Huyssteen 1997: 232–33; 1998: 35.

50. Van Huyssteen 1998: 44.

51. Van Huyssteen 1998: 45–46.

52. Van Huyssteen 1998: 41.

53. Van Huyssteen 1997: 179.

54. Van Huyssteen 1997: 168.

55. Murphy 1990.

56. Murphy 1990; Murphy and Ellis 1996: 10–15.

57. Murphy 1996.

58. Murphy 1996: 36–37; 1997: 22, 24–26, 28, 31. See also Murphy and Ellis 1996: 8–10.

59. Murphy 1997: 31.

60. Murphy 1997: 28–29, 31–32.

61. Murphy 1990: 86; see also p. 87.

62. McGrath 2001; 2002; 2003; 2004.

63. McGrath 2004: 13–14, 56–57.
64. Wilson 2003: 956.
65. McGrath 2004: 112, 114.
66. McGrath 2004: 58, 107; emphasis removed.
67. McGrath 2004: 144; emphases removed.
68. McGrath 2004: 146.
69. McGrath 1998: chap. 5; 2004: 154.
70. McGrath 2004: 145.
71. McGrath 2004: 114–15; emphases removed.
72. McGrath 2004: ix.
73. Sanders and Wegter-McNelly 1999: 19.
74. Wilson 2005: 49.

Chapter Eight

God Acknowledged: Refashioned Theology

The empirical approach to theology looks at the world to see what God is like; what does the world in fact suggest about God? That God acts as the great mathematical orderer? The producer of chaos? The great lover? The great tyrant? Or what? This book aims not only to substantiate and elaborate doing theology empirically, but actually to start doing it.

In particular, this chapter turns to an application of the key-theological method as an example. It focuses, to create a prolegomenon for a key-theology, on happiness, one of the chief aims—if not the chief aim—of many people.

Because scientific research suggests how the universe and its facets (including human beings) operate and come into existence, science can—and does—talk about happiness. It suggests how people might increase their happiness, for instance; it also says these strategies have evolved in humans. Key-theological reflection would consider both of these aspects of God at work. The happiness strategies science uncovers thus say something about how a person might live in tune with the work of God. The study of happiness and other human qualities should offer the opportunity to learn about people's spiritual selves and the nature of God in relationship to them.

Another visit to the method of key-theology might help further orient the picture before providing more detail on God and happiness.

TO THINK KEY-THEOLOGICALLY,
THINK SCIENTIFICALLY

This book tries to justify and work out the idea that scientific method leads to truthful knowledge, that theology should follow science's method, and how theology could do this. When theology does do this, it becomes "key-theology."

The subject of key-theology, what it addresses, comprises the world and making sense of living. The object of key-theology, what it centrally refers to, is God.

1. Key-theology peers at the world through the lens called "God," the core idea by which it tries to find meaning and make sense of people's lives and the world.

   Key-theology adopts the empirical or scientific method. Several people have considered this matter or something like it before; the current exploration has pushed prior deliberations about this further, and looked more deeply at the data key-theology entertains. How might key-theologians investigate with science the nature of God? How might they think theologically with the method and results of science? Three more ground rules help apply the scientific method to key-theology, points that especially rely on the work of Ian Barbour:[1]

2. Key-theology focuses on the creation of models.
3. Key-theology depends on experience, some of which is public and repeatable.
4. Key-theology can find inspiration in anything, and every event becomes a potential datum theology can measure itself against.

These last three points about method apply to all the sciences, but the degrees to which each applies vary across the sciences according to their respective aims and peculiarities. The rules also vary by degree from the sciences to key-theology.[2] For instance, a key-theologian builds her or his key-theology from universals (public and repeatable experiences) and shared basic theories, but also in an individualized way according to her or his unique life story, biology, and personal peculiarities. Physics, in contrast, does not usually build its theories in individualized ways. While key-theology differs by degree from many other fields of inquiry, it still follows the same basic method. This—an empirical stance on the nature of God—promotes a radical but exciting theological challenge: What God exists?

What follows develops the above numbered points 1–4 about method. It tries to understand with them something about God and the spiritual nature of human beings.

Questions from a Common Method

Addressable questions that now arise include:

- What types of models ought key-theology to focus on and where might it find them—for example, models like those in physics or like those in history?
- How does key-theology depend on experience—for example, to what extent can the core idea for God within a system of key-theology change if it conflicts with experience?
- To what data ought key-theology especially pay attention—for example, data like those in quantum physics or like those in historical analysis?

The proposed beginning to a key-theology uses happiness to illuminate this method and, in doing so, addresses three more questions:[3]

- How does happiness relate to God?
- How does happiness relate to the spiritual nature of humans?
- How might people become happier in a spiritual way?

TO GAIN KNOWLEDGE OF
PEOPLE'S SPIRITUAL SELVES, USE SCIENCE

The Spiritual Nature of Human Beings

The relationship between happiness and people's spiritual nature continues the discussion. First, for clarification, what constitutes this spiritual nature? The answer to this question depends on the idea of God. The foundational approach taken here reduces approximately to this:

> God is responsible for all that happens and for everything that exists, did exist, and will exist.

This statement takes seriously the oneness of monism; no devil or other reality exists independent of God.[4] Further, God, by being responsible for all that exists and happens, transcends everything; nothing but God transcends everything. It also means every thing and every event is spiritual, including all of each person.

This understanding of God differs from the more typical point of view. Religious thinkers tend to discern a particular aspect of God—love, for example—that they want to associate with the word "God." They reduce God to a facet of everything (but, they judge, the most important facet) or to a being alongside other beings (but, they judge, surpassing all other beings). To recognize God entails that they distinguish God from everything they could or do experience. They approximate the whole in order to know it.

Religious thinkers similarly single out aspects of their being and behavior as especially spiritual; they bifurcate themselves to help them understand and live. Some forms of happiness, for instance, exceed eating favorite foods and other such physical activities; that "extra" constitutes the spiritual in relation to happiness. Western culture thereby artificially isolates a sense of "spiritual" in which the spiritual self refers to a "moreness" that surpasses what people do or are physically.

Does the sense of "spiritual" advocated in this chapter (that everything is spiritual, not the cultural sense of the "extra") empty the word and leave it redundant? Perhaps "everything is spiritual" produces a tautology like "all water is wet." Perhaps it turns spiritual ideas into "nothing but words," as Viggo Mortensen suggests, "words . . . we could just as well do without."[5] Perhaps a fully naturalistic account suffices.

Not so. "Everything is spiritual" contributes something that atheistic accounts may overlook. It emphasizes the importance of subjective experience and the entanglement of God with the world (in a way that needs elaborating). It points to an approach to life and meaning that people usually fail to notice. It starts toward a more wholesome perspective on what comprises the real and significant, the nature of the human self, and how people might behave.

This idea for "God" also allows the key-theologies built from it to feel true because this God symbol feels as though it refers to something that exists. Everything known for sure to exist does exist, and everything known for sure to happen does happen. Most people feel something is responsible for these existences and happenings. That "something" this chapter calls God.

God's relationship with the world therefore impinges on all facets of the world. God makes a difference to the world. Key-theology ought therefore to have something to say to each of the sciences, and each science ought to have something to say to key-theology. Together they ought empirically to develop a theologically informed science and a scientifically informed key-theology.

Key-Theological Use of Science

The above sought a beginning point from which to comprehend the spiritual nature of human beings. Now the discussion can turn to the nature of happiness.[6]

Happiness developed through human evolution. As Robert Wright relates: people "are designed to *pursue* happiness; and the attainment of Darwinian goals—sex, status, and so on—often brings happiness, at least for a while. Still, the frequent *absence* of happiness is what keeps [people] pursuing it, and thus makes [them] productive."[7] People naturally desire it and should seek to achieve it. Striving toward greater happiness continues in each person as an innate drive, and the genes that produce it must help the species under natural selection.

Science suggests how the world, including human beings, operates—including, therefore, what people can do to become happier. Research in social psychology helps divulge this information: it suggests ways to live that increase happiness and it relates conditions under which these ways tend to work.[8] People experience, for instance, what Mihaly Csikszentmihalyi calls "flow," when an activity absorbs them and time flies.[9] In flow, they optimally engage their skills and talents. In flow, they achieve a sense of satisfaction, meaning, purpose, control, and greater happiness. People should open themselves to such scientific findings (noting the qualified nature of scientific results) in their quest for greater happiness. The class of drugs that includes Prozac offers another example of scientific findings that can lead to increased happiness, at least over the short term for some people.

The findings of science tell not only how to become happier but also how to become happier spiritually. This claim may seem odd because Western culture usually applies the word "spiritual" to something other

than the only physical and natural. How does increasing happiness
through scientific ways relate to people's spiritual selves? How is this
becoming happier spiritually? Does taking Prozac constitute a spiritual
activity?

The operation of God produces the world science seeks to describe.
Science, therefore, tells how God works, how the spiritual operates. Science studies the spiritual. In particular, scientific research on how behaviors or drugs promote happiness tells how the spiritual operates vis-à-vis
happiness, and helps in devising ways to increase happiness spiritually.

If happiness raising constitutes the or one of the chief motivations
for humans, the seeking of happiness ought to sit at the core of a key-
theology. To find out about the nature of God means to find out about
the spiritual nature of human beings. It therefore means finding out
about happiness and relating the findings to what else theology might
suggest.[10]

Learning from science about happiness increases spiritual (key-
theological) understanding both in the broad understanding of "spiritual" and in the restricted sense that refers to behaviors surpassing physical activities like eating. This follows because the state of spiritual
happiness involves or equals subjective well-being, which co-occurs
with biological happiness, a particular range of dopamine, serotonin,
and their receptors in the brain.[11] The spiritual and the physical highlight different facets of the same phenomenon but, in principle, view the
same things. Thus, the spiritual can equal the biological (though people
may mistakenly think of the spiritual as different because they consider
it to involve but exceed the biological). Further, the spiritual can provide ways to achieve the biological, ways to raise the level of happiness
measured through biology and psychology. The spiritual can also invoke an ethical dimension. Biological and spiritual happiness so intertwine with and depend on one another as to become inseparable.

Limitations of Following a Natural Desire

Life—especially life lived spiritually—meets more complexity than a
mere, "Three scientifically proven steps to increase spirituality and happiness." The following questions help pursue this recognition. Traditionalists might ask, "If God wants happiness for people, why do they
not feel happy all the time?" Neuro-pyscho-biologists might ask:

- If happiness is biologically important for people, why do they not feel happy all the time?
- Why do people possess the state of happiness?
- Why do people want to feel happy?
- Why do people not want to feel unhappy?
- For what biological reason do people not feel happy all the time?
- Unhappiness does not necessarily equal the lack of happiness. Does feeling no unhappiness equate to feeling happy all the time?
- Why do people possess unhappy feelings that motivate them to want the happy ones?

Part of an answer may follow like this:

- If people felt bountifully happy all the time, they would not desire it. They would take it for granted like the attraction of gravity. So happiness in its degrees and absence serves useful purposes. What are they?
- Like the experience of pain, unhappiness means something needs fixing. It evolved in human beings as an internal warning system that alerts them of danger.
- Paralleling this, happiness functions to say the person is OK, safe, out of danger—it constitutes the involuntary neural and subjective state for when the person does not feel unhappy. The desire for it also evolved into human beings.
- More than an alert, unhappiness also drives people. It impels them automatically to desire and seek happiness rather than to feel unhappy. It pushes them automatically to try to escape unhappiness and the dangers unhappiness represents.
- Pushing people to obtain more and more happiness, however, the drive to escape from unhappiness continues beyond the fulfillment of its immediate goal.

This answer leaves much unanswered. The happiness-spirituality relationship becomes more complex than the biological function of happiness and unhappiness. If happiness evolved in humans, so did aggression and other negative feelings and behaviors. Does pursuing them also constitute a spiritual activity? Further, writing a book could so engross the author that he fails to notice a fire about to consume children trapped in the building opposite; happiness-increasing activities such as flow could absorb a person to the extent she does not see something wrong, something she would otherwise notice and do something about. Ill-pursued or even immoral happiness-seeking exists. A moral dimension pervades happiness seeking, something with which the spiritual also concerns itself and which the above reliance on scientific research did not address. (Key-theology could develop the moral dimension in a similar way to the above approach to happiness, basing it on inherent values in human existence, given the above idea of God and that God acts consistently.)[12]

Making Decisions toward a Balance

A way into this follows a traditional idea augmented with biology. Modern Westerners think highly of freedom. Western culture holds it as a paramount virtue for each individual, for each society, and, increasingly, for other animals and nature. Free will comprises an aspect of human freedom. A dictionary defines "will" as: "The power of making a reasoned choice or decision or of controlling one's own actions." "Free will" equals, according to the dictionary, "freedom of decision or of choice between alternatives."[13] Free will exists and people experience it. That biology and culture influence and direct a person's mind to believe in her autonomy does not deem her free will illusory. But it becomes complex. The author freely chooses to edit the book, though his sense of obligation—under pressure from others and himself to finish before its deadline—in part influences his choice. The idea "free will" can overrate the sense of choice because it often ignores the other factors—biological, cultural, genetic, and coincidental—that influence and sometimes determine how people act, feel, and think. Free will is usually not all or nothing; humans possess a degree of it. How to understand it leads to another discussion.

A perspective on free will starts with evolution: will, including free will, emerges in and as a result of human biological evolution. Free will requires, for instance, self-awareness—that the person can see and consciously weigh up alternatives—a characteristic that seems to arise from the evolved human capacities for consciousness and memory.[14] The degree of self-awareness and therefore ability to choose constitutes a human talent that, in its magnitude, distinguishes humans from other known animals. Because of this gift, free will offers advantages for humanity's survival and the capacity to adapt to different physical and social environments. Because of it, though, life becomes more complex.

People now must choose ways to behave that are best for them, including those that lead to greater happiness. They now must choose between often competing, perhaps conflicting, inclinations, many of which offer positive or desirable values.

Choices allow the person to balance happiness with its competing drives and each person can choose how to achieve that balance. People can ask what "happiness is best for me" means. What is "best for me" also constitutes something human self-awareness enables people to decide—from memories about what their previous decisions led to and from cultural wisdom about what others' decisions led to. They can ask:

> What for me balances happiness and other things, like justice? Where do I place my priorities in life? I can discern the limits to my happiness seeking in each situation; it feels like trying to discern the roots of my self. The "best" way to act emerges from a constant process of discovery, a discovery of what each inclination that competes within me means for me and who I am in relation to it.

This choosing offers another place for science to help. Key-theologians can examine each inclination within its evolutionary and behavioral contexts, results obtained through scientific inquiry. This helps in understanding the inclinations and why people respond in the ways they do. It helps show how to achieve or avoid any of the traits—including happiness—that the person may choose to follow, explore, or avoid. Science allows a pause in the process and an examination of behavior.

Decision making between inclinations becomes significant spiritually because people employ their free will to choose and achieve a balance between them. This unique ability of human beings equals, in more traditional terms, self-awareness at the core of God. Self-awareness constitutes the human image of God. Spirituality (traditionally, God's way for humans) asks people's self-awareness to develop themselves as best they can.

> To live spiritually means to take account of all the aspects of me and to choose the best for me from among them. To live spiritually means to ask what a balance between my inclinations and attributes means, and then to seek it. In particular, if I want spiritual happiness, I should decide what comprises the balance of happiness with the other demands on me (what appears more important for me to choose)—including perhaps that I also seek justice—and try to achieve it.

The passage above that introduced the spiritual side of human beings referred to this discernment and action and called it "moreness." It requires self-awareness and this carries it beyond what the person does physically.

To seek greater happiness is a natural drive, but not one anyone must follow because science or anything or anyone else says so. *Individuals* can decide *if* they want greater happiness and, if they do want it, *how* they might achieve it—possibly with input from scientific research— and *how* they might balance it with other inclinations. In this case, fact does not define value.

TO GAIN KNOWLEDGE OF GOD, USE SCIENCE

To explore and decide between inclinations can add to knowledge of people's spiritual selves. It can also add to what key-theologians know of God. A series of questions and answers helps demonstrate this:

- Where does key-theology find knowledge of God? The universe presents the only face of God people can see or comprehend. Key-theology must inquire of the universe, therefore, to find out about God vis-à-vis humans.
- How does key-theology gain this knowledge from the universe? Science shows how reality functions and offers the best way to understand the universe. It thus tells about aspects of God people can know.
- What aspects of knowledge of the universe pertain particularly to God? What key-theology knows of human spiritual characteristics also comprises knowledge of God and—insofar as key-theology considers them the most important in the universe—scientific understanding of them concerns what lies centrally in God.

Key-theology discovers the nature of God from the spiritual nature of human beings and it discovers that with science. Conversely, the nature of God as it pertains to people's lives constitutes their spiritual selves. Scientific knowledge of people's (spiritual) selves, therefore, fits hand in glove with knowledge of God.

This discussion lends itself to a related question: Since the spiritual nature of human beings includes happiness, does God enjoy happiness too? Might key-theology personify God and say God achieves greater happiness the same way people can? This is ridiculous. On the other hand, the sentence, "God feels happy and wants people to feel happy as well," includes two things:

- It includes, "God feels happy," an ontological statement about God's happiness. Inasmuch as God matches or mirrors the spiritual nature of human beings—whatever the extent to which God transcends theologians' versions of these properties—key-theology can personify God as happy. God is also sad, ill, tired, well, and so on. What do subjective qualities mean when applied to God? This divinized version of the qualities becomes so vague and fraught with difficulties that key-theology ought not to pursue them at this time. Further research into the nature of God with respect to human qualities may, however, give them meaning.
- It also assumes God exists. This entails the idea that God creates the universe, the means by which God does this, and therefore that and how God evolves humanity. An important and evolved thrust of humans urges people to increase their happiness. Key-theology might therefore say God "desires" humans' happiness and "creates" people so they seek it. God "encourages" humans to hunt for greater happiness—in balance with other inclinations—and "tells" each person (for instance, through the results of scientific research) how to do it.

CONCLUSIONS

This book proposes a theological methodology that emulates science's. Drawing on happiness as an example, this chapter starts to develop such a key-theology, but only a suggestion for a beginning because similar investigations to that on happiness would launch a more rounded study. Key-theology might not only use such results of scientific research. It could also frame and put to empirical arbitration new hypotheses that involve theological assumptions and the knowledge science has already. It can thus find out about God using empirical techniques, perhaps even launching itself from traditional categories and puzzles such as morality and teleology. Further, when they study the nature of what comprises a human person, scientists become key-theologians undertaking science of God.

Key-theology can empirically know about God with this book's proposal. Also, the God model used (God is responsible for everything) itself has empirical dimensions. As a hypothesis, factors can infirm it, even if it tenaciously resists this; ending up with a hopelessly inconsistent or irrational "God," for instance, calls the model into question. An alternative exists: nothing need be responsible for everything, not even nature. (If nature is responsible, then nature constitutes the God this chapter assumed.) This hopefully satisfies the empiricist challenge of Kai Nielsen, whose case chapter 3 expounded in depth.

Western society desperately needs such accounts. The usual stories culture teaches about the world and human beings involve the evolution of the universe from the big bang to people as biological beings. These explanations brand as primary both matter and the science that seeks to explain it. The West also needs an equal story that makes human experience primary. Key-theology offers that within the account of evolution by advocating the inseparable intertwining of the spiritual and the physical, the human and the material. Evolution becomes as much spiritual as biological or physical, as the monist approach to happiness shows. Scientific research can generate knowledge of God and people's spiritual selves. Thus, the universe that science explains leaves behind the image of cold and mechanical matter. Matter actually involves endless depths and mystery; it ties intimately with human subjectivity. It is spiritual.

NOTES

1. Barbour 1974. See also Murphy 1990; Peacocke 1984; Sharpe and Walgate 1998.
2. Barbour 1974; Clayton 1989a.
3. Sharpe 1998; Sharpe with Bryant 2005.
4. Sharpe 2000.
5. Mortensen 1987: 197.
6. Sharpe 1998.
7. Wright 1994: 298.
8. Sharpe with Bryant 2005.
9. Csikszentmihalyi 1990.
10. Sharpe and Waters 1999.
11. Sharpe 1998: 303–4.
12. Sharpe 2000.
13. *Webster's New World Dictionary.*
14. McCrone 1991.

Postscript

I sometimes hear that writing about theological method should only come from mature theologians reflecting on their lived experience and what they have been writing and working out over many years. The opposite may be true. Younger thinkers may have more original and creative perspectives. Further, a younger theologian's theological method reflects her or his basic theological presuppositions as much as do the systems produced by mature thinkers. It seems more appropriate to expose those theological presuppositions and their roots in the first place with a thorough analysis of and justification for the methodology adopted. Neither ought the theologian only to look at theological method having done theology. Discussion on method should come preliminarily. Then, based on this, doing theology can start. The finer points of method, or questions of its validity, may arise once doing it.

I live in the center of Oxford, England, beside the River Thames, not far from Folly Bridge. The word "folly" derives from a building, a folly that stood over the bridge and from which Roger Bacon observed the heavens. The theological follies of Oxford's undergraduate and graduate students sometimes seem more to the point than the tired elaborations of its famous dons.

Bacon (1220–1292) lived during medieval times. Modernity remembers him because he promoted experimental science well before its rise to dominance.[1] In 1242, he became the first person in Europe to detail how to concoct gunpowder, and he wrote about spectacles, flying machines, and motorized carriages and ships. His career did not always champion the spirit of empiricism, however; early in his career, he lectured in the Paris faculty of arts on Aristotelian and pseudo-Aristotelian works, with few signs of his impending fixation with science.[2] He helped change how to gain knowledge of the physical world. This book proposes a similar change in how to gain knowledge, this time in how to gain theological knowledge.

I aim to follow the example of Bacon. Bacon's folly intrigues me; the word "folly" in his time had its current meaning, the locals apparently considering Bacon's building a "costly structure" that showed "folly in the builder."[3] Perhaps they also thought of his astronomical observations as a folly, given his radical change to an experimental method. Is my folly this book's proposal of a scientific method for key-theology? It may, after all, not end with received Christian theism. History will judge when as much water has passed under my bridge as has passed under Bacon's.

The social justice contextualization of theology, while extraordinarily important, still ranks second to what constitutes truth and how this emerges from and is responsible to experience. The modern West, in fact the emerging modern global culture, cannot achieve social justice if its belief system(s), however articulated, bases itself on dogma not founded on all of human experience and knowledge, and not open to adjustment as experience shows new aspects of reality.

NOTES

1. Welch 1992: 174–77.
2. *Encyclopedia Britannica.*
3. *Oxford English Dictionary.*

References

Apczynski, John V. 1977. *Doers of the Word*. Missoula, MT: Scholars Press.
——. 1979. Integrative Theology: Polanyian Proposal for Theological Foundations. *Theological Studies* 40:1, pp. 23–43.
Armstrong, Karen. 2000. *The Battle for God*. New York: Ballantine Books.
Austin, William H. 1967. Waves, Particles, and Paradoxes. *Rice University Studies* 53:2, pp. 6–103.
——. 1976. *The Relevance of Natural Science to Theology*. New York: Barnes & Noble Books.
Bambrough, Renford. 1969. *Reason, Truth, and God*. London: Methuen & Co.
Barbour, Ian G. 1960. The Methods of Science and Religion. In *Science Ponders Religion*, ed. Harlow Shapley (New York: Appleton-Century-Crofts), pp. 196–215.
——. 1974. *Myths, Models, and Paradigms: A Comparative Study in Science and Religion*. New York: Harper & Row.
Barnhart, Joe E. 1976. Has God-Talk Talked Itself to Death? *Southwest Philosophical Studies* 1, pp. 9–15.
Basinger, David. 1981. Kai Nielsen and the Nature of Theistic Ethics. *Journal of the Evangelical Theological Society* 24:3, pp. 233–38.
Baum, Gregory. 1971. Styles of Theological Reflection for the Future. *Theology Today* 28:3, pp. 354–59.
Birch, Charles, and John B. Cobb, Jr. 1981. *The Liberation of Life*. Cambridge: Cambridge University Press.
Black, Max. 1962. *Models and Metaphors: Studies in Language and Philosophy*. Ithaca, NY: Cornell University Press.
Bochenski, J. M. 1965. *The Logic of Religion*. New York: New York University Press.

Borhek, James T., and Richard F. Curtis. 1975. *A Sociology of Belief.* New York: John Wiley & Son.

Brown, Harold I. 1977. Objective Knowledge in Science and the Humanities. *Diogenes* No. 97 (Spring), pp. 85–102.

Brown, Ronald. 1977. Creativity, Religion, and Science I. *Theoria to Theory* 11:4, pp. 275–86.

———. 1978. Creativity, Religion, and Science II. Experimentation. *Theoria to Theory* 12 (April), pp. 31–47.

Brown, Sanborn C. 1966. Can Physics Contribute to Theology? *Zygon: Journal of Religion and Science* 1 (1): 14–21.

Brown, Stuart. 1974. [Review of *Skepticism*, by Kai Nielsen (1973c).] *Philosophy* 49, pp. 220–21.

Brownhill, R. J. 1968. Michael Polanyi and the Problem of Personal Knowledge. *Journal of Religion* 48:2, pp. 115–23.

Burhoe, Ralph Wendell. 1975. The Human Prospect and the "Lord of History." *Zygon: Journal of Religion and Science* 10:3, pp. 299–375.

Buri, Fritz. 1968. How Can We Still Speak Responsibly of God? *McCormick Quarterly* 21:2, pp. 185–97.

Burrell, David. 1979. Theology and the Linguistic Turn. *Communio: International Catholic Review* 6:1, pp. 95–112.

Campbell, C. M. 1974. On Kaufman's "Method." Mimeographed paper.

Capps, Walter H. 1972. Reflections on Theological Reconstruction. *The Lutheran Quarterly* 24 (November): 387–96.

Carey, John J. 1975. Ideology and Theology. *Perspectives in Religious Studies* 2 (Spring), pp. 81–95.

Carnes, John R. 1976. Metamathematics and Dogmatic Theology. *Scottish Journal of Theology* 29:6, pp. 501–16.

———. 1982. *Axiomatics and Dogmatics.* New York: Oxford University Press.

Cauthen, Kenneth. 1967. [Review of *The Relevance of Physics*, by Stanley L. Jaki (1966).] *Zygon: Journal of Religion and Science* 2 (June), pp. 203–6.

Charlesworth, M. J., ed. 1974. *The Problems of Religious Language.* Englewood Cliffs, NJ: Prentice-Hall.

Chenu, M. D. 1959. *Is Theology a Science?* Faith & Fact Books, vol. 2. London: Burns & Oates.

Clarke, W. Norris. 1976. Analogy and the Meaningfulness of Language about God: A Reply to Kai Nielsen. *Thomist* 40, pp. 61–95.

Clayton, Philip. 1989a. *Explanation from Physics to Theology: An Essay in Rationality and Religion.* New Haven, CT: Yale University Press.

———. 1989b. Disciplining Relativism and Truth. *Zygon: Journal of Religion and Science* 24: 315–34.

———. 1997. *God and Contemporary Science.* Edinburgh: Edinburgh University Press.

Clifford, Paul R. 1968. The Factual Reference of Theological Assertions. *Religious Studies* 3, pp. 339–46.

Coburn, Robert C. 1969. A Neglected Use of Theological Language. In *New Essays on Religious Language*, ed. Dallas M. High (New York: Oxford University Press), pp. 215ff.

Colwell, Gary. 1981. The Flew-Nielsen Challenge: A Critical Exposition of Its Methodology. *Religious Studies* 17:3, pp. 323–42.

Comstock, W. Richard. 1971. The Present and Future of Religion. In *Religion and Man: An Introduction*, ed. W. Richard Comstock (New York: Harper & Row), pp. 621–29.

Cooper, Brian G. 1969. Religion and Technology: Toward Dialogue. *Main Currents in Modern Thought* 26: 10–13.

Coulson, C. A. 1958. *Science and the Idea of God*. 11th Eddington Memorial Lectures. Cambridge, UK: Cambridge University Press.

Crow, R. Eugene. 1976. [Review of *Myths, Models, and Paradigms*, by Ian G. Barbour (1974).] *Foundations* 19 (January–March), pp. 92–94.

Csikszentmihalyi, Mihaly. 1990. *Flow: The Psychology of Optimal Experience*. New York: Harper & Row.

Cupitt, Don. 1975. God and the Futures of Man. In *Man and Nature*, ed. Hugh Montefiore (London: William Collins Sons), pp. 180–94.

———. 1976. *The Worlds of Science and Religion*. London: Sheldon Press.

———. 1981. *Taking Leave of God*. New York: Crossroad.

Cushing, James T., C. F. Delaney, and Gary M. Gutting. 1984. *Science and Reality: Recent Work in the Philosophy of Science. Essays in Honor of Ernan McMullin*. Notre Dame, IN: University of Notre Dame Press.

Daly, C. B. 1969. Metaphysics and the Limits of Language. In *New Essays on Religious Language*, ed. Dallas M. High (New York: Oxford University Press), pp. 97–126.

d'Aquili, Eugene G., and Andrew B. Newberg. 1999. *The Mystical Mind: Probing the Biology of Religious Experience*. Minneapolis: Fortress Press.

Davies, Paul. 1983. *God and the New Physics*. New York: Simon & Schuster.

Diamond, Malcolm L. 1975. Introduction: The Challenge of Contemporary Empiricism. In *The Logic of God: Theology and Falsification*, ed. Malcolm L. Diamond and Thomas V. Litzenburg, Jr. (Indianapolis: Bobbs-Merrill Co.), pp. 1–54.

Diamond, Malcolm L, and Thomas V. Litzenburg, Jr., ed. 1975. *The Logic of God: Theology and Falsification*. Indianapolis: Bobbs-Merrill Co.

Dilley, Frank. 1976. The Status of Religious Belief. *American Philosophical Quarterly* 13:1, pp. 41–47.

Dillistone, F. W. 1962. How Far Must Theological Thinking Proceed by Analogy? *London Quarterly and Holborn Review* 187, pp. 253–57.

Dilman, Ilham. 1981. Nielsen on "Wisdom's Philosophy of Religion." *Philosophical Investigations* 4:2, pp. 50–57.

Doppelt, Gerald. 1978. Kuhn's Epistemological Relativism: An Interpretation and Defense. *Inquiry* 21:1 (Spring), pp. 33–86.

Dowey, Edward A. 1958. Tillich, Barth, and the Criteria of Theology. *Theology Today* 15:1 (April), pp. 43–58.

Dulles, Avery. 1976. Method in Fundamental Theology: Reflections on David Tracy's *Blessed Rage for Order*. *Theological Studies* 37:2, pp. 304–16.

———. 1979. Hermeneutical Theology. *Communio: International Catholic Review* 6:1 (Spring), pp. 16–37.

Duthie, Alan S. 1965. Is Theology a Science? *Evangelical Quarterly* 37:1, pp. 3–8.

Eister, Allan W. 1978. Religion and Science in A.D. 1977: Conflict? Accommodation? Mutual Indifference? Or What? *Journal for the Scientific Study of Religion* 17:4, pp. 347–58.

Enç, Berent. 1976. Reference of Theoretical Terms. *Noûs* 10:3, pp. 261–82.

Evans, Donald D. 1968. Differences between Scientific and Religious Assertions. In *Science and Religion: New Perspectives on the Dialogue*, ed. Ian G. Barbour (London: SCM Press), pp. 101–33.

Fawcett, Thomas. 1970. *The Symbolic Language of Religion: An Introductory Study.* London: SCM Press.

Ferré, Frederick. 1974. [Review of *Myths, Models, and Paradigms: A Comparative Study in Science and Religion*, by Ian G. Barbour (1974).] *Religious Education* 69:6, pp. 729–30.

———. 1976. *Shaping the Future: Resources for the Post-Modern World.* New York: Harper & Row.

Feyerabend, Paul. 1975. *Against Method.* London; Atlantic Highlands, NJ: NLB; Humanities Press.

Flew, Antony. 1951. *Essays in Logic and Language.* First Series. Oxford: Blackwell.

Flew, Antony, and Alasdair Macintyre, eds. 1955. *New Essays in Philosophical Theology.* London: SCM Press.

Gallus, Alexander. 1972–1974. A Biofunctional Theory of Religion. *Current Anthropology* 13:5, 15:1, pp. 543–68, 92–99.

Gastwirth, Paul. 1972. Concepts of God. *Religious Studies* 8:2 (June), pp. 147–52.

Geach, P. T. 1974. Fallacy and Proof and the Rationality of Religion. *Sophia* 13:2, pp. 1–4.

Gellman, Jerome I. 1977. The Metaphilosophy of Religious Language. *Noûs* 11:2 (May), pp. 151–61.

Gelwick, Richard. 1975. Discovery and theology. *Scottish Journal of Theology* 28 (4): 301–22.

Gilkey, Langdon B. 1963. The Concept of Providence in Contemporary Theology. *The Journal of Religion* 43:3 (July), pp. 171–92.

———. 1969. *Naming the Whirlwind: The Renewal of God Language.* Indianapolis: Bobbs-Merrill Co.

———. 1970. *Religion and the Scientific Future.* New York: Harper & Row.

———. 1971. Empirical Science and Theological Knowing. In *Foundations of Theology: Papers from the International Lonergan Congress 1970*, ed. Philip McShan (Dublin: Gill & Mcmillan), pp. 76–101.

Gill, Jerry H. 1969. The Tacit Structure of Religious Knowing. *International Philosophical Quarterly* 9:4, pp. 533–59.

———, ed. 1974. *Christian Empiricism.* London: Sheldon Press.

Glenn, Alfred A. 1972. Criteria for Theological Models. *Scottish Journal of Theology* 25:3, pp. 296–308.

Godbey, John C. 1969. Brief Remarks on the Need for a Scientific Theology. *Zygon: Journal of Religion and Science* 4 (June), pp. 125–27.

———. 1970. Further Remarks on the Need for a Scientific Theology. *Zygon: Journal of Religion and Science* 5: 194–215.

Greeves, Frederic. 1972. Theism and Atheism [Review of *Contemporary Critiques of Religion*, by Kai Nielsen (1971a).] *Expository Times* 83:7, p. 217.

Griffin, David R. 1973. Gordon Kaufman's Theology: Some Questions. *Journal of the American Academy of Religion* 41:4, pp. 554–72.

Guthrie, Stewart. 1980. A Cognitive Theory of Religion. *Current Anthropology* 21:2 (April), pp. 181–203.

———. 1993. *Faces in the Clouds: A New Theory of Religion.* New York: Oxford University Press.

Hall, Thor. 1974. Theodicy as Test of the Reasonableness of Theology. *Religion in Life* 43:2 (Summer), pp. 204–17.

Hamer, Dean H. 2004. *The God Gene: How Faith Is Hardwired into Our Genes.* New York: Doubleday.

Hanson, R. P. C. 1972. A Marginal Note on Comprehensiveness. *Theology* 75:630 (December), pp. 631–36.

Hardy, Alister. 1966. *The Divine Flame.* London: William Collins Sons.

Hartt, Julian N. 1977. *Theological Method and Imagination.* New York: Seabury Press.

Hazelton, Roger. 1977. Theology and Metaphor. *Religion in Life* 46:1 (Spring), pp. 7–21.

Heim, Karl. 1953. *Christian Faith and Natural Science.* London: SCM Press.

Hennelly, Alfred T. 1977. Theological Method: The Southern Exposure. *Theological Studies* 38:4 (December), pp. 709–35.

Hesse, Mary. 1975a. On the Alleged Incompatibility Between Christianity and Science. In *Man and Nature*, ed. Hugh Montefiore (London: William Collins Sons), pp. 121–31.

———. 1975b. Criteria of Truth in Science and Theology. *Religious Studies* 11:4 (December), pp. 385–400.

Hodges, H. A. 1978. *God beyond Knowledge*. Ed. W. D. Hudson. London: The Macmillan Press.

Hoffman, Robert. 1970. On Being Mindful of "God": Reply to Kai Nielsen. *Religious Studies* 6 (September), pp. 289–90.

Hook, Sidney. 1975. For an Open Minded Naturalism. *Southern Journal of Philosophy* 13:1 (Spring), pp. 127–36.

Horton, Robin, and Ruth Finnegan, eds. 1973. *Modes of Thought: Essays on Thinking in Western and Non-Western Societies.* London: Faber & Faber.

Howe, Leroy T. 1971. Theology and Its Philosophical Commitments. *Scottish Journal of Theology* 24:4 (November), pp. 385–406.

———. 1974. [Review of *Myths, Models, and Paradigms*, by Ian G. Barbour (1974).] *Theology Today* 31:3 (October), pp. 270–72.

Idinopulos, Thomas A. 1972. The "Ultimate Cosmic Agency." *Christian Century* 89:25 (28 June), pp. 719–21.

Jaki, Stanley L. 1966. *The Relevance of Physics*. Chicago: University of Chicago Press.

———. 1974. *Science and Creation: From Eternal Cycles to an Oscillating Universe.* New York: Science History Publications.

———. 1975. A Hundred Years of Two Cultures. *University of Windsor Review* 11:1 (Fall–Winter), pp. 155–79.

———. 1978. *The Road of Science and the Ways to God*. Edinburgh: Scottish Academic Press.

Jastrow, Robert. 1978. *God and the Astronomers*. New York: W. W. Norton & Co.

Jones, Hugh O. 1978. Gordon Kaufman's Perspectival Language. *Religious Studies* 14:1, pp. 89–97.

Kaufman, Gordon D. 1957. Philosophy of Religion and Christian Theology. *Journal of Religion* 37:4 (October), pp. 233–45.

———. 1968. *Systematic Theology: A Historicist Perspective*. New York: Scribner's Sons.

———. 1972. *God the Problem*. Cambridge, MA: Harvard University Press.

———. 1975. *An Essay on Theological Method*. Missoula, MT: Scholars Press.

———. 1976. Christian Theology and the Modernization of the Religions. *Bangalore Theological Forum* 8:2 (July–December), pp. 81–118.

———. 1978. Theological Method and Indigenization: Six Theses. In *A Vision for Man: Essays on Faith, Theology, and Society*, ed. Samuel Amirtham (Madras: The Christian Literature Society), pp. 49–60.

———. 1993. *In Face of Mystery: A Constructive Theology*. Cambridge, MA: Harvard University Press.

King, Robert H. 1973a. *The Meaning of God*. Philadelphia: Fortress Press.

———. 1973b. The Conceivability of God. *Religious Studies* 9:1, pp. 11–22.

King-Farlow, John. 1979. Nielsen and Penelhum on Agents outside Space. *Religious Studies* 15:1 (March), pp. 79–82.

King-Farlow, John, and William Niels Christensen. 1972. *Faith and the Life of Reason*. Dordrecht, Holland: D. Reidel Publishing Co.

Kirkpatrick, David D. 2004. Wrath and Mercy: The Return of the Warrior Jesus. *The New York Times* Section 4, Week in Review (Sunday 4 April), pp. 1, 6.

Klein, Kenneth H. 1974. *Positivism and Christianity*. The Hague: Martinus Nijhoff.

Klinefelter, Donald S. 1973. God and Rationality: A Critique of the Theology of Thomas F. Torrance. *Journal of Religion* 53:1 (January), pp. 117–35.

Konyndyk, Kenneth. 1977. Verificationism and Dogmatism. *International Journal for Philosophy of Religion* 8:1, pp. 1–17.

Kordig, Carl R. 1968. On Prescribing Description. *Synthese* 18, pp. 459–61.

——. 1971. *The Justification of Scientific Change*. Dordrecht, Holland: D. Reidel Publishing Co.

Kress, Robert. 1979. Theological Methods: Praxis and Liberation. *Communio: International Catholic Review* 6:1 (Spring), pp. 113–34.

Kuhn, Thomas S. 1970. *The Structure of Scientific Revolutions*. 2nd ed. Chicago: University of Chicago Press.

Langford, Thomas. 1966. Michael Polanyi and the Task of Theology. *Journal of Religion* 46, pp. 45–55.

Leatherdale, W. H. 1974. *The Role of Analogy, Model, and Metaphor in Science*. Amsterdam and New York: North-Holland; Elsevier.

Livingston, James C. 1973. [Review of *Contemporary Critiques of Religion*, by Kai Nielsen (1971a).] *Thomist* 37 (April), pp. 396–404.

Lonergan, Bernard J. F. 1972. *Method in Theology*. New York: The Seabury Press.

Louth, Andrew. 1983. *Discerning the Mystery: An Essay on the Nature of Theology*. Oxford: Oxford University Press.

Lovell, Bernard. 1979. *In the Centre of Immensities*. London: Hutchinson & Co.

MacCormac, Earl R. 1976. *Metaphor and Myth in Science and Religion*. Durham, NC: Duke University Press.

Machan, Tibor R. 1977. Kuhn, Paradigm Choice and the Arbitrariness of Aesthetic Criteria in Science. *Theory and Decision* 8:14 (October), pp. 361–62.

MacIntosh, Douglas Clyde. 1919. *Theology as an Empirical Science*. New York: The Macmillan Co.

MacKay, Donald M. 1974. "Complementarity" in Scientific and Theological Thinking. *Zygon: Journal of Religion and Science* 9:3, pp. 225–44.

MacLaren, Elizabeth. 1976. *The Nature of Belief*. London: Sheldon Press.

Macquarrie, John. 1970a. On Gods and Gardeners. In *Perspectives in Education, Religion, and the Arts*, ed. Howard Kiefer and Milton Munitz (Albany: State University of New York Press), pp. 105–15.

———. 1970b. Philosophy of Religion (a Response). In *Perspectives in Education, Religion, and the Arts*, ed. Howard Kiefer and Milton Munitz (Albany: State University of New York Press), pp. 157–62.

———. 1979. Existentialism and Theological Method. *Communio: International Catholic Review* 6:1 (Spring), pp. 5–15.

Margenau, Henry. 1947. Western Culture, Scientific Method and the Problem of Ethics. *American Journal of Physics* 15:3, pp. 218–28.

———. 1950. *The Nature of Physical Reality*. New York: McGraw-Hill Book Co.

———. 1955. Knowledge, Faith, and Physics. *Main Currents in Modern Thought* 11, pp. 108–10.

———. 1960a. Science, Philosophy, and Religion. *Dalhousie Review* 39:4, pp. 447–61.

———. 1960b. Truth in Science and Religion. In *Science Ponders Religion*, ed. Harlow Shapley (New York: Appleton-Century-Crofts), pp. 100–116.

———. 1964. *Ethics and Science*. Princeton, NJ: D. Van Nostrand Co.

Martin, J. A., Jr. 1972. Review Article: The Future of Empirical Theology. *Religious Studies* 8:1 (March), pp. 71–76.

Martin, James Alfred. 1966. *The New Dialogue between Philosophy and Theology*. London: Adam & Charles Black.

Martin, Michael. 1978. Theological Statements, Phenomenalistic Language, and Confirmation. *Religious Studies* 14:2 (June), pp. 217–21.

Martland, Thomas R. 1963. The Relating of Scientific and Religious Interpretations. *Journal of Bible and Religion* 31 (April), pp. 124–28.

Mavrodes, George I. 1964. God and Verification. *Canadian Journal of Theology* 10:3, pp. 187–91.

McClorry, Brian B. 1974. [Review of *Skepticism*, by Kai Nielsen (1973c).] *Heythrop Journal* 15, pp. 80–81.

———. 1975. [Review of *Ethics without God*, by Kai Nielsen (1973d).] *Heythrop Journal* 16, pp. 74–77.

McCrone, John. 1991. *The Ape that Spoke: Language and the Evolution of the Human Mind*. New York: Morrow.

McFague, Sallie. 1982. *Metaphorical Theology: Models of God in Religious Language*. Philadelphia: Fortress Press.

McGrath, Alister E. 1998. *The Foundations of Dialogue in Science and Religion*. Oxford: Blackwell Publishers.

———. 1999. *Science and Religion: An Introduction*. Oxford: Blackwell Publishers.

———. 2001. *A Scientific Theology. Volume 1, Nature*. Edinburgh: T&T Clark.

———. 2002. *A Scientific Theology. Volume 2, Reality*. London: T&T Clark.

———. 2003. *A Scientific Theology. Volume 3, Theory*. London: T&T Clark.

———. 2004. *The Science of God: An Introduction to Scientific Theology*. London: T&T Clark International.

McLain, F. Michael. 1969. On Theological Models. *Harvard Theological Review* 62:2, pp. 155–87.

McMullin, Ernan. 1974. The Two Faces of Science. *Review of Metaphysics* 27:4 (June), pp. 655–76.

Meland, Bernard E., ed. 1969. *The Future of Empirical Theology*. Chicago: University of Chicago Press.

Miles, John A., Jr. 1977. Burhoe, Barbour, Mythology, and Sociobiology. *Zygon: Journal of Religion and Science* 12:1, pp. 42–71.

Miller, David L. 1974. *The New Polytheism: Rebirth of Gods and Goddesses.* New York: Harper & Row.

Miller, James B. 1972. Theological Modeling and Experimental Theology: A Call for Theological Responsibility. *Zygon: Journal of Religion and Science* 7:1, pp. 20–29.

Mitchell, Basil. 1973. *The Justification of Religious Belief.* New York: Seabury Press.

Montgomery, John Warwick. 1966. The Theologian's Craft. *Concordia Theological Monthly* 37, pp. 67–98.

Morrow, Lance. 1979. In the Beginning: God and Science. *Time* 113:6 (5 February), pp. 69–70.

Mortensen, Viggo. 1987. The Status of the Science-Religion Dialogue. In *Evolution and Creation: A European Perspective*, ed. Svend Andersen and Arthur R. Peacocke (Aarhus, Denmark: Aarhus University Press), pp. 192–203.

Murphy, Nancey. 1990. *Theology in the Age of Scientific Reasoning.* Ithaca, NY: Cornell University Press.

———. 1996. *Beyond Liberalism and Fundamentalism: How Modern and Postmodern Philosophy Set the Theological Agenda.* Valley Forge, PA: Trinity Press International.

———. 1997. *Reconciling Theology and Science: A Radical Reformation Perspective.* Kitchener, ON: Pandora Press.

Murphy, Nancey, and George F. R. Ellis. 1996. *On the Moral Nature of the Universe: Theology, Cosmology, and Ethics.* Theology and the Sciences Series. Minneapolis: Fortress Press.

Muser, Donald W. 1977. Two Types of Scientific Theology: Burhoe and Nygren. *Zygon: Journal of Religion and Science* 12:1 (March), pp. 72–87.

Needham, Rodney. 1972. *Belief, Language, and Experience.* Oxford: Basil Blackwell.

Negrotti, M. 1971. Scientific Method and Legitimation of Sociology. *Scientia* 106:9-10, pp. 836–61.

Newberg, Andrew B., Eugene G. d'Aquili, and Vance Rause. 2001. *Why God Won't Go Away: Brain Science and the Biology of Belief.* New York: Ballantine Books.

Nielsen, Kai. 1958. Religion and the Modern Predicament. *Humanist* 18:1, pp. 12–31.

———. 1960. Can a Way of Life Be Justified? *Indian Journal of Philosophy* 1:3, pp. 164–74.

———. 1961a. Is God So Powerful That He Doesn't Even Have to Exist? In *Religious Experience and Truth: A Symposium*, ed. Sidney Hook (New York: New York University Press), pp. 270–81.

———. 1961b. Some Remarks on the Independence of Morality from Religion. *Mind* 70:278, pp. 175–86.

———. 1962a. On Speaking of God. *Theoria* 28:2, pp. 110–37.

———. 1962b. "Christian Positivism" and the Appeal to Religious Experience. *Journal of Religion* 42, pp. 248–61.

———. 1962c. Morality and God: Some Questions for Mr. Macintyre. *Philosophical Quarterly* 12:47, pp. 129–37.

———. 1963a. Eschatological Verification. *Canadian Journal of Theology* 9:4, pp. 271–81.

———. 1963b. Can Faith Validate God-Talk? *Theology Today* 20:2, pp. 158–73.

———. 1964a. An Examination of an Alleged Theological Basis of Morality. *Illif Review* 21:2, pp. 39–49.

———. 1964b. Linguistic Philosophy and "The Meaning of Life." *Cross Currents* 14:3, pp. 313–34.

———. 1964c. God-Talk. *Sophia* 3:3, pp. 15–19.

———. 1965a. God and Verification Again. *Canadian Journal of Theology* 11:2, pp. 135–41.

———. 1965b. Religious Perplexity and Faith. *Crane Review* 8:1, pp. 1–17.

———. 1966a. On Fixing the Reference Range of "God." *Religious Studies* 2:1, pp. 13–36.

———. 1966b. Linguistic Philosophy and Beliefs. *Journal of Existentialism* 6:24, pp. 421–37.

———. 1967a. God as a Human Projection. *Lock Haven Review* 9, pp. 58–63.

———. 1967b. On Believing that God Exists. *Southern Journal of Philosophy* 5, pp. 167–72.

———. 1967c. Wittgensteinian Fideism. *Philosophy* 42:161, pp. 191–209.

———. 1968a. Religion and Naturalistic Humanism: Some Remarks on Hook's Critique of Religion. In *Sidney Hook and the Contemporary World: Essays on the Problematic Intelligence*, ed. Paul Kurtz (New York: The John Day Co.), pp. 257–80.

———. 1968b. Comments on Empiricism and Theism. *Sophia* 7:3, pp. 12–17.

———. 1969a. The Significance of God-talk. *Religious Humanism* 3, pp. 16–21.

———. 1969b. Language and the Concept of God. *Question* 2, pp. 34–52.

———. 1970a. Humanism and Atheism. *Religious Humanism* 4, pp. 29–33.

———. 1970b. In Defense of Atheism. In *Perspectives in Education, Religion, and the Arts*, ed. Howard Kiefer and Milton Munitz (Albany: State University of New York Press), pp. 127–55.

———. 1970c. The Intelligibility of God-talk. *Religious Studies* 6:1, pp. 1–21.

———. 1970d. On Being an Atheist. *Personalist* 51, pp. 99–105.

———. 1970e. On the Logic of Revelation. *Sophia* 9:1, pp. 8–13.

———. 1970f. The Primacy of Philosophical Theology. *Theology Today* 27:2, pp. 155–69.

———. 1970g. On Waste and Wastelands (a Response). In *Perspectives in Education, Religion, and the Arts*, ed. Howard Kiefer and Milton Munitz (Albany: State University of New York Press), pp. 117–26.

———. 1971a. *Contemporary Critiques of Religion*. London: Macmillan.

———. 1971b. *Reason and Practice: A Modern Introduction to Philosophy*. New York: Harper & Row.

———. 1972a. Religion and Commitment. In *Religious Language and Knowledge*, ed. Robert H. Ayers and William T. Blackstone (Athens: University of Georgia Press), pp. 18–43.

———. 1972b. Is Empiricism an Ideology? *Metaphilosophy* 3:4, pp. 265–73.

———. 1972c. The Coherence of Wittgensteinian Fideism. *Sophia* 11:3, pp. 4–12.

———. 1973a. God, Necessity, and Falsifiability. In *Traces of God in Secular Culture*, ed. George F. McLean (Staten Island, NY: Alba House), pp. 273–306.

———. 1973b. Agnosticism. In *The Dictionary of the History of Ideas: Studies in Selected Pivotal Ideas*, ed. Philip P. Wiener (New York: Charles Scribner's Sons), vol. 1, pp. 17–27.

———. 1973c. *Skepticism*. London: Macmillan.

———. 1973d. *Ethics without God*. London: Pemberton Books.

———. 1973e. Arguing about the Rationality of Religion. *Sophia* 12:3, pp. 7–10.

———. 1973f. Religious Truth-claims and Faith. *International Journal for Philosophy of Religion* 4:1, pp. 13–29.

———. 1974a. The Making of an Atheist. *Humanist* 34:1, pp. 14–15, 18–19.

———. 1974b. Empiricism, Theoretical Constructs, and God. *Journal of Religion* 54:3, pp. 199–217.

———. 1974c. Reductionism and Religious Truth Claims. *Dialogos* 27, pp. 25–37.

———. 1974d. God and the Postulated Entities. *Southern Journal of Philosophy* 12:2, pp. 225–30.

———. 1974e. Religious Discourse and Arguing from Ordinary Language: Some Meta-Theological and Meta-Philosophical Remarks. *Metaphilosophy* 5:2, pp. 106–12.

———. 1974f. Truth-Conditions and Necessary Existence. *Scottish Journal of Theology* 27:3, pp. 257–67.

———. 1975a. Religious Perplexity and the Study of Religion. *Philosophy in Context* 4, pp. 98–110.

———. 1975b. Metaphysics and Verification Revisited. *Southwestern Journal of Philosophy* 6, pp. 75–93.

———. 1975c. Secularism and Theology: Remarks on a Form of Naturalistic Humanism. *Southern Journal of Philosophy* 13:1, pp. 109–26.

———. 1975d. Facts, Factual Statements, and Theoretical Terms. *Philosophical Studies* 23, pp. 129–51.

———. 1976. Talk of God and the Doctrine of Analogy. *Thomist* 40:1, pp. 32–60.

———. 1977a. Religiosity and Powerlessness. *Humanist* 37:3, pp. 46–48.

———. 1977b. On Religion and the Grounds of Moral Belief. *Religious Humanism* 11:1, pp. 33–34.

———. 1978a. On the Rationality of Radical Theological Non-Naturalism: More on the Verificationalist Turn in the Philosophy of Religion. *Religious Studies* 12:2, pp. 193–204.

———. 1978b. Comparative Religion and Revealed Truth. *Religious Humanism* 12, pp. 89–90.

———. 1979a. Radical Theological Non-Naturalism. *Sophia* 18:2, pp. 1–6.

———. 1979b. Necessity and God. *International Journal for Philosophy of Religion* 10:1, pp. 1–23.

———. 1980. Wisdom and Dilman on the Reality of God. *Religious Studies* 16:1, pp. 49–60.

———. 1981a. Christian Empiricism. *Journal of Religion* 61, pp. 146–67.

———. 1981b. Does God Exist? Reflections on Disbelief. *Free Inquiry* 1:2, pp. 21–26.

———. 1981c. Philosophical and Religious Commitment: A Response to Dilman. *Philosophical Investigations* 4:2, pp. 58–60.

Nielsen, Kai, and Raziel Abelson. 1967. History of Ethics. In *The Encyclopedia of Philosophy*, vol. 3, ed. Paul Edwards (New York: Macmillan Publishing Co.), pp. 81–117.

Nishi, Shunji F. 1974. Toward a Prolegomenon to an Apologetic Theology. *Anglican Theological Review* Supplemental Series No. 4 (September), pp. 92–123.

Novak, Michael. 1968. What Is Theology's Standpoint? *Theology Today* 25:1 (April), pp. 37–51.

Nygren, Anders. 1972. *Meaning and Method: Prolegomena to a Scientific Philosophy of Religion and a Scientific Theology*. London: Epworth Press.

Oakes, Robert A. 1976. "God": An Observational Term? *Modern Schoolman* 54:1 (November), pp. 43–56.

Oakes, Robert J. 1972. Is "Self-Validating" Religious Experience Logically Possible? *Thomist* 36:2 (April), pp. 256–66.

Ogden, Schubert M. 1966. *The Reality of God and Other Essays*. New York: Harper & Row.

——. 1972a. The Reformation that We Want. *Anglican Theological Review* 54:4 (October), pp. 260–73.

——. 1972b. What Is Theology? *The Journal of Religion* 52:1 (January), pp. 22–40.

——. 1975. "'Theology and Falsification' in Retrospect": A Reply. In *The Logic of God: Theology and Falsification*, ed. Malcolm L. Diamond and Thomas V. Litzenburg, Jr. (Indianapolis: Bobbs-Merrill Co.), pp. 290–96.

Olson, Edwin A. 1982. Hidden Agenda behind the Evolutionist/Creationist Debate. *Christianity Today* 26:8 (23 April), pp. 26–30.

Ott, Heinrich. 1967. The Problem of Non-objectifying Thinking and Speaking in Theology. *Journal of Theology and the Church* 3, pp. 112–35.

Pannenberg, Wolfhart. 1972. The Nature of a Theological Statement. *Zygon: Journal of Religion and Science* 7 (1): 6–19.

——. 1976. *Theology and the Philosophy of Science*. London: Darton, Longman, & Todd.

Peacocke, Arthur R. 1984. *Intimations of Reality: Critical Realism in Science and Religion*. Notre Dame, IN: University of Notre Dame Press.

——. 1990. *Theology for a Scientific Age: Being and Becoming—Natural and Divine*. Signposts in Theology Series. Oxford: Basil Blackwell.

——. 1993. *Theology for a Scientific Age: Being and Becoming—Natural, Divine, and Human*. Enlarged ed. Theology and the Sciences Series. Minneapolis: Fortress Press.

Penelhum, Terence. 1971a. *Religion and Rationality*. New York: Random House.

——. 1971b. *Problems of Religious Knowledge*. London; New York: Macmillan; Seabury.

Peter, Carl J. 1973. A Word on Behalf of *Method in Theology*. *Thomist* 37:3 (July), pp. 602–10.

——. 1979. A Shift to the Human Subject in Roman Catholic Theology. *Communio: International Catholic Review* 6:1 (Spring), pp. 56–72.

Peters, Karl E. 1976. Presuppositions of Scientific Theology. *Perspectives in Religious Studies* 3:2, pp. 140–49.

Polanyi, Michael. 1959. *The Study of Man*. Chicago: University of Chicago Press.

——. 1964. *Personal Knowledge: Towards a Post-Critical Philosophy*. New York: Harper.

Polkinghorne, John. 2001. [Review of *Sleuthing the Divine: The Nexus of Science and Spirit*, by Kevin Sharpe (2000).] *Theology Today* 58:2 (July), pp. 264–66.

Porteous, Alvin C. 1973. [Review of *God the Problem*, by Gordon Kaufman (1972).] *Religion in Life* 42:1, pp. 131–32.

Pratt, Vernon. 1970. *Religion and Secularization.* London: Macmillan.

Pugh, George Edgin. 1977. *The Biological Origin of Human Values.* New York: Basic Books.

Putnam, Hilary. 1979. The Place of Facts in a World of Values. In *The Nature of the Physical Universe. Nobel Conference, 12th, Gustavus Adolphus College, 1976,* ed. Douglas Huff and Omer Prewett (New York: John Wiley & Sons).

Quay, Paul M. 1974. A Distinction in Search of a Difference: The Psycho-Social Distinction between Science and Theology. *The Modern Schoolman* 51:4 (May), pp. 345–59.

Quine, W. V. O., and J. S. Ullian. 1970. *The Web of Belief.* New York: Random House.

Rahner, Karl. 1975. *Theology, Anthropology, Christology,* transl. David Bourke. Theological Investigations, vol. 13. London: Darton, Longman, & Todd.

Ramberan, Osmond G. 1978. Nielsen, Ethics, and God. *Religious Studies* 14:2, pp. 205–16.

Ramsey, Ian T. 1964. *Models and Mystery.* Oxford: Oxford University Press.

Reardon, B. M. G. 1955. Christian Dogma and Scientific Method. *The Congregational Quarterly* 33:3 (July), pp. 204–15.

Reese, William L. 1979. Reductionism and Kai Nielsen. *Dialogos* 14:34, pp. 111–14.

Reist, Benjamin. 1979. The God of the Contexts: Theology-in-Context and the Doctrine of Creation—Clues from the Thought of Michael Polanyi. In *Toward Theology in an Australian Context,* ed. Victor C. Hayes (Belford Park, South Australia: Australian Association for the Study of Religion), pp. 113ff.

Robbins, J. Wesley. 1972. Professor Gilkey and Alternative Methods of Theological Construction. *Journal of Religion* 52:1 (January), pp. 84–101.

Robinson, John A. T. 1963. *Honest to God.* London: SCM Press.

Root-Bernstein, Robert Scott. 1981. Revelation or Reason? The Creationist-Evolutionist Controversy Reconsidered. Council for the Advancement of Science Writing, New Horizons in Science, Nineteenth Annual Briefing, 11 November. Columbus, OH.

Rottschaefer, William A. 1985. Religious Cognition as Interpreted Experience: An Examination of Ian Barbour's Comparison of the Epistemic Structures of Science and Religion. *Zygon: Journal of Religion and Science* 20:3 (September), pp. 265–82.

Runzo, Joseph. 1975. [Review of *An Essay on Theological Method,* by Gordon D. Kaufman (1975).] *Theological Studies* 37, pp. 685–87.

Ruse, Michael. 1982. A Philosopher at the Monkey Trial. *New Scientist* 93:1291 (1 February), pp. 317–19.

Ruse, Michael, and Edward O. Wilson. 1986. Moral Philosophy as Applied Science. *Philosophy* 61:236, pp. 173–92.

Sachs, Mendel. 1976. On the Complementarity of Science and Religion. *Humanist* 36:6, pp. 45–46.

Sanders, Fred R., and Kirk Wegter-McNelly. 1999. [Review of *The Foundations of Dialogue in Science and Religion*, by Alister E. McGrath (1998), and *Science and Religion: An Introduction*, by Alister E. McGrath (1999).] *CTNS Bulletin* 19:2 (Spring), pp. 17–21.

Scharlemann, Robert P. 1973. Theological Models and Their Construction. *The Journal of Religion* 53:1 (January), pp. 65–82.

Schillebeeckx, Edward. 1968. *The Concept of Truth and Theological Renewal.* Revelation and Theology vol. 2. London: Sheed & Ward.

——. 1974. *The Understanding of Faith: Interpretation and Criticism.* London: Sheed & Ward.

Schilling, Harold K. 1962. *Science and Religion.* New York: Charles Scribner's Sons.

Schindler, David L. 1979. Theology and the Historical-Critical Claims of Modernity: On the Need for Metaphysics. *Communio: International Catholic Review* 6:1, pp. 73–94.

Schlesinger, George. 1977a. *Religion and Scientific Method.* Dordrecht, The Netherlands: D. Reidel Publishing Co.

——. 1977b. The Confirmation of Scientific and Theistic Hypotheses. *Religious Studies* 13:1 (March), pp. 17–28.

Schroeder, Edward. 1979. A Book Worth Discussing: David Tracy *Blessed Rage for Order. Currents in Theology and Mission* 6 (April), pp. 105–10.

Scott, William T. 1970. A Bridge from Science to Religion Based on Polanyi's Theory of Knowledge. *Zygon: Journal of Religion and Science* 5 (March), pp. 41–62.

Sharpe, Kevin. 1978. *Science Is a Mythology.* Melbourne, Australia: Melbourne College of Divinity, Theol. M. Thesis.

——. 1979. Theological Method and Gordon Kaufman. *Religious Studies* 15, pp. 173–90.

——. 1982a. Stanley L. Jaki's Critique of Physics. *Religious Studies* 18:1, pp. 55–75.

——. 1982b. A Mathematical Metaphysics: A Language for Qualities and Quantities, the Humanities and the Sciences. *Speculations in Science and Technology* 5:3, pp. 229–38.

——. 1984. *From Science to an Adequate Mythology.* Auckland: Interface Press.

——. 1991. Relating Science and Theology with Complementarity: A Caution. *Zygon: Journal of Religion and Science* 26:2, pp. 307–13.

————. 1998. The Sense of Happiness: Biological Explanations and Ultimate Reality and Meaning. *Ultimate Reality and Meaning* 21: 301–14.

————. 2000. *Sleuthing the Divine: The Nexus of Science and Spirit.* Minneapolis: Fortress Press.

Sharpe, Kevin, with Rebecca Bryant. 2005. *Has Science Displaced the Soul? Debating Love and Happiness.* Lanham, MD: Rowman & Littlefield.

Sharpe, Kevin, and Jonathan Walgate. 1998. Theology Can Use the Scientific Method and Still Be Theology. Presented at the C. S. Lewis Summer Institute, Oxford.

————. 2003. The Emergent Order. *Zygon: Journal of Religion and Science* 38 (2) June: pp. 411–33.

Sharpe, Kevin, and Brent Waters. 1999. The Laws of Life: Grounding Spiritual Truth in Science. *Science & Spirit* 10 (3): pp. 10–11.

Shea, William M. 1976. Revisionist Foundational Theology. *Anglican Theological Review* 58 (3): 263–79.

Shute, G. J. 1973. Language, Truth and an Incoherent God [Review of *Skepticism*, by Kai Nielsen (1973c).] *Expository Times* 84:8, pp. 248–49.

Slater, Peter. 1973. Christian Talk of God. In *Traces of God in Secular Culture*, ed. George F. McLean (Staten Island, NY: Alba House), pp. 345–79.

Smith, Huston, with Samuel Todes. 1969. Empiricism: Scientific and Religious. In *The Future of Empirical Theology*, ed. Bernard E. Meland (Chicago: University of Chicago Press), pp. 129ff.

Soskice, Janet Martin. 1985. *Metaphor and Religious Language.* Oxford: Clarendon Press.

Sponheim, Paul. 1975. [Review of *God the Problem*, by Gordon D. Kaufman (1972).] *Dialog* 14:1, pp. 65–66.

Swimme, Brian. 1996. *The Hidden Heart of the Cosmos: Humanity and the New Story.* Maryknoll, NY: Orbis Books.

Taylor, Paul W. 1961. Justifying a Way of Life. *Indian Journal of Philosophy* 2:6, pp. 163–75.

Teilhard de Chardin, Pierre. 1959. *The Phenomenon of Man.* London: William Collins Sons.

Thagard, Paul R. 1978. The Best Explanation: Criteria for Theory Choice. *Journal of Philosophy* 75:2 (February), pp. 76–92.

Thom, René. 1975. *Structural Stability and Morphogenesis: An Outline of a General Theory of Models.* Reading, MA: The Benjamin/Cummings Publishing Co.

Thomas, Owen C. 1973. *Introduction to Theology.* Cambridge, MA: Greeno, Hadden & Co.

Thomma, Steven. 2004. Analysis: Deepest Divide Is Over Values. *Rochester Democrat and Chronicle* (Sunday 11 April), p. 7A.

Thompson, William. 1972. Theology's Method and Linguistic Analysis in the Thought of Langdon Gilkey. *Thomist* 36:3 (July), pp. 363–93.

Thorson, Walter R. 1968. A Concept of Truth in the Natural Sciences. *Themelios* 5:2, pp. 27–39.

Tillich, Paul. 1967. *Systematic Theology: Three Volumes in One*. Chicago: University of Chicago Press.

Tooley, Michael. 1975. Theological Statements and the Question of an Empiricist Criterion of Cognitive Significance. In *The Logic of God: Theology and Falsification*, ed. Malcolm L. Diamond and Thomas V. Litzenburg, Jr. (Indianapolis: Bobbs-Merrill Co.), pp. 481–524.

Torrance, Thomas F. 1969a. *Theological Science*. Oxford: Oxford University Press.

———. 1969b. *Space, Time, and Incarnation*. Oxford: Oxford University Press.

———. 1971. *God and Rationality*. Oxford: Oxford University Press.

———. 1972. Newton, Einstein, and Scientific Theology. *Religious Studies* 8:3 (September), pp. 233–50.

———. 1981. *Divine and Contingent Order*. Oxford: Oxford University Press.

Toulmin, Stephen, and June Goodfield. 1961. *The Fabric of the Heavens*. London: Hutchinson.

Tournier, Paul. 1957. *The Meaning of Persons*. London: SCM Press.

Townes, Charles H. 1966. The Convergence of Science and Religion. *Zygon: Journal of Religion and Science* 1: 301–11.

Tracy, David. 1974. The Task of Fundamental Theology. *Journal of Religion* 54:1, pp. 13–34.

———. 1975a. *Blessed Rage for Order*. New York: Seabury Press.

———. 1975b. Theology as Public Discourse. *Christian Century* 42:10 (19 March), pp. 280–84.

———. 1977. Modes of Theological Argument. *Theology Today* 33:4 (January), pp. 387–95.

———. 1991. *The Analogical Imagination*. New York: Crossroad.

Trethowan, Illyd. 1966. In Defense of Theism: A Reply to Kai Nielsen. *Religious Studies* 2:1, pp. 37–48.

Trigg, Roger. 1973. *Reason and Commitment*. London: Cambridge University Press.

———. 1980. *Reality at Risk: A Defense of Realism in Philosophy and the Sciences*. Brighton, England: The Harvester Press.

van Buren, Paul M. 1972. *The Edges of Language: An Essay in the Logic of a Religion*. London: SCM Press.

van Huyssteen, J. Wentzel. 1997. *Essays in Postfoundationalist Theology*. Grand Rapids, MI: William B. Eerdmans Publishing Co.

———. 1998. Postfoundationalism in Theology and Science. In *Rethinking Theology and Science: Six Models for the Current Dialogue*, ed. Niels Henrik

Gregersen and J. Wentzel van Huyssteen (Grand Rapids, MI: William B. Eerdmans Publishing Co.), pp. 13–49.

———. 1999. *The Shaping of Rationality: Toward Interdisciplinarity in Theology and Science*. Grand Rapids, MI: William B. Eerdmans Publishing Co.

Welch, R. 1992. The Possibility of Knowing the Ultimate: Francis Bacon on the Fulfillment of Natural Inquiry. *Ultimate Reality and Meaning* 15: 172–84.

Whitehead, Alfred North. 1925. *Science and the Modern World*. New York: The Macmillan Co.

Wiebe, Don. 1974a. On Kaufman's Problem God. *Religious Studies* 10:2, pp. 189–98.

———. 1974b. Science, Religion, and Rationality: Questions of Method in Science and Theology. Lancaster: University of Lancaster, Ph.D. Thesis.

———. 1976. Explanation and Theological Method. *Zygon: Journal of Religion and Science* 11:1, pp. 35–49.

Wiles, Maurice. 1974. *The Remaking of Christian Doctrine: The Hulsean Lectures 1973*. London: SCM Press.

Wilson, Bryan R. 1974. *Rationality*. Oxford: Basil Blackwell.

Wilson, Edward O. 2005. Can Biology Do Better Than Faith? *New Scientist* 188:2524 (5 November), pp. 48–49.

Wilson, Jonathan R. 2003. [Review of *A Scientific Theology, Volume 1: Nature*, by Alister E. McGrath (2001).] *Journal of the American Academy of Religion* 71:4 (December), pp. 955–58.

Winslow, Donald F. 1977. Maurice Wiles and the Remaking of Christian Doctrine. *Anglican Theological Review* 59:2 (April), pp. 197–212.

Wisdom, J. 1944. Gods. *Proceedings of the Aristotelian Society* 45, pp. 185–206.

———. 1953. *Philosophy and Psychoanalysis*. Oxford: Blackwell.

Wittgenstein, Ludwig. 1968. *The Blue and Brown Books*. New York: The Macmillan Co.

Woods, G. F. 1958. *Theological Explanation*. Welwyn, Herts: James Nisbet & Co.

Wright, John H. 1979. The Method of Process Theology: An Evaluation. *Communio: International Catholic Review* 6:1 (Spring), pp. 38–55.

Wright, Robert. 1994. *The Moral Animal: The New Science of Evolutionary Psychology*. New York: Pantheon.

Yandell, Keith. 1968a. Empiricism and Theism. *Sophia* 7:3, pp. 3–11.

———. 1968b. Reply to Nielsen. *Sophia* 7:3, pp. 18–19.

Index